The Fall and Rise of Mackenzie King: 1911-1919

The Fall & Rise of MACKENZIE KING: 1911-1919
by F. A. McGregor

Macmillan of Canada / Toronto / 1962

Designed by Leslie Smart

Printed in Canada
by The Bryant Press Limited

To I.C.F.

Acknowledgments

Had the subject of this book not left such a wealth of material in the day-to-day entries in his diaries and in the vast volume of his personal and other correspondence, the book could not have been written. Many other sources have of course been consulted. My first acknowledgment, however, must be to Mackenzie King himself, for his own contribution has been greater than anyone else's. My apologies to him if in a few places I have revealed more than he would have of incidents in his personal life, and have thereby invaded the privacy which he always took such pains to safeguard.

The idea of writing such a book as this grew out of circumstances which are described in the prologue. Dr. R. MacGregor Dawson, whose political biography of Mackenzie King was published in 1958, suggested that an extensive memorandum which I had prepared for him might be the basis for a separate volume. Later, Dr. Frank H. Underhill, as well as Walter B. Herbert of the Canada Foundation, encouraged me to think that the draft might be developed into a useful book. Their recommendation to Dr. John E. Robbins of the Social Science Research Council of Canada resulted in the Council's authorizing generous financial assistance which made possible the preparation of the manuscript. To these friends, and to the Research Council, I am deeply grateful, as I am to John M. Gray, president of the Macmillan Company of Canada, whose friendly interest in the work at every stage has done so much to stimulate action and overcome discouragements. I offer my warm thanks, too, to my fellow literary executors, W. Kaye Lamb, Norman A. Robertson, and J. W. Pickersgill, for their sympathetic interest and helpful advice. I am also indebted to Professor Frederick W. Gibson of Queen's University for his kindness in giving me access to his extensive and detailed papers, as yet unpublished, on Mackenzie King's part in the politics of the period.

It has been my good fortune, in the task of collecting and checking data, to have had the expert research assistance of Miss Jacqueline Côté (Mrs. Blair Neatby) and Miss Lillian Breen (now secretary of the Canada Council). Their co-operation has been deeply appreciated. Since their retirement from the Public Archives and from Laurier House, Mrs. Eileen Bond has responded in the same spirit to every call for archival assistance.

F. A. McGREGOR

561 Echo Drive, Ottawa
July, 1962

Contents

Prologue

This is the story of a remarkable interlude in the career of a Canadian statesman. The defeat of the Liberal government in September 1911 might well have meant the end of the political career of William Lyon Mackenzie King. It turned out to be rather the beginning of a long hiatus. For eight years he lived a life which varied from actual lack of employment to full and highly-paid activity as economic counsellor, guide, and close friend of John D. Rockefeller, Jr., and as adviser on industrial relations to several of the largest corporations in the United States. The period ends with his return to political life in August 1919, when he was elected leader of the Liberal Party. This meant the end of one career and the resumption of another.

Eight years represent but a short span in the life of a man who lived for over seventy-five. Mackenzie King's life between September 1911 and August 1919, however, was so completely different from his life in the first ten and the last thirty years of his political career that a fairly detailed account of what he thought, said, wrote, and did within that period should add greatly to our understanding of the whole man. The possibility of a return to politics never left his mind, and contacts with Canadian political leaders were frequent, but for five years out of the eight, from 1914 to 1919, he was almost completely absorbed in the study of labour

problems and in his work as confidential adviser to John D. Rockefeller, Jr.

Of the first fifty years of Mackenzie King's life, R. MacGregor
Dawson in his book *Mackenzie King — a Political Biography 1874-
1923* gives a comprehensive picture. It is a political biography,
however, and the author's space for any one period was limited,
particularly for a period that can be described as largely non-
political. The enormous volume of material — diaries, correspondence, and other records — made it necessary for Dr. Dawson to
have help from research assistants who would concentrate on
particular periods or fields of study. As one of Mr. King's literary
executors, and also as one who had been with him throughout
most of this non-political period, I undertook to examine the raw
material relating particularly to labour policies in the years 1911
to 1919, and to prepare a memorandum for the biographer's use.
What might have been a 'memorandum' turned out to be a treatise
of four or five hundred pages, chiefly devoted to industrial relations but with occasional excursions into fields political and personal, and into years before and after the 1911-19 period. In
volume it was far beyond MacGregor Dawson's requirements,
but even though he could compress much into little space, he
could use relatively little of what I had prepared. He agreed, as
did my fellow literary executors, that a fuller account of what
happened between 1911 and 1919, even though it might involve
occasional repetition, should be given in a separate volume. This is
that volume.

II

My memories of Mackenzie King stretch over the period of more
than twoscore years that ended on Saturday evening, July 22,
1950, when he lay dying in his well-loved home at Kingsmere.
Saying farewell to him then, I thought of the day of our first
meeting, when he was a young man of thirty-four years and I a
youth just turned twenty-one. That day, in July 1909, was the

beginning of an association, and a friendship, that had much to do with the shaping of my life. It was a relationship of which I have always been proud. Our meeting came about in this manner: I had just completed my freshman year at McMaster University and had returned to the Post Office Department for summer work in the office of W. J. Johnstone, who served as accountant for two departments, Post Office and Labour. In the latter capacity he had frequent contacts with Mackenzie King, who had been deputy minister of labour until he resigned in June to become the minister. A secretary was required for the new deputy, F. A. Acland, and Johnstone was asked if he could recommend any promising young man for the post. He did — I was his nominee. I was properly excited when an interview was arranged at once with the new minister, even more excited when I was told to report for duty immediately, or as soon as the new Civil Service Commission confirmed the appointment.

By good fortune, as it happened, my first assignment was to serve for several weeks in the minister's own office. This gave opportunity for many new experiences. The first adventure was to act as secretary to the minister when he attended the annual convention of the Trades and Labour Congress of Canada in Quebec City. It was not a heavy assignment, but it gave me my first opportunity to see my new chief in action and to admire the friendly relations he had established with representatives of the labour movement in Canada. Another experience, even more exciting, came when the minister called on me to accompany him to Montreal, where he was the central figure in the negotiations that followed the Grand Trunk Railway strike of 1910. Here was my first lesson in the art of industrial conciliation, an art in which the instructor had proved himself to be a past master — patient, conciliatory, and impartial, but unswerving when principles were at stake. As a young radical in my early twenties I was intensely interested, and was proud to find that my new boss, intolerant of injustice in any form, was possessed of these qualities to an unusual degree.

There were other aspects of his character that I came to know during my occasional assignments to the minister's office. It was part of his ritual to go to his summer cottage at Kingsmere every week-end. It often happened that work prevented his catching the one o'clock train on Saturday afternoon. In his earlier and less affluent days he had been used to making the trip to his cottage by bicycle. Now, as minister, he employed a horse and buggy and, as I knew more about horses than he, it fell to me to go to Landreville's stables on Albert Street and take charge of the trip. On such occasions Mackenzie King was not in the driver's seat. I can recall few occasions in later years when he handed over the reins to anyone else with so little protest. These long drives through the quiet country-side gave a wonderful opportunity to the impressionable young lad I was then, to learn from an older and wiser man. Conversation, though it tended to be one-sided, never lagged on such trips; the emphasis was always on politics and social reform, but religion, art, and music crowded in. He was an idealist, and I think he was pleased with my enthusiasm for the idealistic profile of his friend Henry Albert Harper that he had written in *The Secret of Heroism*. (He had presented me with an autographed copy of this book on the day I entered the Department of Labour, July 5, 1909.) Mackenzie King was, of course, steeped in politics; I was a novice. He prided himself on being a liberal as well as a Liberal, a reformer as well as a Reformer (the Grits still called themselves Reformers in those days). He appeared shocked when I told him I did not know why, or rather whether, I was a Liberal. The name of Laurier had always been spoken with reverence in our home, but ours was not a politically-minded family — we had been brought up, rather, on theology. Even association with such a mentor as Mackenzie King did not raise my political temperature to the cheering-point (but doubtless it did have some effect because in later years I found myself taking it for granted that 'Tory' was a bad word).

Socialism was one subject, as I recall, that came into our conversations. From his youth up, Mackenzie King had had strong sympathies with 'the working classes', and in his university days in Toronto and Chicago he had enjoyed frequent and long talks with radical labour leaders, some of them ardent socialists. In his talks with them he had normally argued against socialism. While at Harvard he had listened to Eugene V. Debs (head of the Socialist Party) but had not agreed with him. He seemed to be veering from the left to the middle of the road, or, perhaps more accurately, to the left of centre. To make any form of socialism palatable for him, there would have had to be a generous admixture of such ingredients as Christian doctrine and social reform. At this time he had not as yet reached unalterable conclusions, but while he had rejected scientific, state, Fabian, or Marxian socialism, he still had strong feelings of sympathy with some form of Christian socialism or collectivism.

Talks such as these on the way to and from Kingsmere kindled in me a lively interest in the subjects discussed and inspired me to hope that some day after graduation I might take a post-graduate course in labour economics at Chicago or Harvard. But this, the first of my three spells with Mackenzie King, ended in September 1911. That month marked the defeat of the Laurier government on the reciprocity issue; it marked, too, the fall of Mackenzie King. He fell to rise, but his recovery did not begin until the summer of 1914. It was then, soon after the turn of the tide, that I joined him again.

My second association with Mackenzie King began in December 1914 and lasted until the summer of 1925. No longer in Parliament, he had been engaged by the Rockefeller Foundation to undertake, on a world-wide scale, a comprehensive study of the problem of industrial relations. It was generally agreed that for a task of such magnitude an elaborate organization would be established; but Mackenzie King had no grandiose ideas about organization — he was content with the appointment of a single assistant, a secretary. If Mackenzie King was elated by the prospect of an opportunity beyond anything he could have dreamed of — and he was —, I, when I received an invitation from him to be that secretary, was overwhelmed. Since I was planning in 1914 for post-graduate work in labour economics at Harvard or Chicago, I was delighted to let my plans give way to a course far more realistic and less theoretical, under a man who had been chosen as an outstanding specialist in the field of industrial relations. The new life turned out to be all I had hoped for. It was a wonderful experience for an untravelled youth to accompany his chief on his many visits to New York, Washington, Chicago, and other industrial centres, and later to England and the Continent. It was, too, a rare privilege to come to know John D. Rockefeller, Jr., with whom Mackenzie King established such warm personal relations, and to travel with them both through the dreary coal-mining areas of Colorado, into the mines and into the miners' homes, and to have even a secretary's part in the transformation of human relations that resulted from those visits. Similar interest in a new approach to the labour problem was being shown by heads of some of the largest industries in the country, such as the two Bethlehem companies, the Standard Oil group, General Electric, International Harvester, and others. What an opportunity it was to 'listen in' on the discussions of important policies by important people — to participate in the writing of Mackenzie King's book, as well as to have occasional contacts with leading personalities in Canadian public life. A post-graduate course indeed! A travelling fellowship of a very unusual kind! Here was a chance to assimilate much of what might be termed 'higher learning' while performing the more prosaic tasks of a secretary.

III

All this was terminated abruptly, on August 7, 1919, when Mackenzie King was elected to the leadership of the Liberal Party, and my course in labour economics was superseded by one in practical politics. Immediately the staff of one was doubled, then trebled. Additional clerical assistance had to be provided for the new Leader of the Opposition, but there was still a minimum of staff, office space, and equipment, with the resultant stress and strain on all concerned. When in December 1921 Mr. King became prime minister, and the change was made to the prime minister's office, work, staff, and hours had all, of course, to be increased. It became a time of enormous pressure for everyone. In neither establishment were the orthodox Civil Service hours of nine-to-five found to be appropriate; something more like nine-to-eleven was necessary to keep abreast of the work. Mackenzie King never felt under any obligation himself to observe union hours, nor did he — or we for that matter — expect that members of his staff would impose such restrictions on themselves. I can recall that when, several years later, I turned to other work, I could not suppress a certain sense of guilt when I left my new office before darkness had fallen. He was a prodigious worker, but I, as secretary, had a somewhat lower opinion than he of his ability to organize his day. He could be prompt in his attendance at Cabinet meetings and sessions of Parliament, but secretarial tempers were sorely tried when it came to arranging times for interviews. I recall one future Cabinet minister who swore he would never try again ('swore' was the right word). On occasion, even his staff had to fight like outsiders for necessary consultations with him on matters which he alone could decide. Many things had to be done and said in his name without his specific instructions, and reasons for the Chief's inability to meet appointments had to be invented on the spur of the moment. This, of course, was part of the technique of a secretary, and normally he backed us up in our attempts to provide such needed protection.

While he could be exceedingly kind at times in his personal relations with his staff, he could never quite conceal his opinion of them. Even the best of them failed at times to provide the support he felt a prime minister should have. The search for the perfect secretary always ended in futility, and unfortunately the incumbents, even the best of them, were not unaware of his feeling of their inadequacy. Sometimes the criticism came by a circuitous route, sometimes it was direct. I can recall, more than once or twice, the direct approach, a withering comment about some shortcoming, ending with the comment, 'The Lord knows, McGregor, I am not criticizing.' The withering comment must have been misunderstood. Another trial to his staff was the too-often-repeated reference to a missing document as 'the most important document of the whole session' — or of the whole trip.

May I correct one story that has found its way into print. Blair Fraser, in *Maclean's*, and others have charged that in a fit of temper I shied a volume of Hansard at the Chief — some have said it was an ink-well — and they add, as if in exculpation, that I missed him. I resent this criticism of my marksmanship. What really happened was that at the end of a long and trying political tour in 1924 I carried into the P.M.'s office a large sheaf of papers that required his attention. We had both been working under tension, and when my appearance was greeted by some unfavourable comment, which again I must have mistaken for criticism, I threw the whole bundle of papers toward the ceiling with a loud cry, and retreated to my office with ungracious haste. It must have startled and disturbed the P.M. He recognized it as the foreshadowing of a nervous breakdown — which, fortunately, never occurred. His understanding and sympathetic consideration were shown in the provision he made, first, for a long leave of absence; then for a visit with him to Atlantic City where he planned to do some uninterrupted work on the Speech from the Throne; later for a trip to England on a quasi-official mission; and, finally, for my appointment to a post in the Civil Service which was to absorb my interest for the next twenty-five years.

IV

Much of this talk of personal relations between principal and secretaries may be trivial (the Lord knows, Mr. King, I am not criticizing). It is, however, revealing of some aspects of his personality: his passion for exactness, his desire to have everything that was done for him performed with the same painstaking care that he himself exercised, his attention to detail and observance of protocol, his disregard of personal considerations when there was work to be done. I myself never thought of Mackenzie King as a slave-driver in the days of his prime-ministership, though I have heard of such criticism. Most of us drove ourselves. It might have been resented if the Chief had not been a hard worker. He was. But some of us felt at times that first things did not always come first, that some of the time taken for long letters to friends, for example, might have been better spent on talks with important people. When December came, we could not help feeling that Christmas cards, outgoing and incoming, held too high a priority. The selection of cards had to be a personal matter; it took time, yet could not be assigned to a personal secretary. The lists of hundreds of names had to be revised every year, with more additions than deletions. Some cards could go out with only a signature; others, many others, had to carry an appropriate personal greeting. There was, too, the inflow of hundreds of greetings. Was it any wonder that there were times when we cursed the man who invented Christmas cards?

Thinking back, I am not sure of our wisdom. After all, he needed relaxation, needed to keep in touch with out-of-town friends who in his lonely life meant much to him. If we had been wiser I think we would have been less critical, too, of the time he spent on his hand-written personal letters. To the bereaved he could write the perfect letter of deeply-felt sympathy, as many a family can testify. He had the right words of comfort to say when he made personal visits at such times, and he made many such visits. It all revealed a tenderness and human sympathy that contrasted strangely with the image of him in the public mind as a man aloof, formal, unsympathetic. In this image there were elements of truth. He could be all these things, but he could also be charming, gracious, and genuinely friendly. There were times, too, when he could be 'the life of the party'. He was a man of many moods, ranging from habitual seriousness to occasional lightheartedness and even jocularity. Who has not heard of the contradictions that made up the complexity of the Mackenzie King character!

One thing we did not begrudge was the time he spent in writing up his diary. That was a stupendous task, undertaken often at the end of a hard day, when his study lamp was the only one left burning. His biographers will never cease to be grateful for this lightening of their labours, for this wealth of source material. Nor did we feel anything but respect for the devotional period with which each day began — the reading of the scriptures, prayer, and meditation, usually inspired by passages from his vade-mecum, *Daily Strength for Daily Needs*. It was not a perfunctory Bible-reading excercise: he could memorize passages as he read, and his frequent pencil notes in the margins of his favourite fourteen-volume version often reflected his own thoughts about what he had been reading. Sometimes these notations merely recorded the day, perhaps an anniversary, on which the passages had been read. He could be moved by the prayers which others had been inspired to write; but when he prayed, as the diaries reveal, he was on his knees and the language was from his own heart.

His early training and ambition had prepared him for a life demanding prodigious energy, but he did need relief from the strain and stress of politics. This he found by withdrawing himself, completely, into the quiet of his study at Laurier House or the seclusion of his cottage at Kingsmere. He has often been pitied for the loneliness of his life, and he was lonely, but at the same time he found rest and contentment in solitude. He needed to be alone to build up reserves of physical, nervous, and spiritual strength. He needed, just as much, other kinds of relaxation such as other men, similarly overburdened, found. But one could never imagine him sitting back in the lounge of his club, sipping a cocktail, smoking a cigarette, swapping stories with the boys, or drawing himself up to the table for a foursome at bridge. He profoundly disliked all card games. A stigma of sin clung to them, certainly the sin of time-wasting. There was, perhaps, at least a trace of self-righteousness in his attitude toward this and other human foibles which he himself did not share.

This is not to suggest that he lived a monastic life outside of working hours. He would accept, though often reluctantly, an invitation for a social evening. Dancing, frowned upon by the strictarians of earlier generations, was something he enjoyed immensely, and without any qualms of his Puritan conscience. He was not a graceful dancer, but he was an enthusiastic one. It was the part of social life he enjoyed most — the companionship, the rhythmic movement of the waltz, the exercise.

Smoking was a habit Mackenzie King never acquired for himself and only very reluctantly condoned in others. The handsome carved box on his library table at Laurier House which contained his father's pipes must have been, however, a continuing reminder to him that smoking, or at any rate pipe-smoking, was not a sure sign of moral obliquity. In his later years he became more tolerant of it. He did not discourage it at Laurier House parties, but he forbade it in Cabinet meetings. As for smoking by women, this was something he could never countenance.

Oddly enough, he seemed to be less intolerant of moderate — very moderate — drinking, than of smoking. His conscience could sanction the one for himself but not the other. In my early days with him I thought of him as the nearest thing to a teetotaller. In his later years he permitted himself wine at dinner and the occasional Scotch or rye for other than purely medicinal purposes; but he did not 'drink his wine with a merry heart', because he was never able to rid himself of an overhanging sense of guilt. Such abstemiousness as his, generally practised, would spell bankruptcy for the distillers and brewers.

While he was no musician himself he did find relaxation in the world of music. He listened to classical music with pleasure and appreciation. He disapproved of and disliked ultra-modern music (as he did ultra-modern painting), even the kind that was less than 'ultra'. The 'good old songs', and of course hymns, came high in his repertoire. No Sunday evening was complete without a session of hymn-singing, beside his mother's piano in the library at Laurier House or on the verandah of the summer home of his Kingsmere neighbour, the beloved Mrs. F. M. S. Jenkins. His choice could run to hymns of the Moody-and-Sankey type, but among his favourites were 'Lead, Kindly Light', 'Unto the Hills', and 'O God of Bethel'. He knew them all by heart.

The world of sport provided for him less in the way of relaxation than the world of music. He was seldom even a spectator at such games as hockey, baseball, rugby, or soccer. He never attempted golf or curling, but in his youth he had enjoyed tennis and soccer; he had been a good runner, too. In his thirties and forties he did a great deal of horseback-riding — surely an ideal form of relaxation after a day at his study table. He was equally enthusiastic about long walks in the country, and his walking companions (William Wilfred Campbell was one of them) had to step out to keep pace with him. In the summer at Kingsmere, in addition to long walks through the woods and canoeing on the lake, there was a never-ending task of clearing brush near his cottage, hard manual work that was always topped off with a swim before dinner. These vigorous forms of exercise contributed much to his excellent physical health.

Through all the years of his public life — and indeed from his earliest days — a strong religious faith played a vital part in his life. Foremost amongst his beliefs was his faith in a future life. How sadly critical he was of Sir Wilfrid Laurier's inability to see that death did not end all. He himself believed implicitly in the survival of human personality, the certainty of a divinity guiding the affairs of men, including his own affairs. 'The Unseen Hand', 'Destiny', so frequently referred to in his diaries, were realities to him. Mystic that he considered himself to be in his thirties and forties, he was intensely interested in psychic phenomena and the mysteries of clairvoyance. He had not far to go to embrace the belief that meant so much to him in later years when he felt that he succeeded in communing, directly or through a medium, with the departed spirits of his mother and father, of Sir Wilfrid Laurier, and of a host of others, some of whom he had never known. There are no clear indications that in the early years he believed he could communicate with those 'beyond the veil', but there are occasional foreshadowings of such a belief. He had his own way of interpreting ordinary phenomena as signs or messages or portents from the unseen world. To him, guardian angels were invisible realities. One incident, and his comments on it, recorded a few months after his mother's death, reveal the tendency of his mind toward an ultimate acceptance of spiritualistic philosophy:

> In my morning walk I saw a little robin on a tree, and stopped to talk with it, it appeared quite tame, and I kept talking to it as I used to to dear mother when she was so ill. In a little while it began to chirp a regular song. Then I talked again for a while & it came nearer, and sang to me again. I kept wondering if it might be a voice from the one most dearly loved and I asked it to sing again. To my delight it did the third time. Then I said good-bye — & it too flew away. I sometimes wonder if those we love do not control the spirits of birds & the fragrance & beauty of flowers & cause them to cheer & speak to us. Why should it not be so. The [in] visible are the great realities of life.

Why should it not be so too, he must have wondered, that a sensitive soul could learn to communicate with those he had loved long since and lost awhile. Years later he was certain that he could.

In spite of this deep and sincere interest in things of the spirit, and in spite of his very genuine devotion to St. Andrew's Presbyterian Church, which he attended faithfully during all his years in Ottawa, his financial support of it was limited. Nor was his name ever included, at least not with any high hopes, in the 'special names' lists of campaigns for funds for charitable or cultural objects. His lack of liberality in these and other directions can be attributed in considerable part to an ingrained fear that his resources might not be sufficient to meet the financial reverses which every political leader must be ready for. Such a reverse did occur in 1911 with the defeat of his party and himself. At that time financial difficulties had overtaken his family and he had to assume almost complete responsibility for their support. The memory of family hardships was always a painful one and a constant warning against any recurrence in the new family he hoped some day to establish. Even more impelling as a motive for saving was his recognition of the necessity of building up reserves as a bulwark against any threats to his freedom and independence in the political career on which his heart was set.

V

In 1925 I was not able to return to the pressures of the prime minister's office, and for the next twenty-five years my contacts with Mackenzie King were few. The world was his parish then, and I had a little corner of the domestic economy to worry about — as Commissioner of the Combines Investigation Act and, during most of the war years, as a member of the Wartime Prices and Trade Board in charge of the enforcement of the board's regulations.

In the nineteen-thirties and -forties, as already noted, Mackenzie King's work, and even mine, prevented anything but the most casual personal contacts between us. One incident is worth recording, however. One evening in August 1941 he telephoned me to say good-bye just before embarking on his first airplane flight overseas. He was plainly nervous and apprehensive. It was not every plane that reached the other side in wartime, and he had serious misgivings about this trip. His concern was so grave that he had rewritten his will that day, so he told me, and (this came as a complete surprise to me) had named me as one of the two executors of his estate; the Royal Trust Company was the other. Two literary executors, as I learned later, were appointed — H. R. L. Henry, then one of his secretaries, and myself. Fortunately no executor was needed for several years. While at the time I was deeply impressed by the honour, I soon forgot all about it, assuming that the will was drafted hurriedly and that more appropriate provision would be made later for the administration of the estate.

VI

It was not until 1949, after he had given up the prime-ministership and retired from the political scene, that I was again brought into a close relationship with him. The Rockefeller Foundation, early

that year, had made a grant of $100,000 to assist him in the prepara-
tion of his memoirs, which the trustees felt would be of permanent
historical value. They were particularly impressed by the value
of the diaries, which covered in detail a period of fifty-eight years
of his life and included all kinds of records of important interviews and conferences, much of it material which could not be
obtained from any other source. (This grant should not be con-
fused with the personal gift of approximately $100,000 in shares
which John D. Rockefeller, Jr., had made to him shortly after his
retirement from the office of prime minister, in honour of his
seventy-fourth birthday, December 17, 1948.) Mr. King told me
of the grant, in a telephone conversation in April 1949, and asked
me to join him in this, his last great enterprise. The offer came
at a crucial time in my work as Combines Investigation Commissioner, and with regret I had to decline. We both knew of others
who would meet the requirements and he said he would approach
one of them. I assumed that he had been successful, but before
the end of the year, after I had found it necessary to resign from
my Civil Service post, I was surprised to find that no one had been
chosen, and that, because of continued illness, no progress had
been made on the memoirs. Mr. King renewed the invitation and
this time I gladly accepted.

So began my third period of association with Mackenzie King,
on January 1, 1950. It was a discouraging prospect, for it soon
became obvious that the Chief's strength was not equal to the
task of any continuous writing. Some beginnings were attempted
and tentative plans for the book were discussed, but little was
accomplished. I expressed more than once my concern about the
lack of headway, and more than once was given the same answer,
'Why worry about it, McGregor, the book is practically written.'
I envisaged the possibility of manuscripts tucked away in one
of his many cupboards, or in steel filing boxes hidden under beds,
or in what used to be called 'the dark room'. But he made his meaning clear one day when he said, 'Why, the whole story of my life
is in the diaries, fifty-eight years of them.' It was a clear indication
that he thought of the diaries as the basic record of his life. He

hoped to make his own selections and to weave this material into an autobiography that would be authentic because it would be his own. That was an ambition he never achieved. On the day of his death, July 22, 1950, nothing had been committed to paper other than a few notes about his early years with his family in Berlin (now Kitchener), Ontario.

One thing of value had been accomplished, however, and that was the making of a new will. I had been surprised and concerned to discover, when I reported for duty on New Year's Day, that the will hurriedly drawn up in 1941, before his departure for England by plane, had not been changed. Much of my time for the next two months was spent in discussing the language of the new draft. He knew in a general way what he wanted to do with his estate: legacies for his family, friends, and staff, and bequests of Laurier House and his properties at Kingsmere to the nation. The gift of $100,000 from Mr. Rockefeller, which he had kept intact, would provide for scholarships, this amount to be augmented by the residue of his estate. He found the greatest difficulty in deciding on details; even more difficult was the task of framing his wishes in language that satisfied him. His friend Leonard W. Brockington, and G. O'Neill Lynch, Ottawa manager of the Royal Trust Company, were called in as confidential advisers. He discussed with them freely every proposal he had in mind, and, with Dr. Brockington particularly, the language of several passages of his own drafting which he was anxious to improve. His work was not done in any orderly fashion; in scribbled notes on many scraps of paper he jotted down what he wanted to say, but he preferred to keep them as loose notes. In disregard of his wishes in this respect, however, I did piece together these fragments, written mostly in his own hand, into a single document of several pages. The draft turned out to be generally suitable. It was, of course, subjected to further legal advice and more revisions of his own, but ultimately the will was signed and it remained virtually unchanged to the time of his death nearly five months later.

In the will three trustees and executors were named: the Royal Trust Company, Duncan K. MacTavish, and F. A. McGregor; and four literary executors: Norman A. Robertson, J. W. Pickersgill, W. Kaye Lamb, and F. A. McGregor. A Board of Scholarship Trustees was also established, consisting of Dr. L. W. Brockington, Dr. F. Cyril James, and Dr. Norman A. M. MacKenzie.

Much of what I have just recounted concerns the forty-odd years in which I knew Mackenzie King. It is of the years between 1911 and 1919, however, that more needs to be written. They were exceedingly important and fruitful years, but because he was out of Parliament and consequently very much less in the public eye, relatively little has been told of his accomplishments; indeed, they were years that might be described as the unknown years. They began with what might have been the collapse of his political career in 1911 and nearly three years of utter discouragement; then the restoration of hope and faith in himself and recognition by others of his genius in another field of endeavour; and finally his triumphant return to political life in Canada and the fulfilment of the dreams of his earliest years. The story of his fall and rise in the years 1911-19 is an exciting one.

CHAPTER 1

The Ten Years before the Fall

If the whole course of Mackenzie King's life were to be shown in the form of a chart of progress and reverses, the year 1911 would appear as the peak of a series of advances, and also as the starting-point of a downward trend to life on very much lower levels. September 21 was the dividing point, the day of the Canadian general election which resulted in the defeat of the Laurier government and of Mackenzie King in his own constituency. Between this fall in 1911 and his ultimate rise in 1919 he turned, after months of depressing unemployment, to work for which his earlier experience as a labour expert had qualified him. But he was never able to suppress the stirrings of political ambition; he clung always to the hope that he could return to the life he had found so fascinating before the collapse of 1911. Both aspects of his new life in the later period can be seen in truer perspective if viewed against the background of that earlier decade.

Mackenzie King had been carrying on post-graduate studies in Europe when, in June 1900, he received a cable from Sir William Mulock, then postmaster general, inviting him to become editor of the *Labour Gazette* in the newly established Department of Labour. He was then a young man of twenty-five years. Sir William, an old friend of the family, had been impressed by the quality of the work King had done while at the University of

Toronto, investigating sweat-shop conditions in the garment-mak-
ing industry, and knew that he could give him the assistance he
needed. After some debate in his own mind King accepted the
offer and Mulock's high opinion of him was soon confirmed. Within a few weeks of taking up his work in Ottawa he was appointed
the first deputy minister of the new department. In his eight
years in this capacity he made an enviable record for himself
in the settlement of industrial disputes, in drafting new labour
legislation, notably the Industrial Disputes Investigation Act of
1907, and in taking the initiative in scores of measures designed
to improve the lot of industrial workers. He took an active part
in many community enterprises — not in municipal politics, but
in church and cultural organizations, and in social welfare agencies.
He was one of the founders of the Canadian Club of Ottawa in
1904; he was its first vice-president and was chosen president in
the following year. The social life of the capital provided diversion
from his official duties; as an eligible and engaging young bachelor
he was always a welcome guest. But his conscience did not permit
him much idle merriment. On one day he refused about six invitations, and this was after a week that 'was like the ragged edge of
Hell, with its fringe of wasted nights'. This was only one of many
such outbursts. More satisfying to him were the many long and
high-minded talks with Henry Albert Harper, his closest friend in
university days, whom he had brought into the department soon
after its establishment. They worked together, and lived together,
until Harper's tragic death in December 1901. (In *The Secret of
Heroism*, which Mackenzie King wrote as a tribute to his friend,
he included many revealing extracts from Harper's diaries and
letters.) He was a frequent guest at Rideau Hall and he enjoyed
the friendship of Lord and Lady Minto and their daughters. With
Earl Grey, Minto's successor as Governor General, he enjoyed an
even more intimate relationship which continued long after Grey's
term of office ended. It was through Earl Grey that he met Violet
Markham, who was visiting Rideau Hall in 1905, and who was to
become one of his closest friends. Altogether, Mackenzie King

established himself in the Ottawa community as an important person, a citizen of some account — one of the most promising political figures of the time.

From early boyhood Mackenzie King had had a lively interest in politics and it was obvious from the first that this interest would thrive in the Ottawa atmosphere. Parliament had dissolved the week before he arrived and the general elections followed in November; but the new Parliament met in February and he had his first opportunity to watch proceedings from the gallery of the House of Commons. Fortunately Sir Wilfrid Laurier was the principal speaker and he was at his best. He was moving a message of condolence and loyalty to the new sovereign, King Edward VII, who had succeeded to the throne on the death of Queen Victoria on January 22. As he leaned over the gallery railing, Mackenzie King was enthralled:

> It was a beautiful oration. The language chosen with care to a word, and thought pure & deep, the theme sustained throughout, eulogy without profusion, deserved praise without fulsome flattery. He spoke without a note & really without hesitation. He did not speak very loudly, however, & to a degree seemed to have exhausted a little of his spontaneous force beforehand. I watched him before he began to speak & while calm in manner as he always is he was nevertheless like a warhorse pawing the turf for a start, ... I was greatly charmed with his reference to the rebellion [of 1837] which I fully expected was coming.

This, his first opportunity to hear Laurier in Parliament, stimulated what had long been his secret hope for a parliamentary career for himself: 'As I hung over the barrier from the upper gallery & listened to him I felt the keenest ambition to be beside him on the floor of the House.' He was not impressed by the calibre of other men in the Commons — Borden's speech was rather flat and very ordinary. There was little of real oratory to be heard, and, listening, he felt no fears as to his own abilities 'if opportunity presented to serve this country in Parliament'. But his ambition carried him farther, not only to membership in the House of

Commons, but to leadership: 'For Grandfather's sake I should like to lead, for his sake & the sake of the principles he stood for.'

Such a hope could be confided to the secret pages of his diary and nowhere else, except, perhaps, to his mother. Even to her, several months later, it was disclosed only in a whisper:

> I whispered to mother that I believed, that if opportunity came in the future I might become the Premier of this country. She pressed my hand & said nothing, then said that perhaps I might. If I ever do, or come near to such a mark, it will be to her life & her love that I have done so.

It was her ambition as well as his that he should 'carry on the work of his grandfather', that one day he should rise to the prime-ministership of Canada. This must have been in their thoughts while J. W. L. Forster was working on her portrait in front of the Kingsmere fire-place. This painting, still in the place of honour in the library at Laurier House, shows Mrs. King with a volume of Morley's *Life of Gladstone* in her lap, opened, as her son later acknowledged, at the chapter bearing the title 'Prime Minister'. It would have been folly for Mackenzie King to admit, even in private conversation, that he entertained such an ambition, but many an astute political observer, within a very few years, was to make the same prediction, sometimes to his pleased embarrassment.

II

During his years as a civil servant he nursed these aspirations but knew that, if they were ever to come to anything, much would depend upon Laurier's attitude toward him. In his years as deputy minister, particularly in the later years, he had frequent contacts with Sir Wilfrid and a genuine warmth developed in their relationship. Basically it was one of hero-worship with occasional disillusionment on the one side and, on the other, warm encouragement tempered by occasional impatience or aloofness. The year 1904 was to mark an upsurge in Mackenzie King's interest in politics as a career for himself. Any words of approval from Laurier heightened that interest, but his very sensitive nature could also magnify out of all proportion any sign of indifference. He was exceedingly unhappy, for example, when Laurier failed to make any comment on a speech he had made at the Ottawa Canadian Club in January. Sir Wilfrid had made 'a fine speech' and Mackenzie King, then vice-president of the club, had followed with a speech that 'took well' though he himself thought it lacked animation and buoyancy and that it was too earnest to elicit much applause. Robert L. Borden, then leader of the Conservative Party, had complimented him on his 'eloquent speech', but Sir Wilfrid had said nothing at the time, and when they met later downtown and in the prime minister's office there was still no comment. Silence on the subject suggested to Mackenzie King intentional slight and seemed to confirm a fear he sometimes had that Laurier felt some sort of antipathy towards him. The incident rankled in his mind for days. He wanted to keep Sir Wilfrid 'as an unshattered idol', but for the time being he felt at least a mild questioning of his hero's infallibility.

His mind had been troubled as well at this time by Sir Wilfrid's attitude toward the labour movement and its leaders. The Prime Minister did not seem to share his own sympathy with the trade union cause. One incident disturbed him. He had arranged with Sir Wilfrid to talk with A. B. Low, a leader in the trade union movement in whom he himself had great confidence. Sir Wilfrid's reception of Low was lacking in warmth, and this inclined him 'to feel that at heart Sir Wilfrid has not much sympathy with Labor. He is an aristocrat at heart, rather, I think, than a democrat in regard to this class of the community. There was not much warmth in him towards this man, and I feel that to be true of his attitude towards the wkg. classes.' As he came to know the Prime Minister better he changed his mind about Sir Wilfrid's attitude toward labour. An interview two years later, in 1906, gave him great pleasure and satisfaction because it revealed a greater sympathy with and appreciation of labour than he had expected: 'I had always felt he was a little afraid of the possible effects of demagoguery & of antagonizing Capital but I see he is a true Liberal in his belief in and willingness to *trust* the people. I am happy too in this, that it promises much for the future in the way of enabling me to count on sympathetic assistance on Sir W's part in shaping the Labor side of the Liberal program, & really effecting thro' this Gov't measures which will affect the welfare of the wkg. classes.'

Sir Wilfrid may have failed at times to say the right words of encouragement, but King's ambition was not stifled nor was his faith in himself weakened: 'I see that with patient work,' he wrote in his diary, 'I could make myself a power with which men & the nation must reckon.' One 'fault or impediment' he could admit to himself, 'the tendency to shirk the necessary work', but this obstacle could be overcome: 'I must free myself & be strong. If I do there is no position in this country I may not with reason aspire to. The lack of means seems an effectual barrier, but most of our great men have been poor.'

He spent many an hour reading Charles Lindsey's *William Lyon Mackenzie*, the story of his grandfather's life, and J. S. Willison's *Laurier and the Liberal Party*. This was stimulating reading. His faith in Liberalism was strengthened and his admiration of Laurier increased. He thought Laurier's current speeches reiterated much of what he had said earlier in his career: 'This is perhaps inevitable, once launched as a leader the day for gaining intellectual capital is past.' He applied the lesson to himself as a potential future leader: 'I must learn this, I must learn now is the time to become prepared or the day will pass & the opportunity not be known.'

William Lyon Mackenzie had always been an inspiration to him. As he reread now the record of his grandfather's fight for responsible government, he could hear the call to carry on the work Mackenzie had begun:

> Truly we are reaping the fruits of the struggles of our fathers. Few men can say that with equal truth as myself. As I read grandfather's life I feel more & more what in truth is my place & call in the history of this country. I begin to feel as in my earlier days the hand of Destiny guiding me to a Future that has been planned. There is a command clearly to carry on the tradition and the

work grandfather commenced, the welfare of the great mass of the people. One cannot but feel tho' how paltry in some ways are the obstacles we have today compared with what they were in the early times. I will seek to apply myself more & more & know that only work can secure position which is other than a false one.

In 1904 there were signs that his two major interests, labour and politics, were becoming more closely intertwined, with politics assuming increasing importance. His closeness to his minister, Sir William Mulock, enabled him on occasion to use party means to effect labour reforms, as, for example, when he pressed for a reduction of working hours for the men working on fortifications at Quebec in October 1904. With the general elections only a few weeks away, the men had demanded a nine-hour day. Mackenzie King had some qualms about having political pressure applied, but he considered that the demand of the men was fair and that they were right in choosing this time to press it. 'It is here,' he observed, 'where I think unknown to wkgm. & others I am able to serve a cause which lies at my heart in accordance with what my conscience tells me is a right purpose and act.'

It is interesting to observe the astute way in which he convinced his minister that he, Mulock, had strong labour sympathies and should regard himself as the champion of the working classes. Sir William had upheld him in his advocacy of reforms such as those which established fair wages and reduced working hours on government jobs and which curbed the abuses of the sweating system. Even though still a civil servant, Mackenzie King prepared political speeches on labour matters for his minister. It was natural that Mulock should look to his deputy minister to prepare the case for the Government. It was natural that this particular deputy should welcome the opportunity and should at the same time entertain hopes of some day shooting the ammunition which he had prepared. In his diary entry of October 19, two weeks before the 1904 general election, he wrote:

> . . . spent the morning continuing a labor speech for Sir William which I commenced yesterday. I wrote out yesterday the 'Con-

servative Record' today the record of the Liberals towards Labor.
I felt very strongly that the attitude of the Tory party had been
one of deception pure & simple, while there has been a not in-
considerable amount accomplished by the Liberals through our
Department. I wrote the Minister urging him to have on a table
before him all the documents, relating to the record on each side.
I said if I were an independent man I would resign & get out &
help him. I know he will pay no attention to this remark, which,
however, is true, but I want him to know I have before my mind
an active part in the political struggle of the future.

Sir William did pay attention to his remark and more than once
encouraged him to keep in mind a future in public life. On one
occasion they got to the point of discussing a possible constituency:

I sat by Sir Wm. after he had gone to bed in his bunk. We spoke
of North Toronto & he said he thought it could be won if a man
would live there & begin to nurse the constituency at once. I
could not help feeling he would gladly let me be the man were I
independent, & with all my heart I wished I were for that reason.
I would rather represent a Toronto constituency than any other
in prlmt.

Sir William gave him more positive encouragement in later years,
even though he had retired from the Cabinet in the fall of 1905.

III

Earl Grey, who had become Governor General in September
1904, was another source of great encouragement to him in his
political aspirations. It was not Earl Grey, however, or Sir William
Mulock, but Sir Wilfrid Laurier, who had to be moved to action
to enable him to enter Parliament. That one step would be enough
for him at the moment; he would be content if he could be started
on his way to the higher goal. Mackenzie King had yet to learn,
however, that it was 'hard to get Sir Wilfrid to move quickly'. On
a later occasion he remarked to Earl Grey, and Earl Grey agreed
with him, that 'as a politician Sir W. sometimes waited for the
events themselves' (meaning the difficulties were often solved

in the interval, or the occasion postponed itself indefinitely). He could not have described more accurately one of his own favourite techniques to be used in later years as prime minister, when he found that time could remove barriers, solve problems, and heal wounds. Another lesson he learned ultimately — and Sir Wilfrid was giving him his first lesson now — was that a prime minister cannot afford to play favourites if he would hold his colleagues together.

Mackenzie King did not much like the idea of plans for his own future being 'postponed indefinitely'. As for the leadership of the party, that was still a secret ambition and he was willing enough to 'wait for the event itself'. It was written in the stars, he believed, that he should enter Parliament, but he was not always able to resist the impulse to hasten the inevitable. In the meantime, however, he was determined to prepare himself in every way for the high honour which he hoped would come to him. He could be painfully aware of his own shortcomings and of the necessity of stern self-discipline. Birthdays and New Year's Days were often occasions for spiritual or moral inventories and new resolves. On his thirtieth birthday he wrote:

> I would like to play a useful part in my country's affairs and on behalf of the mass of the people who make up the nation. I have tried to work faithfully and to think clearly and to abstain from levity in any form, but it has been hard to keep true to this purpose.

Such moments of introspection and self-reproach were many, but moods of self-confidence and ambition were even more frequent. His impatience with Sir Wilfrid's unwillingness to act quickly on his behalf was the occasion for many a disparaging word in his diary. It was all very well for Sir Wilfrid to offer encouragement, to approve in general terms of a political career; but Mackenzie King wanted something more specific. His heart, in fact, was set on three things: a seat in Parliament, the appointment of a minister of labour holding no other portfolio,* and a place in the Cabinet for himself as minister of labour. His still higher ambition was something which he wisely refrained from discussing with Sir Wilfrid at this stage.

He felt more than a glimmering of hope after a long talk he had with Sir Wilfrid on November 4, 1905. He was greeted by the Prime Minister 'in a most friendly way'. He told Sir Wilfrid frankly that he contemplated leaving the Civil Service and if possible entering politics in the near future, if opportunity should offer. He spoke of attractive offers he had received from the United States, but added that he was not anxious to leave, in fact had no thought of leaving, and was determined to stay in Canada. When Sir Wilfrid asked him if he had thought out any plans for himself he hesitated to suggest them lest they might seem too presumptuous. They probably were, for a thirty-year-old civil servant, but he went on to propose, in effect, that the Department of Labour should be made a separate department with a separate minister, that he should be that minister, and that this could be effected by certain readjustments within the Cabinet. Sir Wilfrid listened sympathetically and at the end of this talk remarked that Earl Grey had been right in his comment that 'that young man should be in politics'. There would be difficulties, but they were not insurmountable. It was a great satisfaction to hear Sir Wilfrid say that he was most pleased to know of his willingness to enter public life, but it was infinitely more pleasing to have him add that it would be in the Cabinet that he would want him, and that that would be the real purpose of his entering Parliament. It seemed to King for a moment that his highest hopes would soon be realized. 'I felt pretty tired,' he wrote in his diary at the end of the day, 'but relieved at the new outlook. It is the beginning of a life of work.' To his mother he wrote: 'The interview was all that you or I could wish for and beyond our best hopes. I will tell you all when I see

---

* The postmaster general was also the minister of labour.

you. Suffice it to say at present that from this hour I begin *my political career.*'

IV

Unfortunately things did not work out as planned; Cabinet re-arrangements were not easy to make. Talks with Sir Wilfrid continued, sometimes inspiring hope but more often leading him to believe that it would be better to rely on destiny than on the Prime Minister.

The story of the next two years and more was one of a series of frustrations and postponements, Mackenzie King proposing and Sir Wilfrid disposing. Cabinet shifts were under consideration early in 1906 and King again suggested that his appointment as minister of a separate department of labour would be natural since he had virtually managed it throughout. Sir Wilfrid, surprisingly enough, said he agreed with this but closed the conversation by saying that he 'wd. have the pleasure of talking over the matter again'. It was another postponement, and King began to think he would have to take matters in hand himself, counting on neither Sir Wilfrid nor on destiny:

> My feelings as a result of this interview are that I must watch matters, deliberately get to work to secure this end by legitimate means, not trust to Destiny tho' it may be on my side. . . . Sir Wilfrid may not be forgetful & is not indifferent, but has men pressing him on all sides. By keeping before him in the right way my chances will be improved. I believe public life is to be my lot. I believe that God's purpose in my life is to help to work out His Will in the world in this way. I must seek to realize the greatness of the task, the service to be rendered such a master.

He was still hopeful, indeed confident, that the way to Parliament and to the Cabinet would be opened up at any time: 'It is beginning to look as tho' only a Destiny would determine the end, and this I seem to feel will be so.' That was written at the beginning of February. Six weeks later he felt that within a week or ten days he would know what the future would be. Hopes were still high in September, when he expected that soon he would be 'in the vortex of political life'. But in April things were still in the same state of uncertainty, even though Sir Wilfrid, when he had spoken to him of an attractive offer he had received from Harvard University, told him 'not to think of it, that a man with the blood I had in my veins, my talents, etc. had a great future in this country and that I would be lost as a professor, even if I did write books.'

v

Despite Sir Wilfrid's assurances nothing definite was to come of them until well on in 1908. The intervening period was one of exceptional non-political activity, a period of brilliant achievement in settling serious labour disputes, in drafting the Industrial Disputes Investigation Act and other legislation, and in conducting delicate diplomatic negotiations with other countries on Oriental immigration and related problems. These activities might well have diverted his thoughts from his own political objectives, and to some extent they did. His achievements in these fields, however, served his political ends in bringing his name before the Canadian public in a very favourable light, in impressing Sir Wilfrid Laurier anew with his outstanding qualifications, in confirming his confidence in himself as one who could hold his own in dealing with highly qualified political leaders and with complicated issues, and in reassuring himself that 'Destiny' was on his side. Sir Wilfrid's relations with him were more cordial than they had been, but the Prime Minister was still non-committal on the personal issues which Mackenzie King considered vital. Sir Wilfrid must have considered King impatient and King definitely did think Laurier evasive. He was happy to be sent to England in September 1906 to negotiate measures which would prevent strike-breakers from being sent to Canada, even though such a mission meant a long absence from Ottawa. On his mission to England he had commented on his return:

There is no doubt that politically this step is a good one — & it is good politically because good in itself. It is in the interests of justice & fair play, especially to the working classes in both countries. I cannot but feel gratified at the mark of confidence on the part of the Govt. which this is. I am not yet 32, & to be sent to Great Britain to interview the British Ministers, with a view to securing the enactment of legislation at Westminster, & to go as a representative of Canada is a matter of pardonable pride.

VI

No sooner was he home from his English trip than he was forced again to leave Ottawa, this time for a trip to Western Canada to settle a serious coal-mining dispute in the Lethbridge area. On his return he reported to Sir Wilfrid the satisfactory settlement of the strike and received from him instructions, not that he needed them, to go ahead with the drafting of a measure for compulsory investigation. This ultimately took the form of the well-known Industrial Disputes Investigation Act, the drafting of which occupied him throughout the Christmas holidays.

These talks with Sir Wilfrid opened up opportunities for discussions of political affairs. Sir Wilfrid continued to encourage him to think of the possibility of entering public life and mentioned several possible constituencies. As for his ultimate appointment to the Cabinet, that seemed now to be almost taken for granted. To hasten matters Mackenzie King made an unusual proposal: that he might be taken into the Cabinet as a minister without portfolio and given the Department of Labour without salary. Sir Wilfrid agreed that the labour problem was the great question; that it needed to be handled by a man who understood it; that he, Aylesworth, or Lemieux could not master it with all they had to do; that only one like himself who had given years of study to it could hope to do so. The talk was inconclusive, but encouraging. It was no wonder that Mackenzie King felt he was on 'the threshold of a noble and useful life of public service and endeavour'. His diary entry on New Year's Day confirmed this expectation:

> Before this year is out I expect to be in public life — it will be a
> strenuous year whatever comes, but I am prepared to leave all in
> the hands of the Almighty, who has His own plan & work for me
> to do.

In the summer of 1907 rumours were circulating that Mackenzie
King might shortly be taken into the Cabinet, a step which the
Ottawa correspondent of the Toronto *News* referred to as necessary because of the dearth of Cabinet material in Parliament. It
was unfortunate for Mackenzie King that the dispatch from
Ottawa, so generous in its references to himself, should have dis-
paraged at least three of Laurier's older ministers from Ontario,
men who in the opinion of many had outlived their usefulness.
Naturally the incident aroused much resentment and jealousy.
Adverse feeling was so strong amongst the ministers concerned,
as well as others who hoped to be ministers, that Sir Wilfrid had to
tell Mackenzie King that it would raise a rebellion in the House if
he took him into the Cabinet just then. Mackenzie King saw the
position clearly but was not utterly crushed. Recognizing that
immediate appointment to the Cabinet was out of the question, he
told Sir Wilfrid that he was not seeking a Cabinet position till he
could demonstrate his fitness for it, and repeated his idea that at
the next session Labour might be made a separate department, with
himself as minister. Sir Wilfrid would not give such an undertaking but said he would continue to favour his entry into Parliament,
where he would be able to demonstrate his fitness. He reminded
him that there would be many chances for speaking in debate,
'that in the House of Commons it did not take a man very long to
find his level, he was either up or down very soon after the start,
that unless I belied all that he expected & my friends believed of
me, & my past record I wd. come to the front rapidly'. Sir Wilfrid
would welcome him as a private member, would assist in securing
a constituency; more than that, he said he would bring on a by-
election in North Oxford if arrangements could be made to have

the seat declared vacant. That would make it unnecessary to wait until the next general election, which would probably be called late in 1908. It looked then as though he might be in Parliament, though not, of course, in the Cabinet, within a few weeks!

VII

Accepting Sir Wilfrid's advice to find his own level in the House before taking on the responsibilities of a Cabinet minister, he argued within himself:

> My best course is certainly not to have preferment till I have demonstrated my worth, till I can get it without the asking and till men in fact will ask of me to accept it. My belief in myself leads me to hope that this will some day be realized. The public will admire me for the courage & spirit I shew in sacrificing a certainty for a great uncertainty at a time when the horizon is dark. No single thing I could do could help me more ... it would be folly in other ways to go into the Cabinet even if a chance offered at once. I know very little about general politics. I have not followed even the newspapers as I should. I know nothing about procedure in the House. I am freer as a member to speak my mind, without considering the necessary restraints of the Ministry, I am not the object of such bitter attack, I can have more leisure — which is the wealth I am most in need of, — time to read, to reflect, to prepare, I can become acquainted with the members of the House, and be master of my time & opportunities as I never could otherwise. Altogether I have reason to thank the Providence which removed the temptation of office. Were it present it might — probably would be seized as a prize, against my own better judgment.

He was not losing sight of the leading role which he was determined to play ultimately, but he was content for the moment with the humbler part of private member, or with the prospect of it.

He had felt strongly for a long time that younger men were needed in Ontario's representation in the Cabinet, but when to some extent this need was met by the appointment of George Graham, aged forty-eight, as minister of railways and canals, he

realized that his own chances of immediate preferment were thereby lessened. From that time on, Graham was to take charge of
party organization matters in Ontario and it was he, rather than
Laurier, who would have to continue the delicate negotiations
which might lead to the nomination for North Oxford.

VIII

He still had warm personal contacts with Sir Wilfrid and Lady
Laurier and made fairly frequent visits to their home. On one such
occasion Lady Laurier had invited him to noonday dinner on a
Sunday with, as their only other guest, a charming and wealthy
young widow whom Sir Wilfrid had decided on as 'the right girl'
for Mackenzie King. It was obviously a match-making venture on
the part of host and hostess. It turned out to be a disappointment to
them, and even though Sir Wilfrid followed up afterwards with
very pointed advice and the point-blank question: 'Why don't you
get married?' he failed in his self-appointed mission. Here, however, was an illustration of the close personal relations that existed
between the two men, the fatherly and friendly interest of the
older man, nearing the end of his political career, in the personal
life of a promising young man approaching a new career in politics,
if indeed that career had not already begun. The diary entry that
night revealed how warmly the affection was reciprocated:

> When I came back to the office tonight I knelt down by my desk
> and . . . remembered in prayer . . . the old Chief Sir Wilfrid, who
> has been like a father to me. . . . As to the choosing of a wife my
> heart alone must control that absolutely. I pray that God may
> guide me in the choice, and order all things to His own best end.
> I have faith that he will.

IX

More interested in political than in matrimonial prospects, Mackenzie King had spent most of that day talking with ministers and
others about ways and means of entering public life. From Rod-

olphe Lemieux (then postmaster general and also minister of labour) he learned that Sir Wilfrid had intimated to him that it was his intention to take him (King) into the Cabinet, perhaps at the end of the session, or at most in a year or two, that he ought to be minister of labour. Lemieux reported that Sir Wilfrid had said that he regarded King as 'a born politician', that he had never presented any situation to him that he had not been able to face squarely or circumvent effectively. Sir Wilfrid, he added, could not have spoken more highly.

When Sir William Mulock was told by King that he was thinking of North Oxford as a constituency, Mulock encouraged him; he was as pleased as if he were his own son, and prophesied that some day he would be premier of Canada. Other friends, notably Senator Robert Jaffray, J. F. MacKay, and J. A. Macdonald, all of the Toronto *Globe*, interested themselves in the North Oxford proposal, but to no avail. The chief stumbling-block, according to George Graham, was the opposition of the older Ontario ministers who could not forget the Toronto *News* article and its odious comparison of Mackenzie King's youth with their advanced years. Sir Wilfrid had to agree that North Oxford was out of the question. It was a deep disappointment to Mackenzie King; he was inclined to feel that 'everything is up'. He planned, however, to hold on, 'smile at misfortune (which I cannot do) & wait patiently for other chances'.

Another chance came soon when a Toronto group pressed him to accept the nomination for East Toronto or West Toronto. King thought the risks were too great, and Sir Wilfrid agreed with him. He told the Toronto men that King was 'too good a man to be slaughtered'. He must, he added, be given a safe seat: 'I want King in Parliament.'

The possibility of the leadership of the Liberal opposition in Ontario was mooted in September. It was only newspaper rumour, but Mackenzie King thought that while in one way this kind of notoriety was objectionable, such references might do some good: 'I have no doubt if I wanted it, I would have little difficulty in securing financial aid toward going into Ont. politics with the hope of ultimate leadership from the start, tho' to be the chosen leader at the outset is absurd & out of the question. Even if offered, it would have no attractions or temptations as against my present work for the Dominion & present prospects there.'

x

Opportunities to further his political interests were more or less neglected in the latter part of 1907 and the early part of 1908 because of the pressure of official duties, including the inquiry into working conditions of telephone operators in Toronto, and an inquiry, again as a royal commissioner, into anti-Asiatic riots in British Columbia. His interest in and experience with problems of Oriental immigration had led him far afield — conferences in Washington with President Theodore Roosevelt and members of his Cabinet, followed by a diplomatic mission to England in which he conveyed to Lord Morley, Sir Edward Grey, and others, messages from the President of the United States, and discussed with them aspects of the Oriental immigration problem which were of grave concern to the two countries as well as to Canada. While this experience, lasting many weeks, kept him away from the Canadian political scene, it added to his stature in the opinion of Sir Wilfrid and his colleagues. It meant publicity, too, which enhanced his reputation in the country, and this in turn had the effect of heightening his political prospects.

On his return to Ottawa Mackenzie King immediately reopened the question of a constituency. They discussed several possible ridings (some that were quite impossible) and finally Sir Wilfrid asked 'What about North Waterloo? ... I would advise you to resign [from the Civil Service] & take the plunge.' Mackenzie King thought well of the proposal but wanted to talk it over first with Clifford Sifton, in whose judgment at that time he had great faith. Sifton had been one of the most forceful of the members of the ministry Laurier had formed in 1896. King noted in his diary at this time that he had found Sifton 'a splendid man to work with, he is so positive & direct & has force, & courage. I feel that Sir Wilfrid is looking to him as his successor & it may not be long after the elections.' Sifton had other ridings to suggest — East Hamilton for one and Ontario North for another — but eventually he agreed that North Waterloo should be the choice.

XI

Sir Wilfrid still balked at committing himself to the Department of Labour idea, something Mackenzie King could not understand: 'Sir Wilfrid I cannot make out,' he wrote. 'He is personally very friendly. . . . I cannot tell whether he is playing me along to keep me where I am, or not.' If Laurier could only see his way to establish the separate department, Mackenzie King was sure he could carry either North Waterloo or East Hamilton, but he feared that Laurier would not yield: 'I can only rely on the Unseen Hand to guide me,' he commented in his diary. The very next entry, however, might have been written in red letters: 'The Unseen Hand has revealed itself and the Prime Minister has said that he will make the Dept. of Labor a separate department of the Govt.' One of his objectives had been achieved. It was the signal for a new release of energy and a decision: 'North Waterloo is the place for me . . . a good fight in a Tory stronghold will win for me the respect of men on both sides of politics.' Sir Wilfrid was delighted, felt confident of the result, and added his blessing: 'You will come to the front at once, you will take a great part from the start, you have the instinct for politics, I know what I am saying.'

Announcement of his intention to go into public life led many friends to question the wisdom of contesting North Waterloo. His Conservative opponent, Joe Seagram, had held the seat since 1896 and it was common talk that Seagram's money and Seagram's whisky presented an unbeatable combination. He himself, tired out almost to the point of nervous exhaustion, experienced a conflict of emotions that ranged from downright fear and temptation to withdraw, to firm confidence that he would come back and be the minister: 'Only as I feel that I am fighting God's battle here below do I feel any happiness in the prospect & endeavour; as I think on the contest itself & public life with its "interminable glare" I shrink with horror from it all. It is repellent in a thousand ways. I feel I shall rejoice whatever the outcome, the step had to be & it will be well over. . . . But I believe I will come back & be the Minister & the work should then be greater than ever.'

The official telegram tendering the nomination reached him on September 21: 'It brought a momentary flow of joy — just a moment then the great depression set in . . . when I get into the fight I expect it to disappear. It is foolish for me to waver or to suffer as I do, had I known I wd. feel the weight of the uncertainty so great I wd. never have entered. But I believe it is all for the best and I leave on the morrow to begin a five weeks' struggle which I firmly believe will mean victory in the end.'

Once into the struggle, Mackenzie King spent five weeks of strenuous campaigning, visiting every village and hamlet in the riding, talking with old friends and making new ones, ringing doorbells, appearing at church teas and other social functions, and, of course, making speeches at every opportunity — he was in his element there. Sir Wilfrid's presence in the riding was a triumph, a high-water mark. All did turn out to be for the best. On October 26, he was elected Member of Parliament for North Waterloo with a majority of 263 votes. Sir Wilfrid was delighted, told him that he regarded his fight in North Waterloo as the most spectacular of the whole campaign, that it would have been a thousand pities if he had not gone into politics, that he had a great future in Parliament.

XII

Sir Wilfrid had assured Mackenzie King that it was his intention to put through the Department of Labour legislation at the first session and that he 'would have to do with the new Dept.'. Neither

move could be made, of course, until after he took his seat in
Parliament. Since Parliament would probably be opened in January, that seemed to be reasonable enough. Other things happened,
however, which made it necessary to postpone all three objectives.
Mackenzie King had been nominated a member of the British
delegation to the International Opium Commission to be held in
Shanghai in February 1909. Asiatic immigration to Canada was also
a problem that could be dealt with effectively only by personal
discussions with heads of government of the three countries principally involved, and with representatives of the British Government. Because of his previous experience in this field Mackenzie
King was marked as the right man for such a mission. It was a
marvellous opportunity for a young man, but for some time he
demurred, feeling that a long absence from Canada might adversely
affect his political future. It would mean also the postponement of
his entry into the Cabinet, for Laurier insisted that he must take
his seat in Parliament before being called to the Ministry. He finally
yielded, however, after Sir Wilfrid's assurance and Earl Grey's
urging.

Broadening his mission to include a visit to India was urged by
Earl Grey, but Sir Wilfrid questioned the necessity of it. Some
discussion ensued between them, and the Governor General won
his point. Sir Wilfrid paid a compliment to Mackenzie King when
he told Earl Grey that he wished they could divide him in half,
send one half to China and keep the other in Canada. It was decided
finally that both halves should go to India as well as to China and
Japan.

This trip around the world, which lasted nearly five months (he
left Ottawa on December 14 and returned on May 9), meant that
the newly-elected Member of Parliament missed all but a few days
of the 1909 parliamentary session. From Mackenzie King's point
of view, this investment of time, this further venture into the field
of external affairs, would pay rich dividends in the future. He had
already made a name for himself as a conciliator in industrial disputes; he was now being given another opportunity to show his

mettle as a conciliator in the larger field of international affairs. He performed in his new role with conspicuous success, securing inter-governmental agreements that were acceptable to all concerned.

XIII

Mackenzie King took his seat in the Commons immediately after his return, but it was not for another ten days, on the last day of the session, May 19, that the Prime Minister introduced a bill to create a portfolio of Minister of Labour. He found the days of waiting intensely embarrassing: he was being talked of and greeted as a minister of the Crown before the event. A natural feeling of elation was tempered by his awareness of an undercurrent of envy or jealousy. There were evidences of marked friendliness on the part of some ministers and some members, but his sensitive nature could detect a feeling of disappointment on the part of some that a much younger man was to supersede them and on the part of others that their chances of preferment were being diminished. At last, however, the great day came, June 2, and he was sworn as a member of the Privy Council and Minister of Labour, the highest-but-one of his life's ambitions.

As a new member and a new minister, he made few speeches in the House in his first session. Parliament opened in November 1909 and prorogued in the following May. The most controversial measure of the session was the government's Naval Bill. He had given some thought to the question and believed strongly that Canada should have a navy of her own. Listening with admiration to brilliant speeches by Laurier and Lemieux, he felt a keen desire to take part in the debate himself. He spent the rest of the night and the next morning 'thinking over arguments' and felt prepared to make 'a telling speech'. He believed that the argument for naval defence would have greater force coming from him than from others, for he was the grandson of a rebel and two-thirds of his constituents were of German descent. He held back, however, concerned about what other members of the Government would think of a new and young colleague taking so important a part. They might be alarmed at the outset, but they did not know what he could do, and he was sure they would be pleased and satisfied when he had concluded. Laurier's advice, when he was consulted, was to be prepared but to wait and see. His speech on naval defence was not made in Parliament, but there were to be other opportunities to use his material on the platform and in the House of Commons at the next session.

He had less compunction about addressing the House, as Minister of Labour, on the subject of technical education, although some of his colleagues questioned the wisdom of the federal government taking any action on a matter that came primarily within the jurisdiction of the provinces. 'My purpose,' he recorded, 'was to make a speech which would *compel* the Government to do something, and I succeeded.' The visible evidence of his success was the establishment of a Royal Commission on Industrial Training and Technical Education.

Of even greater length and greater importance were the speeches he made on the Combines Investigation Bill, which he had drafted in 1909 and which he piloted through the Commons in 1910. In this he had Sir Wilfrid's warm support, but only a grudging acquiescence from W. S. Fielding, Minister of Finance, and some of his other colleagues. The bill was an attempt to curb the current rapid growth of business mergers and monopolies believed to be responsible, in part at least, for the alarming increases in the cost of living that were occasioning much public concern. King had already instituted an extensive inquiry into wholesale prices, and the results, published in 1910, represented the first of a series of statistical studies that led eventually to the establishment of the Dominion Bureau of Statistics.

He had taken the initiative also in other matters that required legislative action. In 1911 he was responsible for the enactment of a measure to prevent the importation, sale, or use of opium other than for scientific or medicinal purposes. Another bill that he sponsored in 1911 was designed to prohibit the manufacture and importation of matches made with white phosphorus, an ingredient

which menaced the health of the workers. The bill was passed by
the Commons but did not reach the stage of final enactment before
Parliament was dissolved (it was put through ultimately by the
Borden Government, in 1914). An eight-hour-day bill to apply
to labour engaged on federal public works was introduced in
1911, but too late in the session to receive royal assent, and
federal legislation on the subject was postponed for years. Altogether his two years in Parliament provided an impressive record
of imaginative planning and substantial accomplishment.

The periods between sessions — the so-called parliamentary
recesses — were not periods of relaxation. Settlement of the Grand
Trunk Railway strike in 1910, for example, the most serious strike
situation in years, had been effected only after weeks of protracted
and exasperating negotiation. He had taken time, too, to participate
actively in international conferences in Europe on uniformity of
labour legislation, social insurance, technical education, and unemployment. He took very seriously his responsibilities as a member
of the Cabinet and was gradually winning the confidence of colleagues many years his senior who had sometimes questioned
Laurier's wisdom in bringing him forward so rapidly. He did not
offend by too vigorous assertion of his own views, but he expressed
himself freely and firmly when he felt strongly on subjects under
discussion. For example, he was forthright in his disagreement with
W. S. Fielding, when Fielding spoke out in Council against a
proposal to have Canada represented in Washington by a Canadian,
rather than by the British ambassador. He thought Sir Wilfrid had
made a mistake in inclining too much to Fielding's view. He was
anticipating a policy of later years when he advocated separate
representation, and he now expressed the hope that the day would
soon come when Canada would have its own representation in
every important country of the world.

XIV

Of all the Cabinet meetings Mackenzie King attended, none raised
questions of more serious portent than that of January 18, 1911.

On that day Fielding presented to Council his first draft of a reciprocal trade agreement with the United States. To most of his colleagues it appeared to present an issue that would be received enthusiastically by the Canadian electorate. Mackenzie King questioned the wisdom of the reciprocity proposals, but as a junior member of Council did not assert himself as energetically as he felt later he should have done; he had assumed that 'everything was about concluded'. He did raise objections, however, on the first day the subject was discussed: 'I spoke out strongly about the danger to Ont. of interfering with mffrs., said that certainly I for one wd. not be returned if we did, & that there was danger in many cities.'

His private thoughts after the Council meeting were along the same lines: 'I must frankly confess I see great danger in whole tariff negotiations at this time. Americans will be lowering tariffs anyway.... I question if we will satisfy the farmers & we may prejudice other interests to the extent of suffering defeat at their hands ... well enough had better be left alone.... If we can get a few natural products free each way well & good, but it is questionable touching mffrs. to any extent.'

Fielding resumed negotiations with Washington and the following week reported that an agreement had been reached. In Council the consensus was that it was 'a most exceptional one for the Dominion, while it was likely to prove equally advantageous to the United States'. Some ministers, including Mackenzie King, felt badly about specific items, from which individuals rather than communities would suffer, but 'taken in a broad way it was believed the agreement wd. be hailed with satisfaction by the country with its free fish for N.S. & B.C., free hay for Quebec, free fruits & vegetables & wheat etc. for the West, free lumber for B.C. & Quebec & Ont.'

Canadian concessions in the way of tariff reductions on manufactured products were exceedingly moderate. The Government had presented a policy which even in Sir John A. Macdonald's time would have been accepted by the Conservative Party. The agreement which Fielding had negotiated would open a market in the United States for Canadian natural products without giving Canadian manufacturers any legitimate and substantial ground for complaint. Even the Conservative opposition in 1911 welcomed it when it was tabled on January 26. 'But suddenly,' to quote from O. D. Skelton, 'the mood changed. Mild assent changed to question, question to criticism, and criticism to a storm of denunciation and fierce attack. Party spirit and party hopes had rallied, lines of attack had opened, a chance of victory had gleamed. What was more to the point, the industrial and financial and railway interests had taken alarm and determined to fight the agreement with every resource in their power. Manufacturers, though for the most part untouched, feared the thin edge of the wedge. Railway magnates dreaded breaks in their long east and west hauls. Bankers, intimately linked by their directorates and their loans with both manufacturer and railway, threw their weight into the same scale.'

Opposition became more ominous when Clifford Sifton again broke with Laurier and assailed the reciprocity programme with all the vigour he could command. His denunciations were particularly effective in Ontario, where he enlisted the support of eighteen Torontonians, 'all eminent in the world of finance, and all attached or semi-detached Liberals'. 'To the Conservatives,' as Arthur R. M. Lower put it, 'his support was worth a battalion.' Sir Wilfrid credited him with being 'the real campaign manager' — not Robert L. Borden, who was still the head of the Conservative Party. It was common talk, too, that Sifton had inspired the 'no-popery' cry in Ontario, a whispering campaign against a French and Roman Catholic premier.

Extreme bitterness marked every stage of the seven-weeks-long campaign that ended on September 21. Money was spent lavishly, but the Opposition, supported as it was by the wealth of manufacturing and financial interests opposed to reciprocity, outmatched Liberal financial resources by three to one. The bogey of annexation by the United States had its influence, as did the waving of the Union Jack and the battle-cry, 'No truck nor trade with the

Yankees.' The Government, supremely confident in July, found itself very much on the defensive in September. It was becoming apparent, particularly in Conservative Ontario, that the swing was definitely and strongly against the reciprocity programme.

Even in Quebec, always a Liberal stronghold, things went badly for the Government. Here it was not because of opposition to freer trade with the United States (in Quebec that was a minor issue). Henri Bourassa summoned all his fiery eloquence to arouse nationalistic feeling in his province against Laurier's naval service policy. The Conservatives had opposed it in the Commons on the ground that it would weaken the bonds of empire. Bourassa now assailed it as a measure that would involve Canada in wars of Britain's making; he could foresee French-Canadian boys being conscripted to man Canadian-built ships for British purposes, serving under British — and presumably Protestant — captains. Thus Laurier and the Liberal Party had to do battle with two forces representing in themselves opposing interests, the unholy alliance of Nationalists in Quebec and Conservative imperialists in the rest of the country.

In his own constituency of North Waterloo, Mackenzie King was carrying on a lone battle against prodigious odds. He was fighting alone, for none of his colleagues in the Government and none of his fellow-members in the House could spare time from their own ridings to give him help; they were fighting for their own lives, their political lives. He was more generous than they in the matter of time, for he yielded, much too readily for his own good, to their calls for assistance. He was recognized as one of the Government's most effective speakers, and he took seriously his new obligations as a Cabinet minister. Within the seven weeks he addressed meetings in seventeen other ridings. Within North Waterloo he conducted a vigorous campaign, but that constituency, unfortunately for him in this election, was a centre of manufacturing industries and the anti-reciprocity propaganda had a strong appeal. But there was another adverse influence he had to reckon with, difficult to deal with because it could not be brought into the open field of controversy. That was the thinly veiled hostility of a large part of the German population of his riding to the Government's naval policy. They knew this was part of Canada's programme to assist Britain in meeting what was even then regarded as Germany's challenge to British naval supremacy; they could not believe there was any ground for fearing Germany's intentions. Mackenzie King had thus to contend with issues that had been non-existent in the 1908 campaign; his majority then had been only a modest one. Under other circumstances, and with other issues, including his own record, victory with a much increased majority should have been a certainty. He was now at the peak of his prestige in the party and in the country, with a brilliant record of achievement behind him and a glowing future ahead. If he himself and the Liberal Party were returned to power, a position of leadership, though not *the* leadership, would be well within his reach and indeed his grasp. But there were two other possibilities. One was personal victory but coupled with party defeat: this would dim his own hopes without extinguishing them but would be a crushing blow to Laurier and Liberalism. The other possibility, defeat for both the party and himself, a fate too dreadful to contemplate, would mean that he himself as well as the party would be cast into outer, and utter, darkness. Excitement ran high and forebodings were many. In the end, on September 21, it was the electorate of Canada and of North Waterloo who made the fateful decision. On that day the voice of the people decreed the overthrow in Canada of the Laurier government and, in North Waterloo, the fall of Mackenzie King.

CHAPTER 2

A Futile Search
for a Seat in Parliament

Mackenzie King's first recorded reaction to the defeat of September 1911 was one of relief from strain; his second reaction, a desire to return to the fight. These seemingly contradictory sentiments were expressed in the same entry in his diary, written in Toronto on the Sunday after the election:

> The sense of relief from the strain of office is almost indescribable. It is the first time for years that I feel as I used to feel when I came first into the civil service. I cannot but believe that defeat is all for the best, and that out of this will come opportunities of a fuller & better life.

Out of his mixed feelings the fighting spirit surged to the top: 'I must confess defeat has made me feel more like fighting than ever, I do not experience any feeling of ingratitude on the part of the people — ignorance and viciousness yes plenty of both, & that is the sad part but points more clearly the need.' Understandably, he was tired after such a strenuous but unsuccessful campaign, but he was determined to make the best of what he hoped would be only a temporary retirement, to prepare for an even more strenuous future. He thought of this in terms of study and travel but realized that even a few months spent in this way would cost money. His funds were low and his income as a Cabinet minister and Member of Parliament was cut off immediately. The solution seemed to be relatively easy — a seat in Parliament:

> If I can get a seat in Parliament I feel that to be the wise thing to do. With the little I have saved, I could get along with the indemnity [it was then $2,500] and have time for reading and study, that seems to me the wisest of all courses.

He had good reason for feeling confident that a seat could be found for him without difficulty: his record in the Department of Labour had brought strength to the administration, he had proven himself in the complex field of international negotiations, had acquitted himself creditably as a minister in the Commons, and, perhaps above all, had done more than any other minister to inject fighting spirit into his Ontario colleagues in the bitter campaign in that province. Surely now, he thought, he was entitled to special consideration — only a word from Sir Wilfrid to one of the newly elected members would open the way to his return to Parliament. There would be difficulty in Ontario because only thirteen of the eighty-five elected members were Liberals, but some successful candidate outside the province, particularly in the West, might be persuaded to resign and thus create a vacancy.

Four days after the election the first meeting of the defeated Cabinet was held. Sir Wilfrid was then in his seventieth year. He had stated positively at St. Jerome, towards the close of the campaign, that if defeated he would retire. The shattered condition of the party, however, and the all but unanimous demand of his supporters compelled reconsideration. Even though Sir Wilfrid went through the formality of tendering his resignation to the party caucus, he had already decided to carry on. No one else in the party could 'get it together'. Sir Wilfrid knew that, and so did the loyal group of counsellors who surrounded him after the battle, to recapitulate, to commiserate — and to plan future strategy. No leader comes out of a losing battle with undamaged prestige, or with the same unreserved confidence of officers and men as he had enjoyed in hours of victory. There was still confidence, but not without some reservations. In Sir Wilfrid's view the issue of race and religion had counted more than the issue of reciprocity. He said he thought the 'Ne Temere' decree and the Eucharistic Congress incident were largely responsible for his defeat in Ontario. (The 'Ne Temere' decree was a declaration by the Roman Catholic Church that in Quebec it had the right to annul mixed marriages. Coupled with it in the public mind was the appearance, at the Eucharistic Congress in Quebec, of the Speaker of the House of Commons and a judge of the Supreme Court of Canada in their robes of office. This was an affront to every Orangeman in the province of Ontario, a justification in their minds of the 'no-popery' whispering campaign.) Sir Wilfrid held to this view in all the post-mortem discussions, though he had to agree with Mackenzie King and most of his colleagues that money and the manufacturers had had much to do with the ultimate result.

II

Sir Wilfrid's first question was: 'How are we to get our ranks refilled? I want my old colleagues back in the House with me,' and he mentioned, by name, Fielding, Fisher, Graham, and Mackenzie King, all of whom had been defeated. Inclusion of his own name was encouraging to King. It was encouraging, too, to know that Sir Wilfrid had now decided against withdrawal. If this announced decision of Laurier's was welcome, his next remark was not, for Sir Wilfrid added, almost as if it were a foregone conclusion, that George Graham would have to succeed him as Leader of the Opposition. In mentioning Graham as his probable successor, Sir Wilfrid was not anticipating any immediate change, but was looking to the future. He added: 'A French Catholic can never again be premier.' When some of his colleagues protested he replied, 'No, in Ontario I am the original sin for which there is no baptism — only a Protestant could win.'

No one would have been more surprised than King, had Laurier mentioned him, rather than Graham, as a probable successor. (His older associates in the Cabinet would have been stunned.) Yet he could not repress a flash of resentment when Laurier expressed this preference for Graham. He would have resented less — indeed he might have welcomed — hearing Fielding suggested, or even Fisher; for one thing, they were both in their early sixties and their tenure of office would not be long. He was their junior by about twenty-five years, and he respected their maturity, their integrity, their serious mien, and their long experience in Parliament; he could gladly serve under the leadership of either, as long as might be necessary. But he had never held Graham in the same esteem, and could hardly tolerate the idea of serving under him. Graham, at fifty-two, was fifteen years older than himself, but he had been in the Cabinet only two years longer, and there had always been an element of rivalry in their relationship.

King knew that Laurier's reference to Graham was not a considered and final judgment: Laurier might think differently later on, and so might Graham. Indeed, Graham, only a few days later, told his colleagues that he had received an offer of the presidency of the Travelers Insurance Company at a substantial salary, that he had felt like dropping out of politics, but that when he saw 'the old man' holding on as he was, he did not have the heart to tell him. Mackenzie King questioned Graham's sincerity in making such statements; he was certain he was holding on because he had the leadership of the party in view. Laurier, too, had had second thoughts, as King was pleased to gather from a conversation a few weeks later: 'He doubted if George Graham could hold the party together — This is ... the first time he has indicated less faith in Graham. Heretofore it has been to have Graham succeed him, but he is finding out that this is not in accord with the views of many.' Of the 'many' who objected to Graham's candidature, three (Lemieux, A. K. Maclean, and W. T. R. Preston) expressed themselves strongly at a dinner party at Lemieux's early in 1912:

> I was surprised to hear Lemieux say he wd. not follow Graham as a leader, that there was a strong sentiment against him as not serious enough. Preston was strong against him. Later tonight

Maclean, M.P. speaking privately to me, was strong against him,
& gave what I thought a proper estimate of Pardee — he referred
to his bad manners, blustering way & being merely a tool of
Graham's. He thought too it was a mistake to look to corporation
funds to carry elections. Lemieux spoke of Fisher, because he
talks Fr. as well as Eng. He is to my mind too old and not broad
enough.

The same attitude toward Graham (again his name was coupled
with that of F. F. Pardee, Liberal whip) was repeated by A. K.
Maclean and F. B. Carvell. The three talked together in King's
apartment in The Roxborough from midnight until three in the
morning and Mackenzie King reported: 'They are very much
down on Graham & Pardee trying to control everything, not
strong in their admiration for G. & strong in their dislike for
Pardee.'

There are good reasons to believe that at this time Mackenzie
King shared the critical views expressed by his friends. Long
before, indeed just after his election to the Commons in 1908, he
had called on George Graham to discuss a possible Tory protest
against his (King's) election in North Waterloo. From Graham he
learned that the protest had probably been suggested to offset a
protest the Liberals were making against another election in the
same area; that he (Graham) was meeting shortly with his opposite
number in the Conservative Party to 'arrange a series of sawoffs'.
Shocked by this evidence of machine politics, Mackenzie King
gave vent to his feelings:

> To my mind this is a poor sort of business. There is a want of
> sincerity about it scarcely befitting the dignity of public life and
> its demands. It is unfair too to men who have put up a clean fight.
> I am out of patience with *machine* politics altogether.

From that time on, or at least until after the Liberal convention
of 1919, Mackenzie King seemed to regard George Graham as
more of a machine politician than a statesman. He did not dislike
him. He admired his fine human qualities, his friendliness, his
wholesome lightheartedness and, perhaps, his unwillingness to take

himself too seriously. These qualities, which were much more characteristic of the one man than of the other, were not, however, the qualities which Mackenzie King considered of first importance in a political leader. For him a leader should be above involvements in petty machinations, temporizing, and fund-raising, all of which seemed to be necessary elements in the management of a political party. He should be cast in the pattern of a Gladstone, should be a man of dignity and deep spirituality, a profound student, a speaker on the grand scale, able to plumb the depths and reach the heights. All these attributes George Graham lacked, and the lack of them was reflected in his speeches. Mackenzie King listened to one of them at a banquet given by Sir Wilfrid for Tom Low and George Graham in the Parliamentary Restaurant. King thought of the banquet as an 'Occasion', but he had a low opinion of Graham's response:

> Graham's speech was a distinct disappointment, his opening remarks were almost of a childish kind speaking of Low's baby & his talks with it & incidents of the kind. He travelled on to Railways, bringing in the C.N.R., said an election might be looked for soon, praised Rowell said he was an 'achievement' meaning 'acquisition' & spoke of the fed'l. govt. cooperating with Province. There was neither dignity nor constructive thought, no appreciation of the fitness of things in his remarks. It was the speech of an ordinary man, who has been in the rough & tumble of a backwoods contest.

Graham's speech and Mackenzie King's criticism of it pointed up the difference between the two men: one was the hail-fellow-well-met type, the other the serious student of public affairs. Graham was at his best at a dinner of the Press Gallery, when the journalists on Parliament Hill give up their professional cares for a night of frivolity. Mackenzie King could not rise to such an occasion. He always did his best — but he suffered. No speaking engagement ever caused him more perturbation; he could not shed his customary seriousness. This is not to suggest that the one man was a kill-joy and the other merely frivolous. Mackenzie King

liked much of the fun, but he was not a fun-maker himself except
on rare occasions. George Graham's genius was jocular but he
could be serious as well. Indeed, while he was never credited with
any oratorical masterpieces, inside or outside Parliament, he
brought sound political judgment and homely horse-sense to bear
on important political issues. Mackenzie King was to speak of
him later, when they were colleagues again rather than competitors, as the man in the Cabinet on whose strength he most
greatly relied.

III

It must have come as a surprise to many of his colleagues, as it did
to Mackenzie King, that Graham, rather than Fielding, should have
been mentioned by Laurier as his probable successor. W. S. Fielding, as one of the old originals of 1896, a member of Laurier's
'cabinet of all the talents', had a high place in Laurier's esteem. Had
Fielding been elected in 1911 Laurier might well have yielded the
reins to him. He was then sixty-two years old (Laurier was sixty-
nine, Graham fifty-two, and Mackenzie King thirty-six). J. W.
Dafoe, writing later about this period, spoke of Fielding as the
'only possible successor to Sir Wilfrid' at this time. He suffered the
disadvantage, however, of not being in Parliament, but Graham too
had been defeated in the 1911 election. Dafoe came closer to the
reason why Fielding was not Laurier's choice when he added:

> Also he was in disfavor as the general whose defensive plan of
> campaign had ended in disaster. His name suggested 'Reciprocity'
> — a word the Liberals were quite willing, for the time being, to
> forget. He was left to lie where he had fallen.

Mackenzie King recognized in Fielding a man as serious-minded
as himself, an experienced and skilful debater, and the soul of
integrity. He had been premier of Nova Scotia for ten years and
federal minister of finance for another fifteen; in both offices he
had established a reputation as a capable and fearless administrator.

Oddly enough, very strong opposition to Fielding had shown

itself in the Maritimes, his own stronghold, principally because of reciprocity, but, in one instance at least, on more personal grounds. At a midnight gathering of party stalwarts from the Maritimes at the old Russell Hotel, where Mackenzie King was the only outsider, Fielding's place in the party was hotly discussed:

> With the exception of Mr. Ross, who was strongly Mr. Fielding's champion, and Campbell who was neutral, the others were strong and even bitter in their denunciation of Fielding. Davis and Logan said he had wrecked the Liberal Party. Ned Macdonald said he would never come to the front again, they all agreed on this.

Speculation went as far as the betting of $100 to $10 that he would not come back within six months. As a neutral, Mackenzie King held the stakes, but before the night was over he destroyed the cheques: 'I told them that as a colleague of Fielding's I could not hold these stakes.'

A more personal reason for Macdonald's bitterness was disclosed in Mackenzie King's comment on the discussion:

> Macdonald is bitter against Fielding because the Treasury Board will not grant a certificate to charter the International Bank ... says he will lose $8,000.... What better could illustrate the gratitude of public life? Where are the disinterested men, and what does the country not owe to men like Fielding who are strong in such situations?

Mackenzie King had not always seen eye to eye with Fielding. He had questioned, for one thing, the wisdom of the reciprocity pact at the time Fielding first proposed it, but he had bowed to the will of the majority. Now, as he considered him as a possible successor to Laurier, he recognized another serious objection: 'Mr. Fielding looks very much used up,' he wrote. 'I should not be surprised if this [the election defeat] were to shorten his life. He is very much overwrought and overworked.' Laurier, too, in spite of his admiration for Fielding and his earlier dependence on him, seemed willing at this time to allow him to disappear from the

scene. In conversation with King 'he agreed Fielding's health and
the feeling against him on the part of maritime province men made
it inexpedient for him to return to parliament.'

IV

There might have been an even more powerful rival for the succession to the leadership if Clifford Sifton had not broken with the
party before the 1911 election. Mackenzie King had been one of his
warm admirers in 1908. Sir Wilfrid had shared this feeling; he had
remarked at one time that 'Mr. Sifton was the master mind in
Parliament. He could discern the current political tendencies, put
his finger on the popular pulse better than any other man in my
experience. His executive capacity was extraordinary.' In 1911,
however, Sifton had thrown in his lot with the Tory party and had
campaigned most vigorously against the reciprocity pact. He had
been the real campaign manager of the Conservative Party and, in
Mackenzie King's opinion, 'the evil genius of the campaign'. Thus
his succeeding Sir Wilfrid was no longer a possibility. It is interesting to speculate, however, on the future of the Liberal Party and
of Mackenzie King had such a dynamic personality taken over in
1911.

V

As matters stood in 1911, Graham and Fielding were the only
others who could have been considered for the role of heir-appar-
ent had the need arisen. Rodolphe Lemieux's name had been mentioned, but he suffered from the disadvantage Sir Wilfrid imputed
to himself — he was French and he was a Roman Catholic. As
between Graham and Fielding and himself, Mackenzie King was
satisfied that his own qualifications outweighed theirs, in spite of
his youth and limited experience. He was not anxious to take over
the leadership at this time — a few years in opposition under Sir
Wilfrid would provide an excellent and much-needed course of

training — but he was eager to be regarded as first in the line of succession.

He had, indeed, many qualifications that Graham had not, and one in particular in which he always took pride — he had a family tradition, he had a grandfather. Other politicians could claim the honour of Scottish descent, but none could have been prouder of his forebears:

> I never cease to be thankful that I am of Scotch descent. I wd. rather have Scotch blood than any other in my veins, & I feel it through & through me. The stock seems to have been of a resolute, strong & enduring kind, & one a man may well be proud of. What it contains of valour and regard for religion I cherish strongly. There is a sterling independence which is worth more than anything else.

To this he added:

> I like the independent way grandfather stood out by himself, with his own belief in himself & consciousness of his own integrity & power to serve, in seeking election for the first time. That is the true way. His resolutions & stand in first parliament he was in shew clearly his capacity & splendid reforming insight — what a pity the rebellion came. Could it have been avoided & the reforms achieved, his memory wd. be without a mar even in the minds of extreme loyalists.

Mackenzie King had never known his grandfather in the flesh — William Lyon Mackenzie died thirteen years before his grandson was born — but Mackenzie King's mother had always kept the spirit of her father alive. She looked to her son to vindicate the memory of her father, the victim, as they both strongly felt, of vicious calumny and gross misunderstanding. Nothing angered Mackenzie King more than aspersions on his grandfather's honour; nothing grieved him more than the recollection of the poverty, frustrations, and disappointments of Mackenzie's life; nothing spurred him more to action and ambition than the memory of one whose unfinished work he felt challenged, or commanded, to carry on. He was proud of his grandfather, proud of his fight for res-

ponsible government and his valiant and even violent defiance of
the Family Compact. Even Mackenzie's years of impoverishment
in exile in the United States, that and the £1,000 bounty on his
head, were marks of distinction, not disgrace; his being expelled
five times from the Upper Canada legislature was an inspiration
rather than a humiliation. William Lyon Mackenzie was always
an important plank in his personal political platform. Now, in
1911, when the question of future leadership was being discussed,
it assumed increasing importance.

He knew his own capabilities, and his faith in his own future
was strong. He could repeat to himself, and did over and over
again, his assurance that he would achieve an important place in
the history of Canada. He had weighed himself in the balance with
his contemporaries and found himself not wanting: 'I am apt to
lose confidence in myself,' he wrote, 'but I can see by testing &
comparing that given the same position I cld. hold my own.'

Sir Wilfrid, in discussing at this time the future of the party,
frequently referred to his own age and the different attitude he
might have taken if he were a younger man. George Graham and
Mackenzie King were both younger men. Both of them may have
recalled a story Sir Wilfrid used to tell of an aging habitant in
Quebec who was approaching death. He had buried two wives,
Rose and Marie, and his friends were asking where in the family
plot he wished to be buried. His reply was: 'Bury me between
Rose and Marie, but cant me a little toward Marie.' Both may well
have been wondering in which direction Sir Wilfrid would ask to
be canted.

One thing that was in Graham's favour was his joviality, as
against a certain aloofness on the part of King; there was a feeling
among the members of Parliament that King considered himself in
some sense superior to them. Long before he entered Parliament,
when he had sat in the Commons gallery in 1901, enthralled by
Laurier's oratory, he had formed a low opinion of the other
members:

> As I saw the calibre of other men there, I have no fears as to my
> abilities if opportunity presented to serve this country well in

Parliament. . . . Borden's speech was flat and very ordinary. There is little of real oratory in the House.

He wrote this in 1901, just after he came to Ottawa. He was still making the same kind of comment in 1912: 'I sometimes tire of the low level and commonplace utterances of our prlmt.' More trenchant was the criticism he indulged in after a visit to the Commons in May 1914:

> This is what I find so disappointing in public life. One knows that the men who are taking part, many of them, are wholly without convictions, may be bought and sold like sheep or hogs, have indifferent morals and are corrupt – not all but many, nothing is sacred to them, and their words are Pharisaical.

Such disparagement of others, though never expressed in public, was only too likely to filter through to the consciousness of those criticized. Liberal members of Parliament may have been aware that this young man felt himself to be at least a cut above them. It is true he was, but that did little to allay resentment. He was welcomed cordially by a few, accepted only reluctantly by others who could not stifle certain feelings of envy and even jealousy, and by still others he was spurned as a self-righteous and egotistical intruder. Even his youth, which should have been an asset, and his rapid promotion, which was the reward of ability and hard work, were held against him by many. Throughout the years, Mackenzie King was acutely aware of these varying attitudes towards him. He was always sensitive to any real or imagined disapprobation, felt cheered by every friendly greeting, and depressed by any sign that could be interpreted as criticism.

VI

Mackenzie King realized that, in view of Sir Wilfrid's expressed preference for Graham as his possible successor, a seat for Graham would have priority over one for himself. Provision for Graham was made, indeed, within a few months, but it vexed Mackenzie King that Sir Wilfrid made no move on his behalf. 'He said he wd. like to see me back, but I have just a little the feeling that he wd. not mind if I were unsuccessful, & I cannot count on him to help me.'

This questioning of Sir Wilfrid's good faith and will to help was the first sign of criticism that later expressed itself, in the privacy of his diary, in stronger language than he would have used under less trying circumstances. It marked the beginning of a campaign of importunity that carried on into the next year, and the next. He pleaded with Sir Wilfrid at every opportunity, urged political colleagues to write to newly elected Liberals who might consider resigning, wrote directly to several members, and arranged for talks with them. His friend Lord Grey, who had just completed his term as Governor General and was still in Canada, passed on to him an impossible suggestion from Armand Lavergne that the Nationalists would let him have a seat in Quebec. Sir Wilfrid read the letter containing the suggestion without a word, then said, ' "Nonsense, I wonder that Lord Grey is so gullible." I said I did not see what power Lavergne had, and Sir Wilfrid said, laughing, "Of course he has none." ' Lavergne had previously made a similar suggestion to Mackenzie King in conversation: 'He said I could tell Sir Wilfrid that if he gave Quebec East to Graham or myself we wd. not be opposed by the Nationalists or by the Conservatives. — Armand, I think, takes himself too seriously and is misled a little by vanity.'

VII

With commendable pertinacity, though sometimes at risk of being regarded as unduly importunate, Mackenzie King followed up every suggestion. An Ontario seat would have been to his liking but, he reflected, it would be very difficult in Ontario because of the small majorities and the few seats. Saskatchewan seemed to him to offer more hopeful prospects, and in this Laurier and Sydney Fisher agreed. He weighed the advantages and disadvantages. He dreaded the long journey and the isolation, but felt there would be more likelihood of success in the West and less danger of stirring up dissent. As an easterner elected in the West, he was sure he could be useful in holding East and West together — something which the bitterness of the reciprocity campaign had shown to be a serious problem for the future. His first approach was to Dr. D. B. Neely, M.P. for Humboldt, Saskatchewan, one of the newly elected Liberals. Dr. Neely expressed willingness to resign in his favour and negotiations seemed to be coming to a head when the offer was withdrawn. Sir Wilfrid had predicted as much when he said to King: 'Neely is an Irishman, don't count on him, he will not resign.'

Regina was another riding in Saskatchewan that might have been available. It was held by William M. Martin, who later became premier of the province and, still later, chief justice. Martin wrote to King offering him his seat, but in the same breath he expressed doubt as to the wisdom of opening it or of importing an eastern man. On this Mackenzie King commented:

> The latter prejudice I think I could overcome by getting around among the people. The former we can talk over when Martin comes down. . . . More and more Saskatchewan seems to me the best province for my purpose, if an election can be carried off at not too great an expense. Regina wd. be preferable to Humboldt in many ways, but more difficult probably to carry.

There seemed to be some prospect of success in Regina, but it was not long before these negotiations, too, petered out.

Even while negotiations were continuing with Saskatchewan members, Mackenzie King was sounding out possibilities in Ontario. He had talked with a friend of his early years, John S. Willison, publisher of the Toronto *News*, which had supported the Conservative party in the election. He asked Willison if he would be willing to say in his paper that it would be in the public interest to have seats found for Graham and himself. Willison gave a reluctant promise of consideration, an answer which Sir Wilfrid, when he was told, interpreted as meaning that nothing would come of it.

East Kent was the first possibility in Ontario that was sounded. The sitting member, D. A. Gordon, had indicated his willingness to drop out, but the Liberal organizer, Alex. Beaton (whom King had always thought of as part of the Liberal machine gang), interposed objections — they had never thought of East Kent as a possibility for King, and in any event it might be difficult to arrange. Sir Wilfrid was of the same mind but was encouraging to the extent of saying that he thought King could be elected in East Kent, but not right away, maybe the next spring or summer. King was not happy about the decision, but he made the best of it: 'I told him I was wholly agreeable to remaining out for a short time though my instinct was to get back as soon as possible.' In the end, however, the door to Parliament through East Kent was closed to him.

It was a humiliating experience (one that he had been through before his first election to Parliament), having to apply now to this person and now to that for opportunity to continue his work in Parliament — doubly humiliating to be unsuccessful in every attempt. He could only envy the Liberal members who surrounded Sir Wilfrid in the Commons chamber. After attending the opening of Parliament on November 16, he could not suppress his feelings of sadness and disappointment:

> I felt disheartened a little as I looked down & saw our men on the other side, few in numbers & the old opposition holding power. How short the time since I entered.... Guthrie & Pardee have themselves placed immediately behind Sir Wilfrid & Carvell to their left. These three men I feel are all jealous of me.... They wd. gladly prevent my re-entering the House.

The one riding which more than any other he would have liked to represent in Parliament was North York, but that seat could not be opened because it was held by a Conservative. Mackenzie King had visited the riding when he was helping the Ontario Liberals in the provincial election campaign, and his spirits were raised by the reception given to him. There was a packed house, and there was real warmth in the welcome. It was his grandfather's old riding, and after the meeting many old Reformers gathered

round to express their congratulations. In his diary that night he
wrote:

> I believe that North York will be my next riding, and that with
> a good campaign I can carry it. I wish I had gotten into it at the
> time Sir William Mulock resigned [he had resigned in 1905!], it
> would be mine today.

North York was to be his next riding, or rather the riding he was
next to contest. But that was not to be until long after he had given
up hope of election to the twelfth Parliament.

VIII

On his return to Ottawa, after an absence of some weeks in this
provincial campaigning, he again called hopefully on Sir Wilfrid.
He found him, he thought, looking very tired and worn, almost
wizened in appearance. They talked of the Ontario election results
and of the new political situation in the Dominion. No time was
lost in getting round to Mackenzie King's personal problem, a seat
in Parliament. When King mentioned the East Kent riding, another
possibility that had been discussed, and said he felt he could carry
it, Sir Wilfrid expressed some surprise. It was a disappointing talk,
leading again to questioning of Sir Wilfrid's sincerity:

> This way Sir Wilfrid sometimes has of appearing to have for-
> gotten all previous interviews and of changing front on them
> many times as circumstances arise is a failing and has lost him I
> fear some of his friends. . . . He can be indifferent to all personal
> considerations as few men can. I feel a little hurt and disappointed
> in this as it makes me realize he is to some degree indifferent as
> to whether I get back into the House or not. However, time will
> tell as to that. 'There is a divinity that shapes our ends' and to this
> Divinity I must trust.

This critical attitude toward Sir Wilfrid changed, for a moment,
when he received a kind letter acknowledging Christmas gifts. In
his letter Sir Wilfrid encouraged him by saying that his own special

wish was that he might soon return to Parliament. 'This is very gratifying,' King wrote. 'It is an open and unmistakable expression of his feeling toward me.'

If Sir Wilfrid's New Year's wishes had dispelled suspicions for the time being, some of his subsequent actions did much to renew them. Mackenzie King had accompanied Sir Wilfrid in February 1912 on a trip to the constituency of South Renfrew, a seat which George P. Graham was to take over a month later. They talked of many things on the journey, but the conversation turned, as it was bound to do, to the possibility of a seat for Mackenzie King. Sir Wilfrid mentioned that a report in the *Citizen* that morning was correct: A. H. Clarke, M.P. for Essex South, had told him he was going to resign, but Sir Wilfrid had asked him not to do so until the fall. 'We might arrange to get you in there,' was his encouraging comment. He felt he could not bank on this new suggestion, for Sir Wilfrid had already encouraged him to think of Humboldt and East Kent but in the end had done nothing to help him.

Essex South was, at any rate, to be the centre of his next hopes. His doubts, which were many, and his hopes, not too sanguine, were expressed in a brief entry in his diary:

> I am in great doubt as to what the outcome would be, with both govts. against me, & the cry of being an 'outsider' & the determination of the Tories to win the next by-election. I would have a desperately hard fight, & great difficulty in winning. Still if offered me, I will probably, almost certainly take the chance. — To lose will be to get a great setback in public life, to win sd. be relatively as great a gain, seeing that I am choosing public life as a calling I must be prepared to win or lose. I will require that the party in the riding should be united on me, and that the party in the House & country will stand well behind me. — I am feeling in much better shape physically — not nearly so depressed. Alas I almost fear it is only temporary. My nature seems subject to waves of depression I can hardly throw off at times.

It came as a painful shock to King, however, to learn that Sir Wilfrid, in spite of having encouraged him to hope for the Essex seat, had personally urged another possible candidate, Mahlon K. Cowan, to stand for the nomination. Mackenzie King was greatly incensed and was even more annoyed when Sir Wilfrid, whom he had approached directly, made an evasive reply. Laurier spoke of Ontario ridings being 'close corporations' and said the matter was really in the hands of the local convention. He added that the convention's choice would probably be Cowan, with John Auldt, another local man, as second choice; that if neither of them accepted, Mackenzie King would probably get the nomination. This was too much — to be relegated to third choice! He replied sharply that he knew the decision really rested with Sir Wilfrid and George Graham, that the convention would do as they wished. He made it clear that if he were to be left to wait for a seat till the next general election he had no intention of devoting himself to party work in the interim. It would be necessary for him, he said, to take up some other line of work — he must avoid at all costs the appearance of doing nothing. Sir Wilfrid sought to soothe him by assuring him he had many friends in the House who were anxious to have him back, that there would be other by-election possibilities, and that in the meantime it would be a good thing to do all he could in the interests of the party by helping with organization work and by public speaking. He mentioned the necessity of work in Ontario especially ('Ontario has gone to smash'). But this kind of work had no appeal for Mackenzie King; he had already given a great deal of time to it, but was determined that his main work should be in the House of Commons.

He later consulted Rodolphe Lemieux and George Graham, both of whom were encouraging, but they talked more about obstacles than about ways of surmounting them. To both of them he declared that he would regard it as a direct slight if he, a former minister, were passed over and no seat found for him. It seemed to him that neither Graham nor Sir Wilfrid was making any real effort to help him; but it was Sir Wilfrid's indifference, and particularly what seemed to King to be his underhanded dealings in connection with the Essex South nomination, that rankled. Lemieux's suggestion that he might be put in charge of the preparation of party literature, at a salary, was met with disdain; he would help if he were in the House, but he would never become a party hireling and they could expect nothing from him if a seat in Parliament were not arranged. Insult was added to injury when Madame Lemieux, who with her husband had approached Sir Wilfrid on Mackenzie King's behalf, reported that Sir Wilfrid had spoken favourably of him but said that he was young and could wait; he thought he was 'in too much of a hurry'. This was another devastating blow, another indication that he might as well give up hope of taking any part in Parliament until after the next general election.*

* As things turned out, no riding was opened for him and he had to sit out that Parliament. He did secure a nomination for North York in March 1913, but there was no opportunity to contest the seat until the 1917 general election.

CHAPTER 3

Futility in Other Directions

For eleven years, as deputy minister and minister of labour, Mackenzie King had been worrying about other people's labour problems; now, he found himself faced with a labour problem of his own. He had been engaged in work that was of consuming interest, work in which he was operating from a solid basis of adequate office accommodation, secretarial assistance, monthly salary cheques, and team-work with colleagues in shaping and carrying out policies. It had been work that suited his temperament, talents, energy, and ambition. It had given him opportunity to institute much-needed social reforms and to make speeches about them. He had achieved what he had long prayed for — a seat in Parliament and a place in the Cabinet. Now, everything — his exciting life and his hopes for the future — seemed to disappear overnight. Out of Parliament, out of the Cabinet, he felt all but completely lost. To be suddenly ejected from the whirl of activities to which he had become accustomed was a new and trying experience. He had always stepped from one thing to another, and always it had been a step up. This was a step down, a step to a very much lower level, and he felt the humiliation and the loneliness of it. 'Tonight,' he confided to his diary, 'spent a short time at the Library of prlmt., felt sad as I walked about and felt in a way the sordidness of the life [presumably parliamentary life] as some men take it.' This period of enforced idleness made him restless and even restive. 'Walking about' was not something he had been used to. He paused on one of his walks to stand in front of a Sparks Street newspaper office:

> As I looked on the account on the bulletin board [referring to a strike of nearly a million railway workers in Britain] I thought with a situation like this there ought to be plenty of work in the world for me, & how odd in a way it was, with the kind of ability I have & service I might be rendering, I should in a sense be walking the streets.

As it happened, he did have something to say about strikes in England before the year was out. But for the moment he, like the British railwaymen, was unemployed.

His unhappy predicament weighed heavily upon him, but the more he reflected on it the stronger became his resolve not to allow himself to be discouraged but to plan definitely to re-establish himself in public life. Perhaps, he meditated, 'this period may help to develop character, that is what is most needed in leadership. If I gain in character and knowledge, the time will be better spent than if it had been lived in office.'

Financial concerns, 'the fear of penury', did, however, continue to haunt him, not so much for himself as on account of his family. He spent the last week-end of 1911 in Toronto with his mother and father and elder sister, Bella, and was distressed to find them in poor health and low spirits. (The other two members of the family, the youngest, were no longer at home: Max was practising medicine in Ottawa and Jennie had married Harry M. Lay, a banker, and was living in Walkerton, Ontario.) Family income, never at a high level, had dwindled almost to the vanishing-point, and this, added to the threat of illness, created an atmosphere of gloom. Mackenzie King was proud of the reputation his father, John King, K.C., had achieved as a lecturer at Osgoode Hall and as an authority on the law of libel (his first book had been published in 1907 and his second was nearing completion in 1911). He had many other reasons to be proud of his father; he had been a member of the University Senate for years; he was a kindly person, a good citizen, an able writer and a scholar. But his law practice in Toronto, established when the family moved from Berlin, was far from successful and helped little to meet increasing costs of living, to say nothing of providing for the inevitable years of retirement. He was not slothful in business, neither was he successful, for he had never been able to build up even a reasonably profitable law practice. Now his sight was failing, total blindness was threatening, and the possibility of an appointment to the judiciary, long hoped for, was becoming more remote than ever. There was even doubt of his being able to retain the lectureship at Osgoode Hall.

In spite of this shadow of disappointed hopes that overcast the small family group, there was an element of rejoicing in every reunion. The homecoming of the elder son in the New Year's season was an occasion for renewal of hope rather than for commiseration over the family's plight. It was a family in which each one enjoyed the companionship of the others. Their love was without dissimulation, they were 'kindly affectioned one to another'. As always, the mother was the centre of everyone's interest, and the returning son spent most of his time in her company. How much more would he have enjoyed that companionship if he could have done more to ease the family burden, and how much greater could be his service to the state if only he could be free of financial worries! These thoughts were in his mind when he wrote on the New Year's Eve:

> After dinner I read aloud to mother from Burns' life. She fell asleep on the sofa as I read & I then closed the book to write up this diary while she still sleeps by my side. I am happy with her, as long as she is about. God grant she may be spared, and that in some way in the New Year or years I may be enabled to do something which will ease her mind, & father's & Bell's from any anxiety for the coming years.

The recollection of his father and his family living continually on the brink of insolvency, and his own experience of financial depression, permanently conditioned his thinking about money.

This was at the bottom of his lifelong caution about money matters, his excessive concentration on the necessity of making adequate provision for the future. At this time, however, he was not wholly without funds. He had a small income from his savings, and financial help came from another source. His benefactor was the Englishwoman, Violet Markham, whom he had met some years before at Rideau Hall. Since then there had been a constant exchange of letters between them — warm-hearted and affectionate on both sides but without any trace of romantic attachment. Few decisions had been made and no family crises had occurred on which she had not been consulted. As early as 1905 she had shared the Governor General's conviction that some day Mackenzie King would be prime minister of Canada. Now, as a staunch and public-spirited Old Country Liberal, she was anxious that such a potential and promising political leader should not be lost to Canadian public life merely through lack of a few hundred pounds or dollars. She was a woman of substantial means and the possession of wealth was a problem that troubled her. She had already helped to meet his election expenses and had sent an extra £200 at the time of his defeat. She now welcomed an opportunity to give further financial help and came forward with a promise of £300 a year for three years. This, she said, was not only for the sake of Mackenzie King but for what she thought of as the future of Canada.

II

In spite of this generous contribution to his and his family's needs, Mackenzie King's income was still not sufficient to meet the demands made on it. It was imperative that he find some kind of gainful employment. This did not mean, however, that he was ready to accept the first opportunity that came his way. He dismissed peremptorily the thought of making connections with any business corporation: 'I will not take a business opening, to work for a corporation — however lucrative the offer, — the making of money has no attractions for me.' To Miss Markham he wrote, on October 11:

> I think I know the value of the service I am capable of rendering this country and I do not wish to have my energies, because of mere necessity in its different forms, turned into channels the fruits whereof may be only increased dividends to some industrial or other concern and a living for myself.

'Business,' he said in a letter two months later, 'is mere money making, and to this I do not propose to devote my talents even if I starve.'

One possible field of employment which he did not regard with complete disfavour was that of writing. He could write, and he wanted to write, but he had no interest in writing for a daily newspaper, even for the editorial page of a Liberal paper. That was his answer to his good friend Joseph E. Atkinson, owner of the *Toronto Daily Star*, who had offered him, four days after the election, an editorial post on the *Star* at $3,000 a year. Nor did he respond with any cordiality to another proposal from Atkinson that he should contribute special articles for which the *Star* would be willing to pay at substantial rates.

Literary work of some other kind might well fill in the time until a return to politics, but even it would be only a stop-gap, and the financial returns would certainly be meagre. He visited New York in January in an effort to make an arrangement with the *Outlook* to be its Canadian editor. He reported later, in a letter to Miss Markham, that he had been successful and that he hoped to do the same kind of work for other journals. It was a disappointment that his very tentative ventures in this direction came to nothing.

Academic work, on which his heart had been set in earlier years, reappeared at this time as another alternative. Three days after the election he had written: 'I feel I would welcome a return to academic work, as affording opportunity of study & reflection. . . . A professorship at McGill might prove attractive, or the presidency of some college.' A chair at Dalhousie University (history or economics) seemed at one time to be a possibility, but nothing came of this.

Entering the Christian ministry was another possibility that occurred to him immediately after the election. He had entertained such an ambition at different times during his university days. Ministers of the gospel have at times, it is true, been transformed into ministers of the Crown, but a shift from Cabinet to pulpit would be a rare occurrence. In any event this was only a fleeting fancy; he proposed and dismissed it almost in the same breath:

> In many ways I would be glad to take a theological course as affording a chance for the highest reality, and contemplation of eternal truths, but I realize I am hardly suited by temperament for the Christian Ministry, and I doubt if for me it is the sphere of greatest usefulness even of Christian work.

One possibility after another continued to crop up in his mind, only to be dismissed. 'What I would welcome most would be an opportunity to travel,' he thought longingly. He told Sir Wilfrid at one time he might go to France for a year. 'My feeling is that I should try in the time immediately ahead to supplement the deficiencies and limitations I have realized while in Parliament, particularly as to becoming better informed on Canadian affairs and history.' But travel and study meant outlay rather than income.

Ability as a public speaker was another of Mackenzie King's assets which he felt he should be able to turn to good account. He had often said he enjoyed public speaking more than anything else, and there is plenty of evidence that his audience shared his enjoyment — at least for the first hour and a half. Numerous invitations did come to him to speak in both Canada and the United States, and throughout 1912 and 1913 he had a fairly heavy programme of both after-dinner speeches and evening lectures. He spoke frequently about the trip around the world which he had made in 1909, on the proposed celebration in 1914 of one hundred years of peace, and on two subjects in which he had made a name for himself — methods of preventing strikes and of dealing with monopolies. Such peripatetic speech-making added little to his revenues; his chief recompense for his addresses before Canadian Clubs, Chambers of Commerce, political associations, and similar bodies was audience applause — applause and (usually, but not always) travelling expenses.

His occasional addresses in the United States on the Industrial Disputes Investigation Act served to keep alive his interest in this field in which he had been so much engrossed. In December 1912 he addressed an audience of about a thousand leading businessmen in New York on the Canadian act, and over 600,000 copies of his address were printed and distributed. In Ohio he addressed meetings in several cities and a bill based on the Canadian act was introduced in the state legislature. In other states of the Union several organizations were urging similar legislation, and the State of Colorado did later adopt it, virtually without change.

III

Throughout this period another project that was much in his mind was that of writing a life of Sir Wilfrid. He had spoken of it to him even before the election, as something he would like to undertake if it had Sir Wilfrid's approval. Now that he had time on his hands he again broached the subject and Sir Wilfrid agreed wholeheartedly, saying he knew of no one he would rather see do it. He felt that Mackenzie King had all the essential qualities: he wrote very good English ('that was the main thing,' he said, 'there were very few men in this country who did'), and he felt, too, that he would be sympathetic and enthusiastic. To relieve Sir Wilfrid's mind of any sense of obligation to him, Mackenzie King stressed the value it would be to himself as it would provide him with an opportunity to study Canadian history from the time of Confederation, and thus help to fit him for future usefulness.

When Sir Wilfrid, in one of their later conversations, asked him how he was getting along financially, Mackenzie King told him of the small private income he had from his savings (it amounted to about $1,600 a year). This was enough, he said, to enable him to live quietly, devote the year to the biography and to a study of political questions, and to have time for a little political work as well. Sir Wilfrid thought well of his plans.

As a matter of fact little or no headway was ever made on the biography. Mackenzie King's enthusiasm for the project seems to have cooled with every indication of a waning of Sir Wilfrid's interest in getting him a seat. The rumour that Sir Wilfrid had supported a rival candidate in Essex South had taken the edge off his keenness. This incident had occasioned the most bitter words he ever used about Sir Wilfrid. In the heat of the moment he declared: 'If that is his friendship, instead of looking after his life, I shall look after my own. . . . I feel in a way that perhaps it is a mistake to work too exclusively on it.'

The subject did come up again early in 1913, after Sir Wilfrid had made some kindly comment about wishing he had him with him in the Commons to help in the debate on the Naval Service Bill. Mackenzie King expressed regret then that he had not been getting on with the biography, and Sir Wilfrid again commented, 'Better wait till I am dead.' Though Mackenzie King protested, and though Sir Wilfrid promised to look out some documents when the session was over, that seems to have been the end of a volume that was never started.

IV

Leadership of the Ontario Liberal Party could have been his at this time if he had yielded to the pressure which prominent Ontario party men had applied a few days after his defeat in the September elections. J. E. Atkinson had been spokesman for the group who approached him. Atkinson had discussed it beforehand with Sir Wilfrid and felt he had an appealing argument when he told Mackenzie King that the proposal had met wholly with Sir Wilfrid's approval.

But if Sir Wilfrid did approve, Mackenzie King did not. He went immediately to Sir Wilfrid and told him that he would rather remain in federal politics, that he was more interested in the larger questions dealt with in Ottawa. This evidently pleased Sir Wilfrid for he said at once that he would like to see him hold to politics in the federal field. Atkinson was not prepared to take 'No' for an answer and returned a few days later to press his case. He used a more subtle argument when he said that he and others were looking to him to become prime minister of Canada, that they did not think George Graham had the stability of character or the training or serious outlook which were needed to fit him for the position. Going into the Ontario House, he contended, would probably mean the premiership of Ontario in eight years, and the man who held Ontario would easily rise to control of the Dominion. Mackenzie King was unmoved. Sir Wilfrid's word of encouragement had strengthened his resolution and he repeated to Atkinson what he had said to Sir Wilfrid about his interest in federal issues, such as Canada's relation to the Empire.

His decision was made and he was satisfied it was the right one. But for weeks he could not help trying to weigh imponderables, balancing certain immediate sacrifices against possible future advantages. He had been forced to decide at a time when he felt completely used up, ready to 'drop out of everything', 'not in shape to make a decision on anything so momentous'. He wondered if he would have felt the same aversion to the provincial proposal had he been wholly rested and in good spirits. In passing up such an opportunity he was taking a course which would influence his future 'perhaps more than any decision, other than that of marriage' that he would ever be called upon to make. Acceptance would have meant an immediate return to politics and, although it would have been at the provincial level, this would not necessarily mean exclusion from the federal arena. Indeed, as Atkinson had argued, it might open the way to the highest place in the councils of the Dominion. In the interval he would be established in a relatively high place in the Liberal hierarchy and would have opportunity to give all his time to politics, which, as he now reaffirmed, was his desire. He realized, even by this time, that there was little hope of his getting a seat in Parliament before the next general election. It was a matter of choosing between a provincial bird in the hand and a federal bird in the bush. It was a big responsibility, and he asked himself 'how many men without anything in the world in the way of occupation, with a relative dislike for other occupations & a desire to give all their time to public affairs, to the country's service, wd. pass such an opportunity by'.

Acceptance would have solved the pressing financial problems which had been causing him so much concern. As Leader of the Opposition in the Ontario Legislature he would have a salary of $5,000 a year plus the $1,500 indemnity, railway passes and other perquisites, and also a secretary and rooms in the Parliament Buildings. He thought of the financial side as the least consideration, 'tho' coming now when I am out of everything, simply spending not earning a cent, it is a serious responsibility to pass it by'. He was thinking especially of the seriously depleted resources of his father and mother. Even for himself, he acknowledged that at times he had 'felt the sting of the absence of position with income, the privation of not being able to invite others to a meal, or to offer readily a carriage to a guest'.

In spite of these 'momentary and fleeting feelings' he was sure he was right:

> To have taken the leadership at this juncture wd. have been to go on with a strain which has not been broken for 10 years & possibly to break under it. I feel I do not know the provincial questions well enough to handle them as a leader thro' a campaign but I believe I could master enough to make a good front & the public wd. be bound to be somewhat lenient; on the other hand, I believe I shall gain in the public confidence & esteem by having a period of opposition. Men think I have gone on rapidly & they are more likely to rally effectively later on, by a brave spirit shewn during adversity, than by further rapid promotion. I may be

wrong, but ... somehow I believe God has a great work for me
in this Dominion, maybe at some time to be its prime minister.

V

Though he had refused the Ontario leadership, with its emolu-
ments, he was persuaded to assume the responsibilities of president
of the Ontario General Reform Association, though it was without
salary. To this post he was elected on October 31, 1911. It provided
him, for one thing, with employment, and served to keep him in
the political field and to bring him into close contact with prominent Liberals throughout the province. As president he had opportunities to assist in the drafting of party policies, to make speeches
in every part of the province, to hold conferences on organization
matters, and, generally, in co-operation with the provincial leader,
to guide party activities into productive channels. Mackenzie King
made full use of all these opportunities.

It was apparent at once to everyone that the new president was
not merely a nominal head. One of his first responsibilities was to
assist in choosing a new party leader, and in this work he was associated with the men who had offered him the leadership a few
weeks earlier. One of the men who had urged him to accept had
been N. W. Rowell, K.C. Now it was Rowell's turn to be subjected to pressure, and he yielded. On the day of his election as
president, Mackenzie King took on the important duties of chairman of the resolutions committee and in this capacity had much to
do with the shaping of the platform which would be the basis of
the party's appeal to the electorate in the forthcoming election
campaign. This kind of constructive work challenged his best
abilities. He enjoyed working with his committee members in the
drafting of the platform, and commented on it, thinking of his
refusal of the leadership: 'I had once or twice a slight feeling of
regret that I had not foreseen this kind of co-operation, and the
joy that is in it.'

Inspired by the enthusiasm of his new associates, he threw himself energetically into a campaign which lasted until election day, December 11:

> I am being looked to with Rowell, to see the fight thro' & to conduct it. Here is clearly an opportunity & no less clearly a duty and to that I must for the present subject other plans, postpone the writing of Sir Wilfrid's life & enter on a new campaign. That I can do with joy once I have material prepared, & to the work of preparation I must now give myself. It is something to have been, without seeking or choice the Chairman of the Committee which shapes the platform on which Liberals thro' the Province will fight during the coming years. It is something at 36 to have refused the leadership of a party in the premier province of the country, & still be looked to as the one to shape & carry on the campaign as the President of the Reform Associat'n of the Province.

As the campaign went on, his confidence in Rowell increased. After a meeting at Massey Hall, Toronto, which both of them addressed, he paid him this tribute in his diary:

> He impresses me as a man of exceedingly fine character, has a good intellect, real ability & sterling worth. He will make a good leader, his health will be his one handicap. He inspires confidence admiration and esteem. If he had time to get around the Province he wd. make a decided impression.

The election did not result in a Liberal triumph. No one expected that — Mackenzie King had thought it would be 'rare good fortune if the party retains what it has'. When the election returns came in they showed a total net gain of four seats, and he commented: 'The results as a whole shew a decided return of the tide toward Liberalism in the Province & this within 2 months after it was at the lowest possible ebb.' He was justified in taking considerable satisfaction from the part he himself had played in the campaign.

His thoughts now returned naturally to possibilities in the federal field:

> I am glad the campaign is over. I have gone through with it day by day, speaking every night for 3 weeks, & three other times

besides, have gained in physical strength & clearness of thought with it all, have kept resolutions made to carry it through without late suppers, talking after meetings, etc. & kept up a pretty good level to the close. Feel I have done my duty to the party & shall draw in now until I see what the party is going to let me do. Graham has secured his seat. I shall wait & see if the coming year brings me mine. I have rec'd nothing save travelling expenses for this campaign & that at a time when I might be making money for myself. All the work has been for another at a hard time & in a campaign from wh. I might easily have been excused. It is bread cast upon the waters, but it will return again I believe after many days.

It was many days, many months indeed, before the bread cast upon the waters showed any sign of returning.

VI

His brief excursion into provincial politics had provided him for a few weeks with work of a kind he greatly enjoyed, but it had not been financially rewarding. The door to federal politics was still closed to him, and none of the other occupations to which his thoughts had turned had captured his imagination. The settlement of labour disputes would have attracted him, but he had given that up in favour of a political career. His work as an industrial conciliator in Canada seemed to be a finished chapter, though a chapter in which he was proud to have been the central figure. He now pondered the possibility of similar work in Great Britain. With this in mind he wrote to Violet Markham on February 13, 1912:

> I have been wondering if there would be any possibility of my arranging to give in England a talk in a few centres on our Industrial Disputes Investigation Act. I have spoken in the States at different times upon it and realized a little. Lord Grey once thought the Government might get me over to assist in the drafting of some measure, but there are other and larger measures in their hands just now.

He recalled an inquiry he had received from Britain shortly before the Dominion elections. Rt. Hon. Sydney Buxton, president of the Board of Trade, had written to him about an epidemic of strikes which Britain had been experiencing, and had asked him for his views on the effectiveness of the Canadian legislation. Mackenzie King's lengthy reply closed with a suggestion that if the 'Home Government' were thinking of introducing legislation along the lines of the Canadian act, he would be very glad to go over to England after the elections for discussion with government and labour leaders. He would be willing also to give one or two addresses, which might be useful in developing public interest in the legislation. Buxton's response was cordial, but he was unable to accept the offer at the time; 'later,' he added, 'it might be very useful.' The epidemic of strikes continued and culminated in the strike of railway workers early in 1912. Reports of that strike sharpened King's interest – he longed to be on the scene, and finally decided that he must go.

A trip to England would serve other purposes as well – needed rest and change and the opportunity of talks with Miss Markham. Through his lecturing he had been making a little money and keeping himself a little before the public, but he was genuinely exhausted, mentally, physically, and emotionally, by this long period of indecision and frustration. He felt the need of a complete rest of the kind he could best find in the solitude of his Kingsmere woods. He spent several weeks there and then sailed for England on July 24.

Unfortunately Buxton's absence from London made meetings with him impossible, but it was even more important to him that he have full discussions with Sir George Askwith, Chief Industrial Commissioner of the United Kingdom. Sir George welcomed this opportunity for a series of talks about Canada's methods of settling industrial disputes, and in the end made arrangements to come to Canada to make a first-hand study of Canada's methods of promoting industrial peace.

VII

Industrial peace, in Mackenzie King's mind, was always linked with international peace. He thought of the causes of unrest in industrial and international relations as basically the same. To achieve peace in either area the application of reason rather than force was vital, with reliance always on an educated public opinion and the development of a spirit of goodwill. These strong convictions were responsible for his lively interest in every movement to effect international peace by conciliatory methods. He had been one of the first to suggest, as he had done at Harvard in 1909, that in 1914 there should be a suitable celebration in Canada and the United States of the hundred years of peace enjoyed by the two countries. This had led ultimately to the formation of a Canadian Peace Centenary Association, and to this organization he had devoted much of his time and interest. Later he was to be responsible for the establishment of an International Conciliation Council for Canada.

VIII

After his return from England, although he was still the president of the Ontario Reform Association, his political activities gradually shifted back from the provincial to the federal arena. His residence continued to be in Ottawa and it was only natural that, with his strong preference for the broader issues, he should become more and more involved in discussions with Sir Wilfrid and his close associates in Ottawa. Senator Jaffray had tried to interest him, in February 1912, in organizing the Ontario constituencies, but he decided against it — he did not want to be a party organizer.

More interesting to him, but still not inspiring, was a proposal he discussed with Sydney Fisher and Sir Frederick Borden, a month later, that national Liberal headquarters, adequately financed, should be established in Ottawa, and that he should take an important part in its operations. At first reluctant to serve as a salaried employee of the party, he finally agreed to do some writing on controversial issues then before Parliament, and for this he was to receive some compensation. Before the end of the year he became further involved. 'To make ends meet,' he wrote to Miss Markham, in November, 'I have taken up the work of organizing a Liberal Information Office.' His work included editing weekly letters, assisting in the preparation of briefs and pamphlets, and supervising the work of party organization throughout the Dominion. It was a full-time occupation to start with ('about the same amount of work as if I were a deputy minister') but he planned that as soon as the office was properly organized he would limit his part to half a day ('and reserve half to myself for reading'). He was making some headway in the direction in which he wished to move: 'Without appearing publicly as such, I am in a way the head of the central organization of the party, this keeps me in touch with all that is going on, and enables me to gain inside information.' As for compensation, he was promised the equivalent of a member's indemnity for the session ($2,500). 'That will enable me', he wrote to his mother, 'to meet my expenses and keep out of debt.'

It was on his initiative that the *Canadian Liberal Monthly* was established in September 1913, and he was its first editor. This twelve-page publication was concerned with federal political issues, but in the last two numbers for which he was responsible (August and September 1914) there was no trace of party propaganda. Both numbers had been written in their entirety by himself after the declaration of war and were devoted to an analysis of the existing international situation.

When war was declared on August 4, Sir Wilfrid had immediately announced a truce to all party strife in the face of the national emergency. Even before war was declared, Mackenzie King had urged him to be prepared to issue such a statement of policy. Sir Wilfrid had been at his summer home in Arthabaska when rumours of war were reaching alarming proportions. He was relying on

Mackenzie King, his only senior lieutenant in Ottawa at the time, to keep him informed of every development, and they were in constant communication by letter and telephone. When dispatches reported that Germany had formally declared war on Russia and had issued an ultimatum to France, Mackenzie King urged Sir Wilfrid to return to Ottawa immediately. He arrived two days later, on a Monday evening, and they worked together until after midnight discussing attitudes and drafting statements. Sir Wilfrid felt, even at this stage, that Britain and Canada would not have to be involved, but he was ready to have Canada's full support pledged if Britain were 'on trial'. He thought of saying that the Opposition would offer 'no obstacle' to anything the Canadian Conservative government might do, but Mackenzie King held out successfully for a more positive stand. During these anxious days he was Laurier's closest adviser. He suggested at their first meeting that his colleagues Sydney Fisher and Sir Frederick Borden be called in; Sir Wilfrid agreed, but added that he 'did not want others'. Daily and nightly conferences continued until Parliament assembled on August 18.

In such discussions of high policy Mackenzie King had shown himself to be in his element. Throughout the period when he was out of Parliament, he had taken an important part in party deliberations, though on less vital issues, and his counsel had been listened to with respect even if it was not always heeded. It had had the effect of establishing him as an important person in the councils of the party. As for Sir Wilfrid, he had been coming more and more to rely on the soundness of Mackenzie King's judgment, and his part in the August conferences had made a profound impression on him. In October, when there were rumours of an impending election, he went so far as to say to him: 'I am not the man to lead & win now, there should be a younger man, you would be the one.' It would be a long time, however, before King could be considered as the man to lead the party, a long time before he could find a place in Parliament.

IX

If futility had marked all his efforts to regain a seat in Parliament or to find the best use for his special abilities, so too futility was to mark all his efforts to attain something else he had longed for for many years — a home of his own. His loneliness was now becoming more and more oppressive. Highly sensitive about the feelings of others towards him, cut off from former parliamentary associations and frustrated in every attempt to restore them, not content with any employment to which he could have turned, he was on the way to a solitariness that might have proved unbearable. Even the social life which he still permitted himself at times seemed to emphasize his loneliness, as he saw with envy the happy companionship other men enjoyed with their wives and families. Desolation could not be spelled out with more pathos than in his own words: 'Went to the Rideau Rink for an half hour's skate at noon, the last I think I shall take this year. I got tired going around by myself, and the place was cheerless.' A visit to the Montreal home of his friend Sam Jacobs, later a Member of Parliament, filled him with envy: 'The sight of Jacobs' little child smiling at his father on Sunday revealed to me the security there can be in an infant's faith & trust in its parent.' It moved him deeply to realize this great lack in his own life, and he wrote: 'To go into politics without marrying wd. be folly. I cannot live that cruel life without a home & someone to love & be loved by. . . . Marry I must.' The kind of home life he had known in his youth was one of similar trust and affection; his father and mother had deserved and won the confidence of their children and had created an atmosphere of warm affection which all its members shared. To establish such another family group was Mackenzie King's fondest hope for his own personal life — he wanted a home, and in it just such another mother as his own to give it character and grace.

What a different person he might have been, how much less egocentric, had he become a husband and a father! With a happy home life, what a different kind of prime minister! The right wife might have fended off the attacks of illness and fatigue which plagued him in his later years, and cheered him on his way to a much more serene old age than he did enjoy. There would have been more entertaining at Laurier House, more merriment and sparkle, a bit more prodigality, the infusion of a dram or two of humour and fun in a life that took everything too seriously. Laurier House would have lost its sombreness and Kingsmere would have been even more a paradise.

Of the personal life of Mackenzie King very little was ever publicly known. That was his own wish, for he was very sensitive to any invasion of his privacy. He was absorbed so completely in public affairs, and his hopes were so concentrated on a future in public life, that there would seem to have been little room left for the cultivation of relationships that might lead to marriage. He did not cut himself off from the companionship of women – far from it, he enjoyed their company immensely – but he seemed unwilling to 'let himself go', as if under the compulsion of self-imposed limitations. He would go so far and no further, seemingly seeking to avoid any private involvements or entanglements that might lead to an irrevocable commitment. It may have been, as many averred, that it was a strong 'mother complex', rather than his preoccupation with politics, that was largely responsible for this holding back. No one could reach the heights of his idealized image of his mother. His devotion to her seemed to exclude the possibility of any rival in his affections. If others were ever to be considered seriously, their qualities would have to be measured against hers.

A point was now being reached, however (he was well on in his thirties), when he felt strongly the need of a radical change in his life: 'If my life is to be what I wish it to be I believe a home is all important.' So he wrote a few days after the September defeat, and he added:

> I feel I should seek to become married. If I can only find the one that will be the helpmate needed through life I will certainly marry. It is a mistake not to. . . . I cannot but believe that this good will come out of the present misfortune.

Earlier in 1911, in January, while he was still a Cabinet minister, he had met at Rideau Hall someone who, he had felt, met all his needs:

> In personal beauty she is the type I admire most, in quiet self-possession, in charm of manner, in happiness of disposition, and above all in real spiritual beauty, she possesses all that one can desire. She is interested in human life, in the saving of men, in the betterment of conditions for the poor. In all that I have most at heart, she is living what I am dreaming of.

He discussed his hopes and plans with Lord Grey and Sir Wilfrid, and both were encouraging. Sir Wilfrid, however, put his finger on one weak spot: 'She is from New York,' he exclaimed, 'the Canadian girls will never forgive you.' Mackenzie King agreed that it would be still better if she were a Canadian, he wished she were, but he explained that she had gone to Labrador to help in Grenfell's work, 'preferring useful service to the pastimes of her surroundings in N.Y.' When Mackenzie King mentioned that perhaps Lord Grey, who had met her in New York, had invited her to Ottawa with the object of bringing the two together, Sir Wilfrid playfully remarked, 'I should think Lord Grey would want you for one of his own daughters.' To this Mackenzie King replied that the British aristocracy was a closed corporation and that he had no wish to become an aristocrat, even if there were an opportunity. He thought a peer of the realm would be the probable lot of His Excellency's daughters. 'Oh no,' was Sir Wilfrid's comment, 'I do not think with Lord Grey that would matter.' First responses were to some degree encouraging, but in spite of the impressive sponsorship and in spite of the ardour with which the suit was presented, the end of this brief encounter came within a matter of days.

Financially, and in some other respects, Mackenzie King had been a better matrimonial prospect in January than he was nine months later. In January he had a substantial income, the prestige of a Cabinet minister, and a glowing future. In October he had none of these. He still retained assets that should count more in the choice of a husband: a fine family background, character and integrity, personal charm, an affectionate disposition; and to these could be added earning power once a suitable opportunity turned up. His thoughts continued to turn to the necessity of marriage:

> A great faith within me bids me trust the future and believe that in its unknown keeping is someone of pure soul and noble purpose who will be given to me to share my life. . . . To go on with the strain of excessive work is to postpone again, till perhaps too late, the finding of the life that is to share mine and on the finding of which so much depends.

His intentions took a more definite turn – it could have been a New Year's resolution – when he wrote on New Year's Eve:

> I have a little leisure, opportunity to make with care & prudence the great step in life – the choosing of a wife – This I hope to do during the coming year. God grant I may, & may He guide me in the choice.

It may have seemed for a moment like an answer to prayer when on the following day, on one of his New Year's Day calls in Ottawa, he met a young woman whose charms very much impressed him. He was greatly pleased, when he talked with Sir Wilfrid, to find that he knew her, had known her 'since she was very very small', and thought her a very fine person. One thing that no doubt pleased Sir Wilfrid was that, this time, the object of his interest was a Canadian. When Mackenzie King told him that he was anxious to settle down, Sir Wilfrid agreed that he should and remarked that he thought he was 'on the right track'. With this encouragement Mackenzie King took the first step by arranging for another talk with the young lady, in Montreal, on his way to New York. 'This is a great adventure,' he wrote. 'I have doubts about it coming to anything, but never venture never gain.'

His doubts were confirmed before the day in Montreal was over. In their afternoon talk 'she was rather nervous or frightened I thought & did most of the talking as if afraid I was going to get on to other topics. I liked her exceedingly, in fact I came away feeling the strength of her womanly character, which is both generous & kind.' She invited him to a dance that evening and they had two dances together:

> We sat out both at her request. Somehow I did not feel at ease, and quite differently than during the afternoon. It seemed to me it was the same with her, at any rate I came away feeling it was not wise to 'follow up' our friendship. There is something lacking. Without that something, nothing else counts. I feel like despairing sometimes & wondering if I will ever see anyone I can truly & deeply love. With Miss 'B',* it would not be a matter of more than a year or two before I wd. be the leader of the Liberal Party in Canada & for that matter, a leading figure in politics in England if I wished it. — But the heart will bind itself alone.

The reference in this context to his future in politics indicates rather clearly that he felt marriage would be politically advantageous, but it also shows that he was not willing to regard political advantage as the first consideration — the heart must first be satisfied. To his mind marriage was a prerequisite to political success; so was financial independence, but of the two, marriage was infinitely the more important:

> I know that if I can find the right one to share my life with, & can be freed from dependence on others, I can be the Leader of the Liberal Party & ultimately Premier of Canada. The party today wants a man to follow Sir Wilfrid. If I were independent I have no fears that I wd. be chosen, without independence it would be a difficult role to fill, and harder of attainment. This year I must decide, either to leave politics altogether or be the framer of future policies, and that decision seems to me to depend on the woman I marry. — Marry I must if I can, it is the right life for a man. I have delayed it already too long.

The Montreal venture came to nothing, but almost immediately his thoughts turned elsewhere. He had planned a trip to New York some time earlier — the Montreal visit was merely a stopover — and

---

* In this, and in later quotations and references, the author has for obvious reasons substituted letters for the names that appear in the diary.

even before leaving the city he wrote about the talks he hoped to have with a young lady in New York whom he had long admired. She too had been interested in Dr. Grenfell's work in Labrador.

> I hope this New York trip may help me to a conclusion. My thoughts turn of late to Miss 'C', and have from the very start. All I am afraid of in that connection is that having been brought up with many comforts, these might be necessary to make life happy for her.

Mackenzie King was diffident about approaching Miss 'C', to whom he had written, but he called on her and her mother and they had a pleasant hour together. She was everything he had remembered and more. Her family, it was true, was affluent and he was not, but to his mind, and to hers, such differences were not worthy of consideration. The meeting was of necessity a brief one, but he was resolved that it should not be the last.

In preparation for this visit to New York, he had written in advance to several old friends and told them frankly what was in his heart and in the back of his mind — that he hoped soon to be married, if he could find the suitable wife. They were all fond of him and were interested in furthering his aims. At the Cosmopolitan Club he met several young people whom his friends had invited, one of them Miss 'D', a young girl whom their hostess referred to as 'a good catch' and whom another friend agreed was 'quite ideal'. The visitor from Canada shared their high opinion: 'I must say I liked her exceedingly, she is vivacious and attractive.' But there were other opportunities ahead of him.

Two old Harvard friends were active on his behalf. One in particular promised he would do anything he could 'to bring off a successful marriage' and they had several long talks about possibilities. He said he had invited Miss 'E' to dinner to meet him and he described her charm and mentioned that she would in all probability be worth ten millions. But he had two other suggestions. One was a wealthy widow, Mrs. 'F'. He had written to Mackenzie King about her earlier in the fall, and now told him that he had spoken to her of him. She was beautiful, inclined to be timid, he said, but he thought his friend would have no difficulty winning her. The other had even more to recommend her. She was Miss 'G' — 'the more he thought of that the better he believed it would be'. Mackenzie King was given an opportunity to meet all these young women and others during the fortnight he spent in New York. It was in many respects, as he put it, 'a wonderful experience'. It did not produce the principal result he had hoped for, but he came back to Ottawa with renewed determination to accomplish what he had set out to do. The women he had met were all beautiful, all high-minded — and all were women of wealth. There is no telling how any one of them would have responded if he had indicated serious intentions, but, as he had told himself some time earlier, the very fact that a woman was wealthy created in his mind an impediment. Financial advantages, like political advantages, should carry no weight when it came to the choosing of a life companion — the heart alone must guide. His prejudice against wealth might, of course, be overcome, if the qualities of nature which he sought — such as character, beauty of spirit, genuine interest in social welfare — dominated the whole personality. This would be a rare combination of all the talents, but he felt that he had found all this in the one person he had had in mind when he set out for New York — Miss 'C'. After his return to Ottawa, reflecting on his experiences, he wrote: 'The one thing on which in my heart I feel no doubt is the beauty of the character and soul of Miss "C". . . . She is one woman who, compare her from any point of view with any other woman, seems to surpass all. . . . If I were an independent man I would speak to her tomorrow, but I am supersensitive on my own position.' He found it difficult to write to her (for some reason would have preferred writing to her mother), but he did write because he wanted to know whether she was interested or not: 'I hardly know what she thinks or feels, but there is no doubt in my mind as to her great worth in every particular. She seems in a way beyond me.'

But his own lack of decision, his inability to make up his mind definitely, seem evident from the fact that on that same day he wrote to Miss 'G', telling her he thought of visiting her city and asking if he might call on her. In contrast with the letter to Miss 'C', he quite enjoyed writing this letter because he felt there was a response in her nature. A little note he had received from her had been frank and without reserve, and this had appealed to him.

In spite of his high hopes, nothing was destined to come of his venture in either of these two directions — perhaps because of a cooling of his ardour, perhaps because of his concern as to financial inequalities — or it may have been because he received insufficient encouragement. He was still forced to go on his way, lonely and unsatisfied, but he continued to hope that his life would ultimately take on a new beginning. His quest for the ideal wife had thus far been a futile one, but he made other tentative approaches in succeeding months. The nearest thing to a commitment on his part seems to have been in 1914, when he was still just under forty, still without remunerative employment. In this case the home of the young lady, Miss 'H', was also far distant from Ottawa, and in the United States, which meant that the courtship, if courtship it could be called, had to be carried on by correspondence. For months they had been writing to each other, and her letters had raised his hopes that at last he had found what he had sought. He decided to try to bring matters to a conclusion through a personal visit. He was excited and hopeful:

> I received this morning a lovely letter from Miss 'H'. It made me very happy and tonight I wrote her asking if I might come to see her next week. How I hope my life may take a new beginning as the result of that visit. . . . My mind is full of next week. How I pray all may go well.

Unfortunately he had waited too long: the letter welcoming his coming visit conveyed, alas, the information that the young lady had recently become engaged to another. Perhaps it had been excess of caution, perhaps a questioning as to the rightness of his decision; or it may have been his lifelong belief that time would solve most problems and that precipitous action often led to dire results, that was responsible for the abrupt ending of this hope. It was a lesson, a disappointment: 'The experience has taught me how unwise it is to let time run on in a matter of this kind.' It was a disappointment, because he found the young lady

> ... all that I believed her to be in character and disposition, kind, generous, sympathetic, frank, and with the truest and noblest purpose. I felt I would never forgive myself for my delay.... We would have been well suited and very happy together, but I have been slow. She has been right in everything she has done, I could not have asked for more, but a week or two or a month might have made the whole difference for the whole of life.

Such keen disappointment, such self-reproach because of his procrastination, is understandable. But more difficult to understand are his seemingly contradictory feelings. Even on the day he received the letter telling him of the other engagement, he was able to write: 'Oddly enough I feel a real sense of relief in the thought that all uncertainty as to the outcome of my visit is at an end.' He did, however, pay the visit and on his way home on the train, although he wrote of his uppermost feeling being a wistful sort of regretfulness, he commented: 'This intermingles oddly enough with a feeling entirely the opposite, one of genuine relief at the thought of a complete freedom.' At least partly responsible for these contradictory feelings was the impression made upon him by the girl's father at their first meeting: 'I should never have been quite happy with Mr. "H". That I feel sure of, and that would have affected the other relationship. The explanation of the delay lies in large part there.' The uncongeniality of this prospective father-in-law, a man of great wealth, may have contributed something to his sense of relief, but a certain holding back, of which perhaps he himself was not wholly aware, made it difficult for him to commit himself whole-heartedly as the crucial moment approached.

This latest venture was not to be his last. Before the night was over (he did not arrive in Toronto until 4.30 in the morning) he recorded a new resolution: 'I am determined to make headway & have a home of my own ere long, if I can manage this. It is all such a mystery. Never will I debate again if I can prevent it.'

Suiting action to the word, he sought immediately to make headway in another direction. On the day he returned to Ottawa, he wrote a letter to Miss 'I', whom he had not met but to whom a close friend had given him a note of introduction some two years earlier. He had heard glowing reports of her and knew that she, too, had been interested in Dr. Grenfell's Labrador mission — an indication in itself of unselfish devotion to a worthy cause. There was to be a college gathering in June in the American city in which she lived and his letter was a cautious inquiry to find out where she would be at that time. If she were to be at home, then he would go. They did meet and he was more than favourably impressed. Indeed they met many times during the next few years and greatly enjoyed each other's company, but their relationship never got beyond the point of warm and understanding friendship.

There were to be other such friendships in his maturer years but at the end of this period, in the late spring of 1914, he was still a bachelor and without any likely prospect of having that status changed.

CHAPTER 4

'A Heaven-sent Deliverance'

If an election had been called in the early months of the war, as had been rumoured, Mackenzie King would have seized any opportunity to find a place for himself in Parliament, where his undoubted abilities could have been put to their best use. He had been seeking such an opportunity for nearly three years, ever since the defeat of 1911, but time and again his hopes had been frustrated. He was gradually becoming convinced, so he wrote to a friend, that 'public life hereafter must be a closed opportunity to me'. Family illnesses and unrequited affections weighed on him; he was engaged on what was little better than 'hack work' for the party, which brought him little income and, worse still, little opportunity to give of his best. He admonished himself for his feelings of depression and tried to put on a brave front before the world. But underlying everything was a pervading unhappiness and disappointment that his new life, so full of promise, should so soon have taken on the appearance of failure. Looking back on the bleakness and frustrations of many months, he summed up all his misery in an exclamation, 'How terribly broken down on every side is the house of life around me!'

Deliverance, however – he described it as a 'Heaven-sent deliverance' – was to come, and from an unforeseen quarter. On June 1, 1914, he received from the Rockefeller Foundation an invitation to come to New York to discuss a major project the foundation was contemplating. This invitation, and the share he was to take in the proposed project, was to open up a new way of life for him for the next four years. Labour and politics had been the two major interests of his life. Their relative importance was now to be reversed, and labour relations were to assume first place: politics, while not wholly displaced, were to be relegated to the background; the politician was to become the industrial-relations consultant — the platform speaker, the board-room adviser. He had had a real triumph in 1907 as author and sponsor of the Industrial Disputes Act; now he was to face new labour problems and shape new plans to meet them.

The invitation had come in the form of a telegram from Jerome D. Greene, secretary of the foundation:

> Recalling our Harvard acquaintance I venture to ask whether your engagements would permit you to advise large interests I represent in regard to present labor difficulties and probable far-reaching studies looking toward the future. If so could you come to New York at our expense this week for preliminary consultation.

Mackenzie King had met Jerome Greene a few years before when Greene was secretary to President C. W. Eliot of Harvard University, but he was not aware of the interests with which he was now connected. He had not known that such an institution as the Rockefeller Foundation existed, and he knew little more about 'the present labor difficulties' to which Greene referred. He had no idea of the nature of the proposals to be made to him, but presumed that the request had something to do with Canadian labour legislation. He expected nothing more than an interview of a few hours and perhaps a request for detailed information about the working of the Canadian Industrial Disputes Act. When, however, he received on the same day a telegram from President Eliot himself, he realized that this was to be no ordinary conference:

> Opportunity offered by request to you from Rockefeller group is immense. You might greatly serve all white race industries and

show way to industrial concord in whole world. I urge that you inform yourself fully about the opportunity and then seize it. Well worth a temporary abandonment of Canadian prospects. Coming from such a source, this telegram caused him to consider seriously what the significance of the invitation for consultation might be. 'From the moment it was received I saw that ... the moment was perhaps the most critical of my whole life.'

The telegram had provided a slight clue to the object of the proposed conference. Jerome Greene supplemented it in a long letter written two days later, in which he disclosed that it was the strike in Colorado about which he wished to consult him — 'not so much with a view to the settlement of that strike as to obtain your advice in regard to a very thorough and, I hope, far-reaching study of the labour question in America'. He explained that he was associated with John D. Rockefeller, Jr., and his father, and represented them in the directorates of several corporations and philanthropic institutions, such as the Rockefeller Foundation, the General Education Board, and the Rockefeller Institute for Medical Research, whose investments aggregated 150 million dollars. The Rockefeller Foundation had been planning, he said, some economic and social studies which might have an ultimate bearing on the solution of the labour problem. If substantial improvements in the relation of capital and labour could be worked out, on a basis compatible with sound finance, the foundation might perform a greater social service than it could render through any of its strictly philanthropic expenditures. Although President Eliot had referred glowingly to future prospects, Greene's letter on the face of it was merely an invitation to a conference to discuss 'a wise approach to this great problem'. He added, however — and this sentence was significant — 'Whether your public engagements or your political preoccupations would make it possible or prudent for you to enter into any continuing advisory relation with this project, must be determined after conference.'

Mackenzie King learned later from Jerome Greene that his name had been suggested to the trustees, presumably by Greene himself, when they were discussing persons they might consult about the scope and objectives of the project and the qualifications of the man or men who would undertake the work or act as advisers. During the discussions it had flashed across Greene's mind that Mackenzie King was the very man to advise on work of the kind. President Eliot, when consulted, had agreed and this had led to the invitation to go to New York for consultation.

'The Colorado situation' was indeed to play an important part in the discussions with Mackenzie King. The Rockefellers had substantial holdings – in fact a controlling interest – in the Colorado Fuel and Iron Company. Here a strike of coal-miners and steel-workers, which involved the employees of this company as well as other smaller coal-mining companies in Colorado, had been declared on September 23, 1913, and the miners were still out on strike in June 1914. The conflict had aroused nation-wide interest. The state militia had been called in, and many lives had been lost in the fighting in which strikers, mine guards, and militiamen were engaged. John D. Rockefeller, Jr., had been kept informed of developments by the company's officers in Colorado and he had consistently upheld their policies. They had refused to recognize the trade union, and he had concurred. He had been bitterly assailed, particularly after the so-called 'Ludlow Massacre' in April 1914, as an absentee owner who failed to use his influence to remove the injustices of which the miners complained and to bring the strike to an end. He was subjected to so much personal abuse on this account in the early months of 1914 that the solution of the Colorado problem had a first place in his mind. The suggestion of Mackenzie King's name at that time was welcomed by him, not as that of a distinguished economist, but as that of a man who could point the way to a solution. It was his wide experience in settling industrial disputes that had especially commended him to the Rockefellers.

II

There was no hesitation on Mackenzie King's part in accepting the invitation. The meeting was held on Saturday morning, June 6, in the junior Rockefeller's New York residence on West 54th Street. Rockefeller had with him Jerome Greene and Starr J. Murphy, his solicitor. Because of the importance of this first meeting with Rockefeller, some extracts are quoted here from the detailed record which King dictated six months later:

> The conversation was carried on for the most part by Mr. Rockefeller himself, and, as I now recall it, dealt broadly with two topics: firstly, the methods of adjusting industrial differences and maintaining industrial peace; and secondly the wisdom of instituting a course of special studies on industrial problems, and the persons likely to be of most service in prosecuting work of the kind. The Colorado situation was spoken of, though, as I recall, it was expressly stated by Mr. Rockefeller that the question of recognition was the sole one which remained, and that the United Mine Workers, not being an organization which the management felt it wise to enter into an agreement with, they were determined not to yield on this point. Mr. Rockefeller said that, so far as collective bargaining was concerned, he believed in the principle of it, and thought it was quite proper that the men should have some kind of adequate representation where large numbers of them were working together. He asked me whether I could suggest any plan or arrangement which might be adopted with advantage in this connection. I then told him that my experience in personally intervening in industrial disputes had led me to believe that purely economic questions were easily adjusted, that it was the personal antagonisms and matters arising out of prejudice and bitterness and individual antipathies which were the ones which caused the most concern.

Mackenzie King was right in his diagnosis that the troubles in Colorado had arisen from ill-adjusted human relations — prejudice, bitterness, and individual antipathies. Obviously this was not just a relatively simple economic problem: without knowing more of the conditions in Colorado he could not prescribe the remedy at once, but he suggested, tentatively, that better relations could be developed if the managers and representatives of the miners could be brought together in committees to deal with grievances at an early stage, before they became serious. Rockefeller was impressed by his grasp of the problem and his approach to its solution; he pressed immediately for details of the application of such a plan. A more elaborate outline of the proposals was promised.

The conversation then turned to the feasibility of the foundation's instituting an inquiry infinitely broader in scope than the one they had been discussing. Mackenzie King was confident that such an inquiry could be conducted with very great advantage to labour and capital, and also to the public. The problem of finding the man or men qualified for such an undertaking would be a difficult one. He had not anticipated discussing any individuals, but he mentioned a few names that came to his mind, such as Charles P. Neill, former United States Commissioner of Labor; Victor S. Clark, formerly of the United States Bureau of Commerce and Labor; Professor John R. Commons of the University of Wisconsin; John Graham Brooks; Sidney and Beatrice Webb; Sir George Askwith. He promised to give thought to other names and also to prepare a brief outline of what such an extensive inquiry should embrace, and the time and staff that might be necessary.

Later he wrote in his diary:

> I have since learned from Mr. Rockefeller, in conversation, that when I came to New York on that Saturday morning he had not in mind doing other than getting my advice upon the Colorado situation, and the advisability of instituting a study into the labor problem, that during the course of the conversation he was impressed with the manner in which I discussed it with him, and that before the conversation ended he had made up his mind to ask if I would not undertake this work myself. In conversation he said to me, 'You will remember me asking you before we parted to consider the work yourself'. As a matter of fact, I do not think he made the proposal in so many words, but I gathered, as others present also did, that without putting it into concrete language, he was making an offer as direct to me as he thought it was wise to do at the time without further conference with his associates.

After the conference in New York, Rockefeller and his associates were in no doubt about the desirability of concluding an arrangement with King. Jerome Greene telegraphed and wrote to him three days later making a definite proposal that he enlist in the broad study they had discussed, and inviting him to return to New York soon for a further conference. What the foundation had in mind at that stage, he said, was an

> ... investigation of the great problem of industrial relations, with a special view to the discovery of some organization or union, or at any rate of some mutual relationship of capital and labor which would afford to labor the protection it needs against oppression and exploitation, while at the same time promoting its efficiency as an instrument of economic production.

They would like to know what his conditions of service would be, the amount of assistance he would require, what compensation he would expect, and also how long it might take to complete the studies.

About the duration of the inquiry Greene had more to say:

> Of course the problem is so vast and the difficulties are so largely inherent in human nature, that a complete solution is not to be expected in five years or in a generation. On the other hand, it might be expected that hard study for a year or two would yield much light on the problem and particularly on the very question whether such studies could be profitably pursued for a longer or an indefinite time under such auspices and with such resources as the Rockefeller Foundation could provide. These resources would be to all intents and purposes limited only by the judgment of the Trustees as to the limits of profitable investigation along these lines.

The funds of the foundation, he had already said, amounted to more than a hundred million dollars, and almost the entire income was still available for the various projects the trustees might institute.

Greene's explicit outline of what was involved in the foundation's proposal made Mackenzie King realize even more clearly the magnitude of the opportunity opening before him. He replied at once but explained his own political involvements in Canada and also the need he felt for further conference with the foundation's representatives. Before accepting the offer he expressed his warm appreciation of the honour done him in asking him to undertake a work 'fraught with such far-reaching possibilities'. In his diary he wrote: 'I doubt if ever an opportunity of such magnitude was set forth in more generous terms than the proposal made in his letter.'

He could not have written so enthusiastically about the proposal had his personal contact with John D. Rockefeller, Jr., and his father not convinced him that his deeply-rooted prejudice against millionaires was not justified as far as they were concerned. He was immensely impressed by their sincerity and public spirit.

III

But he still had some misgivings about such a radical change in his plans for the future. He could not lightly lay aside his belief, long held, that it was foreordained that he should become prime minister of Canada. Less than a month before, Sir Wilfrid had spoken words of encouragement. If, now, alliance with the Rockefellers meant separation from Laurier, there could be no such alliance. That seemed to be the first consideration in his mind. When he consulted Sir Wilfrid (the first person with whom he spoke fully) he told him that he had in mind also another consideration – his obligation to North York:

> This being my grandfather's old constituency made it impossible for me not to consider my obligation in this connection very carefully, and made me particularly anxious, even should I not continue in politics, to at least carry that riding at a general election.

Sir Wilfrid was reluctant to advise him. He knew of Mackenzie King's personal circumstances, but felt sure that King would not think of giving up politics except from dire necessity. He spoke in admiring terms of young Mr. Rockefeller, saying that he had thought the position publicly taken by him in regard to the Western troubles was a sound and fearless one and just.

In odd moments between political speeches and conferences, King consulted several other friends of long standing. Sir William Mulock was completely in favour of acceptance:

> He said his advice would be to abandon the thought of politics altogether ... he hoped in negotiating with the Rockefellers I would not place my services at too small an estimate ... that I should ask for $20,000 a year and a written contract for ten years. With this amount he thought I could save and by living quietly accumulate enough to come back into public life later on, should I still so desire, but he was quite emphatic about dropping politics altogether in the interval.

Hon. Sydney Fisher, a former senior colleague in the Laurier administration, opposed the idea because of political considerations. He said that:

> Sir Wilfrid had told him he thought I might come to regret the decision if I made it, that I might realize there was before me the opportunity of being the Leader of the Liberal Party in Canada, and that while the older men were still on the scene, this might not be immediately possible, it was almost certain that later on, if I were to continue in politics, this chance would come my way.

Colonel John G. Foster, United States Consul General in Canada, with whom King had very friendly personal relations, favoured acceptance:

> I think [he] almost despaired of me when I argued against so doing on the score of it appearing to be an exchange of opportunities of public service for a financial consideration, and the betrayal of labor interests to which I had from the outset devoted my life.

Wilfred Campbell's only comment was that he 'did not like the idea of my severing connections with Canada and abandoning the political prospects ahead of me'.

Other old and influential friends were encouraging, with only an occasional warning against separating himself from Canada and its opportunities. The danger he would run of becoming involved in 'Big Business' was also pointed out. This, of course, Mackenzie

King felt very strongly himself. To his brother, Dr. D. Macdougall King, who then was a patient in a sanatorium in Denver, Colorado, he wrote: 'Did it mean allying myself in any way with the "interests" as a solicitor might, I need scarcely say that nothing would have tempted me to consider a proposal of the kind one way or the other. This, however, is wholly different.' Macdougall King's reply was what he might have expected:

> I can't but urge you against making any business arrangements with the 'interests'. With your clean-cut conscience, it cannot possibly be lasting and it will brand you with the laboring classes for the rest of your life, whether you deserve it or not, as being the tool of the Rockefellers. There is a pretty mess to clear up in this country and the very heart of the Colorado Fuel and Iron Company has to be changed and millions of dollars sacrificed by them before things will be right in the sight of God.

When he cabled to Violet Markham for her advice, he said it would mean life work and giving up Canadian politics and added: 'Would source affect probable service?' She knew better than most of his friends what his family and political circumstances were, and having these in mind advised by cable that he should accept 'if independent self-respecting terms arranged'. What she had in mind in adding this condition was clarified in a long letter written on the same day. She wrote:

> It all depends on the terms, Rex — nobody must be able to say Rockefeller has bought you and you will speak with his voice in future. I am sure this can't be so as you would not have considered the offer....
>
> Your material success would be dearly purchased at the loss of a fragment of personal independence, but I repeat it, if the conditions leave you free to work as you will, — to attack capital if necessary to destroy trusts and monopolies — if this is so I can see no harm whatever in your following this new path which you may tread to the great benefit of mankind.

She went further in her letter:

> Frankly I don't like millionaires of the Rockefeller type. One

wonders what he is after with a proposal of this kind. It is difficult to think a man like that can really care about ideal conditions of labor or the higher life of the workers.

The first horrid thought which went through my mind was whether this was an attempt to buy you. If so I would rather see you begging your bread than attain success through such a source. But I felt on reflection that the very fact that you have considered this proposal shows that it must have come to you in an honourable self respecting way. Otherwise you would have been the first to turn from it in disgust.

I could not bear the idea that your liberty of thought or action or service should be at the mercy of such a man as Rockefeller — that you should part with one atom of your independence.

But, if he is really genuine and sincere in his proposals, if this is a case of honest study and honest work then I see no reason why you should not accept and serve in this new direction as well as you have done in the past.

Violet Markham's critical attitude toward the Rockefeller connection would have been less critical had she known John D. Rockefeller, Jr., or known more about him. She came in later years to realize that her mental picture of him in 1914 was a sadly distorted one. At the moment she was concerned, too, about the suggestion that this would mean giving up Canadian politics altogether:

And when you say a life work isn't that looking too far ahead? Why should you not do this job for 10 or 12 years and then come back into Canadian politics? I mind very much losing you to the Empire — I don't want to see you permanently annexed by America!

On the whole, however, her advice was to accept:

In view of the obstacles and discouragements you are confronted with at this moment of your political future I do think this offer may point the way to a new and happy and interesting life and one which will enable you to provide as you could not otherwise for the necessities of your dear ones.

If he had entertained any misgivings about the decision to accept, this letter would have dispelled them. The questions she raised were answered: he was convinced of the sincerity of John D. Rockefeller, Jr., he was stimulated by the magnitude of the project, and he would insist on a way being left open to return to Canadian political life. He was satisfied that Rockefeller was not deserving of the reproach commonly applied to men of great wealth, but his political sense forced him to realize that it would be difficult to convince the Canadian electorate, and particularly the labour element, that his new sponsors were as high-minded as he had come to believe. He realized that association with the Rockefellers, even with the Rockefeller Foundation, would have its disadvantages, would be misunderstood and misinterpreted, and would be used against him politically, indeed might impair his political future. He debated very carefully whether he would be wise in entertaining the proposal at all: 'I felt that once associated in any way with the Rockefeller concern, my future in politics would be jeopardized.' He 'would have rejected it utterly had the offer come to enter the service of the Standard Oil industry and not to work under a foundation where money was held in trust'.

He knew also that absence from the country would militate against his chances politically, particularly if it were misrepresented that he was working for Standard Oil in another country. It might be due wholly to prejudice, 'but prejudice was a factor which a public man had constantly to be taking into account'.

There was substance in every argument he considered, pro and con. He was dazzled by the prospect of the new life that was opening before him, and was convinced that he should enter upon it. At the same time he could not refrain from counting the cost, weighing the advantage of immediate acceptance against the danger to his whole political future. He spent many worrying days and nights before he returned to New York for a second conference, this time with John D. Rockefeller, Sr., and his son, in the family home in Tarrytown. Before they finished their conversations he gave his final commitment and agreement in principle was reached.

IV

Even after he had finally given his acceptance, thoughts of future political attacks continued to plague him. He told Mr. Rockefeller in December that

> ... in accepting I had had to consider that I was prejudicing my political future for all time to come, that my battles henceforth would be not with the political issues but against the Rockefeller prejudice, that I wd. not be harangued against as a Liberal politician but as a 'Standard Oil man'. Still I felt I was not going to be governed by prejudice, and had decided on this basis.

It was not until August 13, however, after some further negotiations with Murphy and Greene, that the executive committee of the foundation passed a resolution whereby he was 'appointed to make a comprehensive study of industrial relations'.

He did not accept unconditionally. He had two reservations on which he was insistent: one, that he should retain his Canadian citizenship, and the other, that he must be free to participate in Canadian politics as opportunities arose.

His attitude on these vital points had been made clear at the conference at Tarrytown:

> I spoke of my association with Sir Wilfrid and North York, and mentioned that if acceptance of this proposal meant severing my connection with Sir Wilfrid before another election I did not think I could entertain it. To this Mr. Rockefeller, Jr. replied, 'We would only think the less of you, Mr. King, if you did not consider matters of this kind.' Mr. Rockefeller, Sr. . . . could see no objections to my continuing in politics, but that as a matter of fact there might be advantages in my so doing . . . there might be distinct advantages in talking with men in other countries, through being also a member of the Canadian Parliament.

Mackenzie King then mentioned one political commitment he had already made which he felt must be fulfilled. This was to accompany Sir Wilfrid on a proposed trip to the Canadian West in August and September. Mr. Rockefeller readily agreed to this, with the understanding that on his return from this trip he would be prepared to give his full time to the work of the foundation. It would be much less than full time, of course, if an election were called and if Mackenzie King were returned to Parliament. In that event he would have to withdraw for perhaps four or five months. This was specified in his letter of confirmation, but, he added, during that period he would of course accept no salary from the foundation.

His place of residence was to continue to be in Ottawa, but a letter from Starr Murphy suggested that 'if hereafter you were to become continuously in residence in New York for such a period as would materially modify the situation this question would then be subject to reconsideration and readjustment'. The situation was never 'materially modified'. The Roxborough, Ottawa, continued to be Mackenzie King's headquarters throughout his association with the foundation, even though the trips to New York were many and the several visits to Colorado prolonged. Several months later, when the foundation offices were moved from 26 Broadway to 61 Broadway, he was assigned quarters on the fifty-ninth floor. They were never occupied by him; he visited the suite once or twice, but office furniture was never installed. When he visited New York he preferred to do his work, other than attendance at conferences, in a single room in the Harvard Club on West 44th Street.

v

When the question of remuneration came up, Mackenzie King, recalling his conversations with friends in Canada, suggested that $15,000 a year might be a proper figure 'in view of offers I had rejected in the past and the risk I would now be running of giving up a political career'. He repeated that he would forgo all salary for such time as he would give to public work in Canada. Rockefeller replied that they had decided they could not think of offering him less than $10,000 a year; but that they had not thought they could remunerate work for the foundation on the same basis as if it were business. His compromise suggestion of $12,000 a year was acceptable to Mackenzie King, and that point was settled. In his letter of confirmation Rockefeller added: 'If after further and mature reflection you feel that $15,000 is the proper figure, it is our disposition to be guided by your wishes in the matter.' Mackenzie King noted in his diary:

> I might, had I wished to do so, had securing myself financially been the main consideration, have expressed my willingness to give my undivided time to the work of the Foundation for a period of five years, at the rate of $15,000 a year and necessary travelling expenses, and have secured an agreement on that basis. Accepting $12,000 instead of $15,000 with an understanding that I would forgo pro rata remuneration for the time spent in politics, I view in the light of a financial sacrifice for the sake of opportunity of independent public service.

VI

The duration of the inquiry, or rather the duration of Mackenzie King's association with the foundation, was not made definite, but estimates ranged all the way from a year to a lifetime. The possibility of a continuing connection, after the study of industrial relations was completed, had been suggested by Rockefeller:

> It may be that it is better for an agreement to be entered into at this time for a year only, the year to begin with your active assumption of work in the latter part of September or the first of October. . . . My feeling is that the one year agreement would be the simplest and that before the expiration of the time, both you and we would be very much better able than now to discuss the further and more permanent relationship to which we are looking forward.

This was confirmed in Mackenzie King's account of his talk with Murphy and Greene on July 2:

> It was agreed, therefore, that the term of our arrangement to be formally entered into was for a year, with the understanding that it was the hope of the Foundation and my own hope that in the

interval events would so shape themselves as to make our association one which it would be of mutual advantage to continue over a number of years.

Violet Markham had suggested ten or twelve years and then a return to Canadian politics. But Mackenzie King realized that every year away would make re-entry into political life that much more difficult. A businessman might move back and forth, but a politician, particularly one who was ambitious for leadership, had to think of the attitude of voters to a man whose political foes might describe him as an expatriate, if not unpatriotic. On the whole a short-term commitment, one from which he could withdraw if political possibilities developed as he hoped, seemed to be the wise course. He would have to live in a state of uncertainty, making the best of the immediate very attractive opportunity but always hoping for a return to that other field which was so much closer to his heart.

In one of the conferences with the Rockefellers about the nature and form of the projected inquiry Mackenzie King was asked if he would like a board or a committee to advise with. He was very definite in rejecting such a suggestion:

> I replied that I should accept the whole responsibility myself, as I would not hesitate to advise with anyone whom the Foundation might wish, but that I felt it would only prejudice whatever work I might strive to do were I in any way, either rightly or wrongly, restricted by the known attitude of individuals who might comprise such a board. Mr. Rockefeller Sr. said at once 'You are quite right in that; do not have a board.'

Some of the foundation trustees had anticipated that the new venture, replacing an earlier idea of a Bureau of Economic Research, would call for an organization, perhaps a very big organization, with a staff of directors and research assistants. Mackenzie King would not commit himself on this point, preferring to let events determine his course. He did say, however, in a letter to Sidney Webb in England, written on November 9, that when he had gathered a certain amount of information on the most profitable paths of inquiry he would begin to set a staff of investigators to work. Then if changed conditions permitted he would probably extend inquiries begun in America, to other countries. But this was not a final decision — he was still feeling his way.

When the foundation announced his appointment on October 1, the statement declared that 'in spirit and method the investigation of the problem of industrial relations will be like that carried on by the Rockefeller Institute for Medical Research'. The analogy was frequently used. He wrote to his brother, for example:

> What I have suggested is that the work should be commenced in a way which will enable it to develop in time into an institution doing for social diseases what the Rockefeller Institute for Medical Research is doing for human diseases.
>
> If successful that work will far outrun the lives of each of us and the service it is likely to be to mankind is too great even to contemplate.

The key to the parallel between the work in industrial relations and the work in medical research had been given to King when he read a passage written by Louis Pasteur which he was to quote frequently:

> Two contrary laws seem to be wrestling with each other nowadays: the one, a law of blood and death, ever imagining new means of destruction, and forcing nations to be constantly ready for the battlefield — the other, a law of peace, work, and health, ever evolving new means of delivering man from the scourges which beset him. The one seeks violent conquests, the other the relief of Humanity. The latter places one human life above any victory; while the former would sacrifice hundreds of thousands of lives to the ambition of one.

'It may lead,' he wrote, 'to an Institute on Industrial Relations.'

But it was more the spirit of the Medical Research Institute that was to be emulated than its form or size. He made this clear when he drafted an answer to an inquiry which a federal government agency had addressed to the foundation as to the nature of his investigation. The answer said that the method would be akin to that of the Rockefeller Institute for Medical Research, and added:

In so far as Mr. King's inquiries have to do with industrial controversies, his attitude will be that of a physician who investigates the nature and causes of the pathological conditions with which he has to deal, with a view, if possible, to the discovery of effective remedies.

What . . . is also contemplated is an opportunity of promoting industrial experiments calculated to improve industrial relations in some of the industries in which the $100,000,000, the property of the Foundation, is invested.

As regards organization . . . Mr. King expects as time goes on occasionally to retain expert advice and assistance, but it is not his intention to attempt the organization of any staff, such, for example, as exists in Government Bureaus or Commissions; with the exception of the appointment of Dr. Foerster and a secretary, Mr. King has not thus far made any request for appointments.

Dr. R. F. Foerster of Harvard University had been asked in July to prepare a bibliography. His appointment, and mine as secretary, were to be the only ones, apart from occasional clerical assistance, that were made during Mackenzie King's association with the foundation.

As his work went on Mackenzie King developed a strong dislike of the idea of an 'organization'. He expressed himself strongly after an interview with Dr. J. W. Glen, director of the Russell Sage Foundation:

> In speaking of my work the mere suggestion that it presupposed building up a staff to do such work as gathering statistical data, made me feel irritated. It is life, vital ideas, not material that I am out to seek, and I hope to find this through immediate contacts with men of thought and action, not in building up an organization of pretentious proportions.

VII

Mackenzie King's work under the foundation began on the first day of October. It was obvious, before his 'investigation' was well under way, that it would not follow the conventional pattern of allocating subjects to a coterie of experts, each one keen to build up a staff of fact-finders, or through questionnaires and conferences to amass all the available statistics and expressions of opinion that could have a bearing on his branch of the whole subject. This had never been King's way of working. He was not one to plough through endless briefs and blue-books in order to reach his conclusions. His techniques would not be those of a modern social scientist. He would read widely and talk freely with people in all walks of life. His was a roving commission and the foundation had left it to him to conduct the investigation in his own way. Since his original plans to travel widely had had to be abandoned when war was declared, future plans would have to depend on circumstances — he would not commit himself in advance to any rigid programme or schedule.

Presumably on the orthodox theory that the first step in any research project should be the preparation of an elaborate bibliography, Dr. Foerster had been engaged in mid-July 1914 to prepare a bibliography of publications relating to industrial relations and a directory of organizations and individuals engaged in research in this field. The work was completed in less than four months. About 9,000 cards constituted the bibliography and about 800 the directory. The chief use to which the catalogue seems to have been put was in suggesting topics for elaborate charts on which King worked incessantly for weeks, a kind of preliminary exercise as he pondered the most effective approach to his problem of industrial relations. He was fascinated by this work on the diagrams and enlisted the draughting skill of an Ottawa architect, J. Albert Ewart. What was produced by this combination of lively imagination and master craftsmanship was a series of nine charts designed to illustrate the actions and reactions of various factors and forces (such as discovery and invention, public opinion, education, government) in their bearing on the central problem of effecting right relations within industry. (These charts were ultimately reproduced as an appendix to his *Industry and Humanity*.) It was a highly abstruse presentation of many abstract ideas, something that one could ap-

preciate only with the help of the word-of-mouth explanations of
the author himself. In spite of the inordinate time that was spent on
their preparation, the charts contributed little if anything to a
businessman's, or even a professor's, understanding of the basic
problems of industrial relations and their solution. They probably
served a useful purpose, however, in enabling King to see these
problems in a truer perspective, against the background of broader
movements, national, international, and even universal. His most
effective work was to be done in the handling of concrete issues
that arose in the course of his inquiries.

VIII

The abandonment of politics and the taking up of this new career
meant to Mackenzie King a radical change in the ordering of his
daily life. He began the first day, as was his custom, with his morning devotions; he ended it with the writing of the diary — in itself
almost a religious rite. For a long time, in his morning readings, he
had made notes in the margin opposite the passages he was reading.
Sometimes he made longer comments in his diary, such as: 'This
morning, as yesterday, I got back to the joy of reading my bible
first thing in the morning. This has been the truest help and inspiration to me. This association with that wonderful life and eternal
truth. It comes to me with an ever deeper and profounder meaning.'
Mackenzie King was by nature a deeply religious man. He had inherited something of the mysticism of his Scottish forebears; he
could approve of the solitudes of the monastery; he was deeply
impressed by the quiet devotional spirit of the Quakers. 'As I study
myself,' he wrote in November of that year, 'I find myself more
and more a Quaker. They seem to me to be nearer the spirit of
Christ than other denominations.'

His new, well-ordered life in Ottawa, as he viewed it, was to have
conscientious work as its centre. Its opportunities would be improved by early-morning rising and by avoiding social engagements and pleasures save on the most limited scale. ('I have not

answered the phone even, but kept myself steadily at work all week.') There would have to be some relaxation; he would live laborious days but all delights would not have to be scorned. Horseback-riding came within the category of permissible diversions. ('... the event of today was putting into practice a resolution formed some time ago to take up riding when I could afford it. ... I was not tired or stiff after two hours exercise.') Long rides, even in the coldest winter weather, became an established habit for the end of the day, and he derived an odd sense of companionship from them. ('I talked with the horse most of the way, and enjoyed the ride exceedingly.') Days when he did not ride he took long walks and he found 'skies and fields most companionable'. Social engagements were not wholly given up but they were restricted and took the form mostly of serious talks with friends, reading poetry, and listening to good music. Occasional visits to Government House gave him opportunities of talks with the Duke of Connaught about the war and political questions and with the Princess Patricia about books and the deeper meanings of life. He was surprised to find that the Princess was a firm believer in reincarnation, a belief he himself could not share. In an earlier talk she had told him of her interest in psychic phenomena; she believed, as he did, in the survival of human personality and communication with departed souls.

In public life one responsibility he took seriously was the work of the Canadian Patriotic Fund. He was a member of its executive committee, and was one of five speakers at a 'Patriotic Meeting' at the Russell Theatre (the others were the Governor General, Borden, Laurier, and Foster). It was an honour he greatly prized:

> In the eyes of the public this was company of a high order. It at least has this of satisfaction to me. It shews the point I have reached at the moment of accepting work that may take me out of public life altogether. I do not believe it will. To do this work well and enter into politics as a leader later on is the ambition I secretly cherish.

Official and personal correspondence was, as it always had been and always would be, a time-consuming burden. ('It takes me all my time to keep up with it and at the same time to work on the

planning of the investigation proper.') He was getting along without a full-time secretary and that position was not filled until the
end of the year. For him there were not enough hours in a day, or
days in a week.

Frequent demands on his time came from another source — from
New York — and interrupted the programme of study he had planned for himself. John D. Rockefeller, Jr., was looking to him for
guidance in formulating new labour policies for the Colorado Fuel
and Iron Company and in answering troublesome questions from
governmental quarters about the foundation's motives in instituting
an inquiry of its own into the whole problem of industrial relations.
To advise his new principal on such matters was an opportunity as
well as a duty. On one vital point he had made a good beginning: he
felt that he had succeeded in convincing Rockefeller and his colleagues that investors, even such corporate investors as the Rockefeller Foundation, must share responsibility for labour conditions
in the industries in which they had investments. Acceptance of that
doctrine meant action in the direction of reform. Rockefeller was
eager for such action, in Colorado first and then in other industries
in which his voice could be effective. Such a prospect more than
ever convinced Mackenzie King that he had been right in 'giving
up the other life'. He expressed himself with enthusiasm:

> With the largest capitalist taking the lead in it, what reform may
> we not be able to work out together! I felt more than overjoyed
> & more than repaid for having taken up the work I have & giving
> up the other life. Here is a tremendous field of usefulness, & my
> immediate influence in a practical way is likely to be more far
> reaching in ultimate practical results than it could be in any
> government. This is where the reform to be effective must come
> from. Here is the spring source.

His whole emphasis, in talking with Rockefeller about industrial
relations, was that they were relations between 'human beings'. He
was delighted by the prospect of their working together to have
'changes made voluntarily rather than at the instance of government':

> I told him the key-note of my inquiry was there, it was with life

not machinery or institutions, that if we could together emphasize this note in industry what might we not be able to effect. . . .

Still pleased and excited by the prospects before him, Mackenzie King wrote, a fortnight later, on the eve of his fortieth birthday:

In all that makes for what is most enduring & promising I find myself more fortunate than I have been for many years. That the future has great work and great usefulness in store I feel sure. God grant I may prove worthy of all that has come and been given me.

CHAPTER 5

A Much-investigated State

Developments in connection with the Colorado situation were responsible for a major interruption in his studies early in October. They had not been well started before Mackenzie King was forced to forsake them, and give almost exclusive attention to this particular problem in this particular area. Such a narrowing of the scope of the investigation was in conflict with the imposing and far-reaching programme which the Rockefeller Foundation had authorized in the summer of 1914 and which it had outlined in its formal announcement of October 1, the day Mackenzie King commenced his work. The announcement had clearly stated: 'In no sense will the investigation be local or restricted, or carried on with particular reference to any existing situation, or, for that matter, with reference to conditions in any one country. The experience of the several countries of the world will be drawn upon.' In June King had committed himself to the undertaking and had immediately begun to shape his plans for an inquiry on the contemplated world-wide scale. The war, however, had prevented the investigation from assuming these proportions immediately. Other circumstances now arose which made it unwise to make a beginning even on a nation-wide scale. It had been anticipated that the labour troubles in Colorado would be one subject that would be considered in the broader study, but Colorado demanded his immediate attention and continued to be the centre of his interest for many months. It was a moot question how far it had been responsible in the first place for the establishment of the more comprehensive inquiry. The two objectives had been linked in the original invitation, but 'Colorado', in the negotiations that followed, seemed to be a subsidiary issue, one that might be lost sight of, or taken care of, in the proposed treatment of the universal labour problem of which it was only a part, though not an insignificant part. Indeed the foundation in its formal announcement on October 1 had made no reference to the industrial disturbances in Colorado. But it was the strike there, and the wide publicity given to the armed conflict which was part of it, that had led Rockefeller and the Rockefeller Foundation to give thought to its underlying causes and to seek means of preventing similar disturbances in the United States and other parts of the world. Mackenzie King had not been called in to settle the strike – it had virtually been settled by the time he entered the scene – but he would never have been invited, and the Investigation of Industrial Relations would never have been instituted, if the strike had not occurred.

Colorado was to play such an important part in Mackenzie King's life in his first year with the foundation that some description of the background of events is necessary here. The strike was called, as already noted, in September 1913. In a sense it was a 'wildcat' strike, for the local union of the United Mine Workers of America took this action without the consent and against the advice of the heads of the international union. The national leaders were jealous of the good name their organization had earned in its forceful but law-abiding representation of the interests of the mine workers. The western section of the U.M.W.A., however, had fallen under the influence of a lawless and irresponsible group who had disqualified themselves as leaders because of their resort to arms, internal dissension, intimidation of non-union workers, and complete concentration on the goal of union recognition. They had had much to say, however – and with considerable justification – about the deplorable working- and living-conditions in the

mines and mining areas. It was one of the most fiercely fought
strikes in American history. In the struggle that ensued, the strikers
and their families had been evicted from their homes in the company towns and had established themselves in nearby tent colonies.
A crucial stage had been reached on April 20, when open warfare
broke out in the Ludlow area, a tragic episode which was to become
known as the 'Ludlow Massacre':

> By some mistake or misunderstanding a shot was fired, but
> whether it came from the militia or the tent colony was never
> determined. In any event, both sides were armed, and the battle
> began. It continued until late at night when the militia finally
> captured the camp and set it on fire. Several strikers were killed,
> but the full extent of the violence was not revealed until the next
> morning when it was discovered that eleven children and two
> women had suffocated in the bottom of a cave where they had
> sought refuge from the machine gun fire.
>
> When news of the catastrophe reached the strikers, they were
> incapable of responding to anything but the terrible fact of the
> disaster itself. Tried by a long winter of accumulating resentment,
> and raging now with the horror of this new tragedy, they took
> up their arms to fight a war of extermination. The militia was
> called back to the field, and the union issued a call to arms as
> workers from all over the state joined in the battle. Mines were
> attacked and burned; buildings were looted; and the entire state
> was gripped with the fear of anarchy. Finally, in desperation, the
> Governor appealed to President Wilson for federal troops. Wil-
> son declared a state of insurrection, and on April 30 six troops
> of United States Cavalry arrived in Colorado. The fighting
> stopped, but the possibility of reconciliation seemed now more
> remote than ever before.

When Mackenzie King came into the picture, months later, he
realized that responsibility must be shared by company owners and
managers on one side and by the western leaders of the union on
the other. Even before going to Colorado he had come to some
tentative conclusions:

> The companies were right in not recognizing the United Mine

Workers, in view of the way they attempted to secure recognition and in view of the record they have. They were wrong in the conditions which they have permitted to prevail in Colorado, and to this extent there was a just ground for unrest. Mr. Rockefeller and other directors were right in allowing the managers to decide the question of recognition and backing them in this policy. They were wrong, I think, in not doing more to satisfy themselves that the representations being made by the managers covered the ground satisfactorily, and in not attempting to exert an influence to bring the strike to a speedier termination.

Although popular clamour of the day cast major blame on the Rockefellers, the company in which they were financially interested, the Colorado Fuel and Iron Company, was only one of many companies involved. It was much the largest, however, controlling 300,000 acres of coal and other lands, whereas the next largest, the Victor American Fuel Company and the Rocky Mountain Fuel Company, controlled 50,000 and 31,000 acres respectively. It signified little in the public mind that the Rockefellers had not received a cent in dividends on the common stock of their company from the time they took it over in 1902. They were still represented as wicked capitalists grinding the faces of the poor.

II

In these troubled years Colorado deserved the reputation it had achieved of being 'the most investigated state in America'.* Newspapermen and magazine writers — some of them were referred to as 'war correspondents' — found it a fascinating source of exciting stories. From the inception of the strike, and even before it, one government agency after another had sought to bring the parties together and to establish machinery whereby grievances could be discussed and settled. They all recognized that in the circum-

---

* Labour disputes in Colorado, many of them so serious as to require intervention of the militia, had always been numerous. See Carroll D. Wright, U.S. Commissioner of Labor: 'A Report on Labor Disturbances in the State of Colorado, 1880-1904' (365 pages), and other U.S. Department of Labor reports.

stances union recognition was out of the question. Secretary of Labor W. B. Wilson, who prior to his appointment to the Woodrow Wilson Cabinet in 1912 had been secretary of the U.M.W.A., conceded this. Before the strike was called he had tried to use his influence to prevent the western union leaders from forcing the issue of recognition. After it was called he went out to Colorado himself believing a settlement could be effected if the question of recognition were dropped. He found, however, that the union men were adamant on this point. The companies were equally stubborn in their refusal to agree to an appeal board. Wilson told King many months later that 'had Mr. Rockefeller taken the same stand then that he has taken since, the strike would have ended at that point'.

The head of the state, Governor Ammons, had made repeated efforts to effect an agreement, before and after the strike. At the outset his sympathies had been strongly with the union; indeed, John R. Lawson, the most belligerent of the strike leaders, had been a member of his political campaign executive. Ammons had been highly critical of the companies in 1913, when they declined his invitation for a conference with the men, but before the end of the negotiations his attitude had changed completely. He co-operated with Secretary Wilson, and at one point they had both felt sure of success. The companies had finally agreed to meet a committee of the striking miners as long as they were not union officers. The employees' representatives had agreed with Ammons that union recognition would not be an issue at the conference, but at the last moment they had insisted that it should. The Governor, incensed, accused the miners' committee of bad faith; he felt, as he told Mackenzie King later, that 'it was not conditions but simply recognition of the union that these fellows were fighting for'. Negotiations had fallen flat and within a few weeks open warfare broke out. After that, Ammons could not blame the companies for their decision to have no dealings with these union leaders. Mackenzie King's own comment was:

How very wrong the men must have been when this man, who

started using his office to better their conditions, has come to be the strongest of anyone in his denunciation of their wrongdoing.

Secretary Wilson had continued his efforts and on December 4 proposed a conciliation board composed of representatives of both sides. The situation was developing so seriously that the President of the United States, Woodrow Wilson, felt it necessary to intervene. He wrote to the companies several times urging 'a spirit of accommodation'. The strikers agreed to the proposal of a conciliation board, but the companies refused. They felt they had just been double-crossed by the union, and feared that a conciliation board (with the employees probably represented by three union men) would be forced to consider the question of union recognition, and that even meeting the union men would be construed as union recognition. They were suspicious, too, but without justification, of Secretary Wilson, because of his earlier association with the U.M.W.A. This suspicion had been most strongly voiced by L. M. Bowers, chairman of the Colorado Fuel and Iron Board, an anti-unionist to the core, who, unfortunately, was one of Rockefeller's principal advisers at the time. His advice from Colorado was to fight trade unionism to the last ditch: he denounced the striking miners, and particularly their leaders, as 'disreputable agitators, socialists, and anarchists'. So violently and increasingly reactionary became Bowers' advice to his principals in New York that Rockefeller had ultimately to insist on his resignation.

Throughout this period further investigations and attempts at conciliation were carried on by representatives of the federal Department of Labor. They achieved nothing. In rapid succession, within the year 1914, three separate inquiry commissions were appointed by the federal government (the Foster congressional committee in January, the Davies-Fairley commission in May, the Seth Low commission in December). As if these were not enough, the U.S. Commission on Industrial Relations (the Walsh commission), which had been appointed in 1912, turned its attention to Colorado early in 1914 and conducted an inquiry which was more extensive and intensive than all the others. To these was now to be added Mackenzie King's Investigation of Industrial Relations sponsored by the Rockefeller Foundation.

The Foster committee had been appointed by Congress on January 27, 1914, several months before Mackenzie King had been approached by the Rockefeller Foundation. The chairman, Congressman M. D. Foster, made repeated attempts, by letter and interview, to induce John D. Rockefeller, Jr., to agree to arbitration. Rockefeller maintained the stand he had always taken, that such policies were made in Colorado, not in New York. That had been his answer when he gave evidence before the Foster committee in Washington in April 1914, two weeks before the Ludlow tragedy. It was an attitude which was much criticized, the refusal of an absentee director to accept any responsibility for labour conditions in an industry in which he had large investments. It was an attitude with which Mackenzie King had no sympathy and one which he was finally to induce Rockefeller to forsake. On the issue of trade unionism Rockefeller's testimony, reflecting the attitude of his advisers of that time, had been most reactionary. He had said:

> The owners of the property — and I speak for a large interest — would rather see the properties closed up permanently and lose every dollar of investment than to concede a point which they believe is so absolutely fundamentally against the interest of the workers of this country. It is a principle we are standing for at any cost.

Opposite this statement in Mackenzie King's copy of the evidence appears a large question-mark. Such an extreme assertion, which could be interpreted as reflecting strong antipathy to the whole trade union movement, was to become, later on, the text for a series of sermons from him, as Rockefeller's new adviser on industrial relations.

Foster did not insist that the companies give up their stand against union recognition; in fact he quoted William Green, secretary of the U.M.W.A., as saying publicly that the 'mine workers would waive any recognition of the union or unionizing camps' if the companies would enter into negotiations for settlement of the strike on that basis. In a telegram to Rockefeller, Foster pleaded for the adoption of this course: 'I strongly urge you to do so, and believe that the strike can be settled without recognition of the union and all the other differences can be amicably adjusted. In my judgment, it is your duty to do so.' In his answer Rockefeller repeated that the officers of the companies in Colorado were the only people competent to deal with the question. It was an answer that the Colorado companies welcomed, but one that aroused public indignation because of the implied refusal to take any measures to stop the conflict. It was an answer that Mackenzie King would never have approved of.

The reports of the Foster committee — there were three of them — criticized Rockefeller as 'a long-distance director' who had been indifferent to the conditions of the workers. The committee criticized the companies for their refusal to meet the miners, or to submit differences to arbitration, or 'to accept any settlement that looked to the creation of a committee of grievances or other machinery whereby differences arising in the future between them and their employees could be adjusted'.

When Mackenzie King read the final Foster report he described is as 'a straight campaign document in parts, written with a view to serving political ends at the expense of the prejudice that exists against Mr. Rockefeller'. He was shocked that it made no mention of other mining companies and nothing of the managements, 'but brings in the deliberate assertion that Mr. R. was prepared to use the funds of the company for the purchase of guns and the starving of the miners into submission, rather than arbitrate conditions affecting their welfare; that he was helping Belgians and others liberally, yet doing nothing for some six thousand men in his own employ. Knowing all the facts as I do, I can think of nothing more cruel than this.' No action was taken on the majority and minority reports of the Foster committee, which were not published until March 1915. The committee had made its principal impact through the day-to-day publicity of the oral testimony given by many witnesses.

The Davies-Fairley commission came into being immediately after the Ludlow disaster of April 20 had shocked the nation. Its two members were Hywell Davies, a Kentucky coal operator, and W. R. Fairley, a former official of the U.M.W.A. They spent several weeks in Colorado, attempting mediation and considering possible solutions. In the report they made in September 1914 they referred to the conflict in Colorado as practically 'a state of war, with a temporary peace . . . maintained by the presence of federal troops'. Their chief recommendations were 'a three-year truce', subject to certain conditions including the waiver of any claim for union recognition, the establishment of a grievance committee in each mine, and the appointment, by the President of the United States, of a commission of three to act as referees if grievances could not be otherwise adjusted. President Woodrow Wilson urged 'with very deep earnestness' that these proposals be accepted as a basis for settlement. The union accepted the proposals. The companies, who replied separately, rejected them: they feared that even this, to the United Mine Workers, would have a semblance of recognition. The reply of the Colorado Fuel and Iron Company on September 18 was less outspoken than its earlier rejections had been, a changed attitude which reflected the pressure Mackenzie King was already bringing to bear on both New York and Colorado even before his appointment became effective on October 1. The company's president, J. F. Welborn, in his reply to the commission, claimed that the company was developing an even more comprehensive plan for dealing with its employees than the plan urged by President Wilson. In drafting this plan the Colorado managers had been influenced by a tentative outline of organization which Mackenzie King had submitted to Rockefeller on August 6, but King's proposals were more radical than Welborn was willing to accept. Welborn's adaptation of them did not, in Mackenzie King's opinion, go far enough, but he conceded that he was moving in the right direction.

The Davies-Fairley commission, even though its recommendations were so strongly supported by President Wilson, was unable to bring the parties together. It did much, however, to arouse public opinion, and through it to bring pressure on the companies to produce definite and adequate alternative proposals.

Close on the heels of the failure of the Davies-Fairley commission came the appointment of still another commission, headed by Seth Low, a former mayor of New York and one-time president of Columbia University. The commission was appointed by President Wilson on December 1, 1914. The other members were Charles W. Mills, a Pennsylvania businessman, and Patrick Gilday, a former officer of the United Mine Workers of America. On December 10, even before they had received their official instructions from the President, the Colorado strike was called off. Their mission, however, was not to settle the strike; it was to 'act as a friend of all parties in an effort to bring about a mutually acceptable agreement'. Such an agreement, the President suggested, might follow the lines of the findings of the Anthracite Strike Commission in Pennsylvania. The eastern strike had been satisfactorily settled without recognition of the union.

The Low commission offered its good offices to the Colorado operators, 132 in number. Of these, seventy-one companies, producing sixty-one per cent of the coal mined in Colorado, made a joint reply saying explicitly that 'no useful purpose can be served by your commission going to Colorado'. The replies from the Colorado Fuel and Iron Company and several of the smaller operators were conceived in a very different spirit. By that time Welborn and his associates in Colorado had come to approve, more or less grudgingly perhaps, an outline of a scheme of things along the lines of Mackenzie King's original proposals. Accordingly, Welborn joined with Rockefeller in welcoming the assistance the Low commission had proffered. When the commission made an interim report early in March it was clear that its members had been impressed by the efforts of the company to get into closer relations with its employees and to provide means for the joint consideration of grievances and for their correction. They noted with satisfaction that the company was not referring to its plan as a thing complete in itself but that it hoped it would prove the first step in a movement which would bring about increasingly good results.

Seth Low and his colleagues decided to postpone their visit to Colorado until later in the year. The reasons for the postponement were, primarily, the extremely unco-operative attitude of many of the companies and, paradoxically, the extremely co-operative attitude of the Colorado Fuel and Iron Company, whose new plans could be better judged by their fruits after a few months' operations. The commission had in mind also certain advanced legislation which the new governor (Carlson) had drafted providing for workmen's compensation, regulation of conditions affecting the health of workingmen, and official mediation and voluntary arbitration in case of industrial disputes.

It is worth noting by way of summary that recognition of the union under existing conditions was not favoured by the Foster congressional committee or the other two government commissions (both of which included former U.M.W.A. officers), by President Woodrow Wilson or Secretary of Labor W. B. Wilson, by William Green, secretary of the U.M.W.A., or by Governor Ammons or his successor, Governor Carlson. It was recognized by all that the vital problem was one of bringing the parties together in a relationship which would provide for fair representation of management and men, acceptance by shareholders of certain responsibility for working- and living-conditions, and adequate safeguarding of the interests of the public. It was to this problem that Mackenzie King addressed himself, but before he could get far with the constructive measures he had in mind he had to take into account the intervention of still another government commission, the United States Commission on Industrial Relations.

CHAPTER 6

United States Commission on Industrial Relations

The United States Commission on Industrial Relations had been created by Act of Congress on August 23, 1912. It was composed of nine persons: Frank P. Walsh of Missouri, chairman; Professor John R. Commons and Mrs. J. Borden Harriman, representing the public; F. A. Delano (replaced by Richard H. Aishton in March 1915), Harris Weinstock, and S. Thruston Ballard, representing employers; and John B. Lennon, James O'Connell, and Austin B. Garretson, representing organized labour. In its terms of reference, which were exceedingly wide, the commission was directed to 'seek to discover the underlying causes of dissatisfaction in the industrial situation'. More specifically it was called upon to inquire

> ... into existing relations between employers and employees; into the effect of industrial conditions on public welfare and into the rights and powers of the community to deal therewith; into the conditions of sanitation and safety of employees and the provision for protecting the life, limb, and health of the employees; into the growth of associations of employers and of wage earners and the effect of such associations upon the relations of employers and employees; into the extent and result of methods of collective bargaining; into any methods which have been tried in any state or in foreign countries for maintaining mutually

satisfactory relations between employees and employers; into methods for avoiding or adjusting labor disputes through peaceful and conciliatory mediation and negotiations; into the scope, methods and resources of existing bureaus of labor and into possible ways of increasing their usefulness.

For the first year of its life there had been no occasion for the commission to investigate conditions in Colorado; but when, in September 1913, the strike of coal miners was called in that area and wide publicity was given to it, attention was inevitably focused on a situation which came so obviously within its terms of reference. Members of the commission's investigating staff were assigned to make a preliminary survey of the field, but it was not until a year later that the real work was begun with the examination of witnesses at public hearings.

There is a remarkable parallel between this development and that of the Rockefeller Foundation in the same period. The foundation had been incorporated in May 1913, with wide powers to authorize studies in many directions. It was not until the Colorado coal strike that the president of the foundation (John D. Rockefeller, Jr.) had his attention called forcibly to the problem of industrial unrest. Nearly a year later he was forced to the conclusion that some positive steps would have to be taken by the foundation to determine the underlying causes of such labour disturbances, not only in Colorado, but generally, and to devise ways of eliminating them. It was at this point, in June, that Mackenzie King had been first consulted, though he did not begin his work for the foundation until October. It was no mere coincidence that the Walsh commission's announcement of public hearings on the Colorado situation was made almost immediately after the foundation's announcement of King's appointment.

II

It is understandable that the chairman of the commission should resent the intrusion of Mackenzie King, a Canadian, a foreigner, into a field which the United States Congress had in a sense pre-empted for the commission. Besides, Walsh could foresee, and did foretell, baleful consequences if millions of Rockefeller dollars were poured into a campaign to discredit labour organizations. Even the philanthropic aims of the Rockefeller Foundation as a whole were to him suspect and subject to investigation by his commission. When it became apparent that Mackenzie King was to venture into the troubles in Colorado, Walsh's worst suspicions were confirmed. Possibility of friendly relations, or even toleration, became more remote, and probability of open conflict more certain.

Walsh had already begun to secure evidence to bolster his preconceived conclusion that the Rockefellers were largely if not solely responsible for the deplorable conditions in the industry. He was regarded by many as a demagogue bent on achieving results by fomenting class hatred, and it was evident that Rockefeller was to be made a scapegoat. Walsh regarded Mackenzie King's intervention at this time as an attempt to whitewash his intended victim.

Mackenzie King was convinced of the injustice of the attacks being made upon Rockefeller. In some important respects, however, he saw evidence of wrong-headedness, as in the refusal to meet representatives of the workers or to permit them any voice in determining their own working- and living-conditions; in the too-ready acquiescence of absentee owners in management decisions affecting labour; in the failure to insist on management's taking positive steps to remove causes of grievances; and, generally, in the unwillingness to recognize that investors must bear their share of responsibility for such conditions. In these respects Mackenzie King's diagnosis differed little from that of Walsh's commission. Substantial difference was apparent in the treatments prescribed: Walsh's, to use spectacular methods in exposing evils and inflaming the public mind against the one man whom he chose to hold responsible for them; Mackenzie King's, to convince 'the one man' that he must act boldly in facing new responsibilities, that he must induce the management of the Colorado Fuel and Iron Company to forsake its policies of complete domination, and that he must have machinery established which would provide for at least a measure of labour self-determination. He was certain that, once the principle of representative government was accepted by owners, management, and employees of the Colorado Fuel and Iron Company, it would be developed within the company and, if successful, would be adopted by its competitors. It was to be successful, and was to achieve wide acceptance even beyond the coal-mining industry of Colorado. But Frank P. Walsh and the commission were entitled to a substantial measure of credit for the initial success and ultimate achievement. The publicity inspired by their methods applied an irresistible pressure, a spur to action; it threatened dire consequences if strong remedial measures were not taken. Walsh's spectacular exposure and King's constructive remedies proved to be complementary forces even though hand-in-hand co-operation was not premeditated and could not be effected. For that matter, the strike itself, while it did not end in triumph for the union, contributed importantly to the end result.

III

Mackenzie King's first contact with the commission had been in April 1914, months before he had anything to do with Colorado or the Rockefeller Foundation. He had been called from Ottawa to Washington at that time to give evidence which related almost exclusively to the workings of the Canadian Industrial Disputes Investigation Act. At that time the commission was interesting itself in the strike in Colorado. In its interim report of October 23, 1914, the commission stated that a thorough investigation had been conducted in Colorado and that plans had been made for holding public hearings at an early date. Its interest in Colorado had been quickened when the newspapers carried the story of Mackenzie King's appointment on October 1. Immediately the chairman had one of his officers write to Jerome D. Greene, on October 8:

> He [Walsh] saw an account in the paper of the work you are
> going to do in Industrial Relations. He wishes to find out all
> about this work, your plans and the extent of the work and

everything of that kind. I think it is of tremendous importance to the country. Great foundations are going into philanthropic work and other work which has a great bearing on the great question of industrial unrest.

Walsh was all for arranging public hearings immediately. Within days a subpoena was served on Mackenzie King in Ottawa, where he was working on plans for his own investigation. This first move of the Walsh commission incurred the displeasure of the prospective witness:

> When I got back to my rooms, an officer of the U.S. Commission on Industrial Relations was waiting to serve a subpoena on me to appear before the Commission in Chicago next Tuesday (October 20). There seemed to me to be just a little sharp practice or smartness in this and I told the officer I had already appeared & wd. write the Chairman myself. I then drafted a letter . . . which may help to shew the Commission that I know my job, or rather how to go about it, and also that they have laid themselves open to a lesson in courtesy. I take it that probably one or two of the labor men on the Comm'n., either Lennon or O'Connell, have suggested this, in view of the Colorado trouble, or some feeling of jealousy may have prompted it, the intention being to publicly embarrass me if possible.

John D. Rockefeller, Jr., and Jerome Greene had been served with subpoenas at the same time. But the testimony of all three was not heard till much later, Rockefeller's and Greene's late in January and early in February, and Mackenzie King's not until May.

In the meantime, Mackenzie King left Ottawa for New York and spent many days and evenings with Rockefeller and his advisers preparing answers to elaborate questionnaires submitted by the commission. The questions related to the purposes of the Rockefeller Foundation, Rockefeller's interest in the Colorado situation, and Mackenzie King's investigation of industrial relations. Discussions were many, too, about the attitude Rockefeller should take when on the witness stand. It was a wonderful opportunity for the two men to get to know each other and to appreciate each other's worth. To Mackenzie King it was an opportunity to influence his principal's whole attitude toward his responsibilities as one of the leading industrialists of the country. He did his best to induce him to forsake the traditional Rockefeller attitude of secrecy and extreme caution. He advised, and even preached, in season and out of season, at mealtime, in the office, in walks along New York streets, in the subway, and in the family car. The diary contains many references to such talks. A typical entry was made a few days before the New York hearings:

> We had a very earnest talk coming along in the car. I repeated to him what I have said several times to him, that there appeared no alternative so far as he was concerned, to his being either the storm centre of a great revolution in this country or the man who by his fearless stand and position would transfuse a new spirit into industry. I advised him strongly to nail his colours firmly to the mast at the hearings of the Commission, and said that he must recognize that we were living together in a different generation than the one in which his father had lived, that it was possible, in building up an industry such as the Standard Oil, to maintain a comparative secrecy as to methods of work, etc. and to keep business pretty much to those who were engaged in it. Today, there was a social spirit abroad, and it was absolutely necessary to take the public into one's confidence, to give publicity to many things, and especially to stand out for certain principles very broadly.

In one of these talks Mackenzie King suggested the preparation of a very careful statement of Rockefeller's position on the Colorado situation which Rockefeller could read into the record. The following morning he started to work on the drafting of such a statement. 'In what I am writing,' he confided to his diary, 'I am seeking to bring out the man as I know him myself, and shall try to have him overcome a natural reticence in the matter of publicly revealing his personality.'

This may have been a ghost-writing job, but if Rockefeller followed his usual practice the finished piece was substantially different from the original. Mackenzie King had commented the day before:

> I have observed that in everything that goes out from himself he never lets it pass from his hand until even commas have been accurately inserted. . . . I have seen no man in my life's experience more careful and more genuinely honest in the work he performs.

Mackenzie King's part was not limited, however, to preparing statements of policy and coaching his protégé in doctrines which were new to him. He made appointments for him to have personal talks with commission members including the chairman, Walsh. Before this meeting took place Mackenzie King had a personal talk with Walsh in which he sought to correct false impressions and to uproot the prejudices which he felt Walsh preferred to cling to because of their usefulness in fomenting antipathy. At one point in the interview Walsh declared: 'You have put your finger right on it: I do not know Mr. Rockefeller, Welborn does not know Mr. Rockefeller, the men in Colorado do not know Mr. Rockefeller.' Mackenzie King agreed that Rockefeller was far too diffident, but

> . . . pointed out that this was a limitation which arose through a desire not to appear to be influencing others and from a natural retirement. I compared him with men who were wasting their millions on yachts and horse races and fast living, and said it was to my mind a great injustice that these men should escape all kinds of criticism and even mention at the hands of public bodies like his Commission, while a man that was seeking to discharge his obligations as a citizen with the highest conception of duty should be made a target for abuse.

When the time came for Rockefeller to appear before the commission, Mackenzie King's last words to him were very much in the nature of a sermon. He had heard Hugh Black preach that Sunday morning on the text, 'They made me the keeper of the vineyards, but mine own vineyard have I not kept.' He did not accuse his principal of having failed in his responsibility, but he made the point that

> . . . the people felt that, with his wealth, with the Foundation

and the work he was doing, he was the keeper of great vineyards for the future. Still, they regarded Colorado as his peculiar vineyard at the present time; that it would be the greatest thing he could do in his life to make of that scene of past conflict, a garden where men and women could dwell in happiness; and that he could begin now to make it apparent to the public that it was his intention to take that up as a great piece of work.

IV

With this benediction sounding in his ears, John D. Rockefeller, Jr., made ready for three days of questioning. When he went on the witness-stand on Monday, January 25, the atmosphere was charged with hostility and bitterness on the part of the labour people who attended, and with suspicion and prejudice on the part of the chairman and one or two of his colleagues. The answers to the questionnaires had been given full publicity in the morning papers, 'but their headings were as usual in accordance with popular prejudice'. A week before, Walsh had made 'a violent and irresponsible kind of speech at the East Side Forum'. He took the same belligerent attitude the first two days of the hearings. 'He was really brutal in the manner in which he asked and addressed questions, but it gave Mr. R. a chance to display his innate courtesy and great patience.' Raymond B. Fosdick, in his biography of John D. Rockefeller, Jr., commented: 'Walsh was determined to extract a confession of guilt. His methods were those of a prosecutor rather than an investigator, and before the hearings were completed he had tried the patience not only of the witnesses but of some of his fellow commissioners as well.' John R. Commons, one of the commissioners, told Mackenzie King that 'he thought Mr. R's statement the best thing he had heard anywhere in the way of a pronouncement on the question of unionism'. Garretson's comment to Lennon (both of them labour representatives) was that 'those who thought he was merely his father's son and echoing his father's voice would have to revise their opinions, that he had a mind of his

own, was honest, sincere, of a right spirit, and only needed experience'. Mrs. Harriman thought 'he was the best witness . . . who had
yet appeared before the Commission, that he had made a splendid
impression, and that all the Commissioners had said so'. Mackenzie
King talked later with her and with Frank J. Hayes, vice-president
of the United Mine Workers. Both she and Hayes agreed absolutely that Walsh's manner and questions and methods were unfair,
though they did not think his intentions were necessarily so. On
this Mackenzie King commented: 'The fault is in the breed of the
man and the suspicion which lies at the root of his heart.'

Mrs. Harriman had taken strong exception to Walsh's outbreak
at the East Side Forum a week before the hearings. She told Mackenzie King then that she was very much disgusted with Walsh's
behaviour as chairman of the commission, that she had written the
President telling him she thought Walsh had done both the commission and the President considerable harm, and that Weinstock
and Garretson were also opposed to his random way of talking.
Seth Low and the other members of his commission also expressed
themselves strongly about Walsh.

On the third day of the hearings Walsh's outward attitude
changed. Mackenzie King reported:

> Walsh's tone at the hearings was as different from yesterday as
> possible. Clearly the commissioners had met together and had
> told him they must try to conclude the hearing in the afternoon,
> if possible, and that he must not persist in what the public had
> come to regard as persecuting methods.

V

Up to the time of these hearings Rockefeller had had no personal
contact with leaders of the labour union movement. None of them
had been able to see him; even their letters were unanswered. The
company officials in Colorado had similarly declined to consort
with them and Rockefeller had approved of their attitude. It came
as a shock to them, to his older advisers, and to Rockefeller him-

self, when Mackenzie King took the unprecedented course of arranging for a series of interviews with officers of the United Mine Workers of America, some of them the very men who had made so much trouble for all the mining companies in Colorado: Edward L. Doyle, Jim Lord, and John R. Lawson, western officers of the union, and Frank J. Hayes, vice-president of the United Mine Workers. Mackenzie King invited all four of them to meet Rockefeller in his office in the Standard Oil building at 26 Broadway. Lawson was unable to come, but the three union leaders, in a two-hour session, expressed themselves freely and frankly about their grievances without insisting on union recognition, and Rockefeller was equally frank in saying that he thought most of their grievances could be readily adjusted. He was much impressed by his visitors, they were 'different men from what he had expected to find'. They in turn were impressed by him and more than one expressed the opinion that if they could have talked together earlier in this fashion their differences could have been settled. Hayes admitted frankly that 'he himself had done Mr. Rockefeller a great injustice and that he was ready to do all he could now to restore him to his rightful place in the minds of the people'. The meeting with John R. Lawson, two days later, was less encouraging. Lawson had been one of the more rabid of the union leaders, and both Rockefeller and King had expressed doubt as to his trustworthiness. He seemed to be friendly enough at the meeting, but he left it to take the witness-stand before the commission and there he launched into what Mackenzie King described as a vicious assault upon Rockefeller. 'In this attack he did not hesitate to take a shot at myself when he described me as an alien whose only contribution to labor had been the enactment of a law which rendered workingmen liable to imprisonment whenever they put down their tools.' Such duplicity and misrepresentation were sufficient to confirm King's low opinion of him:

> If there was ever ground for refusing recognition to an organization, Lawson's evidence on the stand, after his talk with Mr. R. and myself, would have afforded it.

A possible explanation of this complete change of front on Lawson's part may be that the attack was part of a prepared speech which he already had in his pocket at the meeting, and which he had not had time to revise before giving his evidence. Neither Mackenzie King nor Rockefeller was prepared, in the circumstances, to take such a charitable view.

Among other labour leaders whom Mackenzie King introduced to his principal at this time, the most remarkable, the most spectacular, was 'Mother' Jones. She was a native of Ireland who had spent most of her eighty-three years as a violent labour agitator, and several months of that time in jail. This elderly white-haired woman had visited every coal-mining camp in the United States and was held in veneration by the miners and in fear by the operators. She had done more than any other labour organizer in the country to rouse the mine-workers to revolt against their 'oppressors', as she called them — the capitalists. In Colorado early in 1914 she had been charged with disorderly conduct and immediately thrust into jail, where she remained for some months without even being given just reason for her imprisonment. Her case and others like it were examples of the conditions which led to violent protest and, in turn, to the investigation by the Foster congressional committee.

She was still in jail when Rockefeller had given his testimony before this committee in Washington in March 1914. This was the woman who now watched him and listened intently as he gave his evidence before the Walsh commission in New York in the following January. At the end of the first morning's session, when Rockefeller had made a profound impression on commissioners and audience alike, the dramatic moment came when Mackenzie King introduced 'Mother' Jones to this man whom she had so often assailed as the arch-enemy of the working classes. Newspaper reporters and photographers were alive to their opportunity, as were the secret police who were on special duty in case some fanatic should create trouble. Surprisingly, the meeting of the two was cordial; it lasted no more than a few minutes, but it was more than a mere formal exchange of courtesies: she told him how really pleased she was to meet him and how pleased she had been with what he had said. Mr. Rockefeller, on his part, as he commented later, 'took a fancy' to her, and they arranged then and there for a further meeting. Before leaving the court-house she upbraided a group of vehement partisans who had taken her to task for shaking hands with him, told them he was really their friend though they did not know it, and added: 'If the working class people and middle class folk had done half as well as he had they would have brought about decent conditions for the workers.'

Two days later Mackenzie King arranged another meeting and he himself brought 'Mother' Jones to Rockefeller's office by subway; Mackenzie King described the interview as one of the most interesting he ever expected to witness. She gave a vivid account of the distressing conditions in Colorado, responsibility for which she and her associates had always attributed to 'the Rockefellers'. She was frank in saying that

> ... she had done all she could to malign him and to turn their batteries on him, that when anything particularly bad was happening, she and others of her class had used the expression 'The Rockefellers are after us', saying that name became synonymous with attempts at oppression. She had thought Mr. R. was a man with a thin, hard jaw, who kept his teeth and mouth firmly compressed and his hands clutching out for money all the time. She imitated as she spoke. 'When I saw you going on the stand, and listened to the evidence, and saw the kind of man you are, I was filled with remorse. I felt I had done you a great injustice.' She went on to say that she would now strive to remove the false impressions she had given; that if he did not do anything, she would, of course, feel free to fight him; but that if he did all she felt he would, she would do all she could to remove these false impressions.

Years after, Rockefeller was to describe her as 'the marvellous, vigorous, courageous organizer of the United Mine Workers of America'.

VI

Mackenzie King was proud of the performance of this man who was both his protégé and his principal. He had some criticisms to offer about his evidence on the first day:

> There were, I thought, three weak spots in his testimony: one was where he was asked about the right of union officials to go into a mining camp, hold public meetings, and distribute literature. He seemed to convey the impression that he did not favor this kind of thing.... Similarly, I thought that when being examined regarding men working in blast furnaces, he evaded coming out openly with the statement that he did not favor work on more than six days a week.... Also, I felt that in talking of conditions in Colorado, particularly the proximity of a saloon to a school and in regard to the right of men to organize unions on a national scale, and, generally, in regard to the kind of conditions that prevail in a 'closed town', he had far too much in mind the possible bearings of these questions on Colorado and the effect it might have on his own officials.

On the latter two points King sent notes to the witness while he was on the stand, and the 'unfortunate expressions' were corrected before the end of the day's hearings. King felt particularly strongly about the responsibility of directors with respect to labour conditions:

> There can be no doubt that, as a director of the Colorado Fuel & Iron Company, he has not sufficiently informed himself of labor conditions there. This is due, not to an indifference to the conditions, but rather to holding too strictly to the accepted guiding principle of business, namely, that men [managers] should be selected for the work and given responsibility and practically unlimited discretion. The day for conducting business in that way is past. Public opinion is becoming too much of a reality, and the interchange of thought among men too considerable to permit men to reap rewards through investments without being responsible for conditions where their money is invested.

In spite of his resentment of Walsh's unfairness and malevolence, Mackenzie King realized the value of the work he was doing, and he was able to write:

> The Government has done a good thing, in appointing this Commission, in helping to bring home the truth. Undoubtedly they have helped to bring it home to Mr. Rockefeller, for such clearly has been the effect of all our work during the past couple of weeks. He has come to see that as a director he can no longer hold to this view, and his evidence, in his general statement today, was an admission of that fact.

Mackenzie King had scored another point in the hearings. Rockefeller had announced his intention to go himself to Colorado, and in the near future, something Mackenzie King had been urging from the very beginning.

In spite of the few 'weak spots' in Rockefeller's testimony, his mentor was enthusiastic about the good impression that had been made:

> When it is remembered that his father has in practice been one of the most secretive of men about his business, that this has been the method in which business men generally have viewed their obligation; when it is remembered that Mr. Rockefeller, Jr. is at present only administering his father's affairs and is not free to act of his own responsibility in complete measure; when further, it is remembered that it has been his father's friends . . . who have been his immediate advisers, the progress which has been made by him towards a modern, progressive outlook is remarkable indeed. What is particularly satisfying about it is the circumstance that every bit of it has been based on conviction. He has said absolutely nothing that he does not with his whole heart and mind believe. . . .
>
> My own feeling is that, not only has Mr. R. given himself a new start with the American public, and particularly with labor, but he has also helped to make an epoch in the industrial history of this country itself. Students will go back to his evidence of today in indicating the period of transition from indifference on

the part of directors to the assuming of obligation by them. . . .
I look forward to seeing Mr. R. ultimately get a great reception
from the workingmen of Colorado.

This truly remarkable change in outlook can be traced without
question to the influence of Mackenzie King, and when it is considered that they had met for the first time only eight months before, it is all the more impressive. Such a result was possible, it
should go without saying, only because of the fundamental goodness and soundness of the human material he had to work with.

Rockefeller had taken the right course in his first day's testimony
before the commission. 'It makes one shudder,' King wrote, 'to
think what an opposite course, or one of indifference and antagonism to the Commission might have meant, not merely for Mr. R.
himself, personally, but for capital generally in the United States,
and for the welfare of the industrial classes. It may be that his
attitude today has helped to save millions of dollars to capital, has
helped to prevent even industrial revolution.'

But this was only a beginning: fine words, expressive of genuine
conviction as they were, had still to be translated into vigorous
action. This would mean a complete change in existing social conditions in the Colorado mining camps; it would mean elimination
of the abuses 'Mother' Jones had described so vividly to Rockefeller at their meeting. Specifically, it would mean

> . . . introducing co-operative stores and doing away with supplies
> furnished exclusively by the Company, opening up closed towns,
> providing recreation grounds, and above all, developing machin-
> ery whereby there would be adequate representation of labor's
> views and participation by the workers in the shaping of condi-
> tions by which they work.

Of these changes the fundamental one was, of course, the provision
for participation of the workers in the shaping of their own working conditions. If it could be made effective in Colorado — and
King was determined that it should be — its influence could extend
'not only throughout America but wherever industry in the way of
large undertakings is carried on'.

VII

The success of the first day's testimony was repeated on the following days and led Mackenzie King to comment:

> Altogether, in his replies, he has shown wonderful political sense
> and sagacity. He has great tact and really would, if he permitted
> himself to undertake it, make a splendid public man. He has all
> the qualities which count to make a true statesman.

Mackenzie King had made a prediction before the hearings opened
that Rockefeller's evidence, listened to in derision at the outset,
would meet with applause at the end:

> That prophecy was literally and absolutely fulfilled. . . . He has
> the admiration of the Commission, of the press, of the labour men,
> and even of many of the Socialists and I.W.W.* workers who
> were most bitter in their hatred against him.

Another prediction, that Rockefeller would form a genuine
friendship with A. B. Garretson, one of the labour representatives
on the commission, also came true. Garretson was president of the
International Order of Railroad Conductors, a good friend of Mackenzie King's from the days of the Grand Trunk Railway strike in
Canada in 1910. Mackenzie King introduced them, and their liking
for each other was spontaneous. The three men had lunch together
a few days later at the Recess Club:

> Garretson spoke with utter frankness and fairness, giving the
> point of view of organized labor in a manner which not only
> appealed to Mr. R. but also convinced him of its significance.
> Garretson told him about conditions in Colorado. He gave both
> of us to understand that it was simply closing the door to any
> kind of communication which had caused most of the trouble
> there. . . . Both he and Mr. R. spoke to each other in terms of
> genuine belief in each other's sincerity, and appreciation of each
> other's point of view. . . . I feel that this friendship between
> Garretson and Mr. R. has been one of the greatest things that it

* Industrial Workers of the World.

has been possible to help to bring about. There is no telling just how much it may mean for the future.

A chance meeting in a subway car had given another opportunity for the two men to understand each other, and for Rockefeller to gain a new appreciation of men he had never known and had always misunderstood. Mackenzie King was pleased:

> Garretson, while frank and blunt in his manner, was pleasant and genuinely cordial. When we left the car, Mr. R. said to me, 'What a splendid man that is: I wish very much my father could meet him. He is the kind of man my father would like very much. Would you think it wise for me to ask him to have a talk with Father?' I said I thought it would, though perhaps he had better let me suggest it in the first instance, which was agreed. He then went on to say that he hoped to have a friend in Garretson all his life, that Hayes had impressed him too as an honest man, and that, as far as he was concerned, whenever a chance offered to back men of that type, he would be glad to do it. It has been a splendid thing, his meeting these labour leaders first hand, as it has been a revelation in character to him.

Those who knew John D. Rockefeller, Sr., might have assumed, too readily, that he would not approve of the new friends his son was making or of the admiration for them he was expressing. As a matter of fact the father knew of everything that was happening. The relationship between father and son was an intimate one, and during this trying week the father was kept informed of every development. He knew, he understood, and he approved. The highlights of each day — his son's testimony, Walsh's belligerency, Mackenzie King's helpfulness, the talks with 'Mother' Jones, Garretson, and the other labour men — all had been reviewed and discussed by father and son as between two close friends. The father had always been proud of his son but never prouder than now. He was entirely satisfied. So pleased was he, indeed, that on the day of his son's last appearance on the witness stand, he presented him with forty thousand shares of Colorado Fuel and Iron Company stock, the equivalent of about $1,000,000. It was a kind of graduation present, his way of showing his approval of the course his son had taken, and of the splendid way in which he had handled himself:

> I think, too, [Mackenzie King wrote] the old gentleman had in mind giving him a freer hand to work out his policy in regard to Colorado. With this amount of stock his own, instead of an amount held for his father, he will now be free to take a much more positive stand in regard to his duties as a shareholder as well as a director.

VIII

Starr J. Murphy, one of the older advisers of the family, was also converted to the soundness of the new approach; he was 'very strong in his endorsation of the whole course, and the significance of it for good in Mr. R.'s life'. He reported, however, the dissent of other members of the older school. Frederick T. Gates, for example, who had been the close adviser of the older Rockefeller since 1891, was tremendously put out about it all, and seemed to think that the new policy of the open door was a gigantic mistake. His advice had always been along these lines: 'In this business you have to live the life of a recluse. Never make friends. Don't join clubs. Avoid knowing people intimately.' Nothing could conflict more sharply than this with Mackenzie King's advice. And the same conflict was apparent in the course which Mr. Gates said he would have followed had he been the witness. In a private memorandum, written with characteristic vigour, evidently to give vent to his feelings, he deplored the 'conciliatory' character of the junior Rockefeller's testimony:

> ... the attempt to parry blows, but not to return them. It may be urged that this policy is the Christian policy. I do not so understand Christ that he adopted any spirit of conciliation toward those who came to him in the spirit of these Unionists.... I would have engaged an array of the most brilliant and able counsel to be gotten in New York — men not afraid, if necessary, to make a scene in court.... I would have demanded in a tone to be

heard way across the continent my legal rights of appearing by counsel and cross-examining witnesses. I would have used every legal method, if necessary that of injunction. I would have called upon the President of the United States in open speech and public letter. I would have exposed the record of this man Walsh. If necessary I would have carried the matter so far as to invite arrest, and I would have resisted arrest, and been carried struggling and shrieking from the court room for the purpose of getting my case vividly, powerfully, before the people of the United States.

Other directors shared to some extent this attitude, but President Eliot, the dignified aristocrat from Harvard, would never have stooped to or countenanced language or actions of such violence. When Mackenzie King met him on Fifth Avenue the next day, he told him he thought things had already gone too far in the direction of the spectacular. He had been shocked and grieved by the way in which the newspapers had played up the 'Mother' Jones episode, with sensational headlines and photographs of the two principals shaking hands and conversing with each other. It had been a mistake, he thought, for Mr. Rockefeller to have had anything to do with 'Mother' Jones. King countered with the argument that something of the kind was essential to help remove the terrific prejudice which existed against Mr. Rockefeller among certain classes whose interests were represented by 'Mother' Jones. Eliot did not seem to realize the seriousness of the situation in Colorado and King spoke to him 'pretty plainly', telling him he thought it was just about as bad as it could be. 'It was a question,' he added, 'not of settling the Colorado matter alone, but of helping to avert industrial war in the country.'

IX

For John D. Rockefeller, Jr., this week of his testimony before the Walsh commission had been an exhausting but triumphant one. He gave full credit to the three men who had been at his side —

Murphy, Lee, and King. He was always appreciative of the help of his associates and was never reluctant to express it. For example, on the last night of the hearings, as he and Mackenzie King parted, recalling that there was to be a further interview with the labour leaders in the morning, he appealed to him: 'Don't fail to be down at the office when these men turn up. I want my god-father there, or I won't know what to do.'

On his return to Ottawa after the conclusion of the hearings, Mackenzie King commented on the proceedings in which he had just taken part:

> This Commission is a hideous contrast to methods of judicial procedure as we are accustomed to them; if democracy means this kind of mob control as it was framed up with the Commission, the press and the United Mine Workers, what is to become in time of the U.S., what of the true friends of labour! It fills me with indignation the whole thought of it; it is like dealing with mud and impurity to have men carry on proceedings in the name of truth and justice in such a manner. There is something in British institutions more valuable than the people under them comprehend. In responsible government and an impartial and high minded judiciary, lies the safeguard of British Liberties. The U.S. has neither (save in its highest courts).

If Mackenzie King's experience in New York in January lowered his opinion of 'American justice' as practised by a quasi-judicial tribunal, it increased his already high regard for the man whom that tribunal had treated unjustly. He wrote to him on February 9:

> No man I have ever known has shown such splendid courage, such unswerving integrity, and such true Christian character, as you have through this fight. I feel my own life to have been strengthened through association with you in the conflict, and I feel that you have done more for all the activities with which your name is associated, for yourself, and for your future, in the three days of your public examination than has been accomplished in as many preceding years. This I find to be the opinion of every man with whom I spoke. . . . It seems to me you will have to lead,

have to be the example, whether you will or no. Your modesty and your humility does not permit you to see this, but those who have your life interests and your life most at heart see it, and it is in the field of industry primarily that this leadership must be conspicuous.

CHAPTER 7

Mackenzie King's
First Visit to Colorado

The Walsh commission had been doing its best to incite public feeling against the Rockefellers, to fix blame on them alone, and to discredit as hypocritical the proposals of the Rockefeller Foundation to sponsor a study designed to allay industrial unrest throughout the country. Long before the commission had started its campaign, indeed at the first meeting he had had with the Rockefeller group in June, King had seen clearly that Rockefeller and the foundation, because of their substantial holdings in Colorado, would have to take prompt and bold measures to set their own house in order. His first impulse then had been to get out to Colorado himself. He had made the suggestion at that meeting and had followed it up on his return to Ottawa with a letter to Jerome Greene. His idea had been that a conciliator be sent to Colorado: 'It would be agreeable if the person chosen were in no way connected with American industry or labor unions, and one known to have experience. . . . A selection of a man outside the country in this way might command the respect and confidence of all parties.'

That proposal had fallen through. In the meantime, on August 6, Mackenzie King had written Rockefeller a long letter suggesting the establishment of boards of conciliation and outlining a method of dealing with grievances; it was the precursor of his plan of industrial representation. After reading this letter, Rockefeller had written to King asking him if he could arrange to 'go to Denver for a few days within the next month or so' to confer with the company's officers if they wished such a conference. He had sent to J. F. Welborn, president of the Colorado Fuel and Iron Company, extracts from King's letter with the suggestion that it might be arranged to have King visit Denver 'for conference privately with you gentlemen'. Welborn and his associates had plans of their own, however, and they did not welcome either the King proposals or a visit from him. With the strike still on they considered the timing would be bad. Welborn wrote:

> It seems unnecessary for him to come to Colorado at this time, for my opinion is that it would be inadvisable to undertake a plan such as Mr. King suggests while the strike is in an unsettled state.... [It] would weaken us with our men; would tend to strengthen the organization with our employees not now members of it; and would, in the minds of the public, be an admission on our part that a weakness, the existence of which we had previously denied, was being corrected.

Rockefeller had sent this reply on to Mackenzie King with the comment, 'I cannot but feel that the Officers of the Company are right in the conclusion which they have reached.' King accepted the decision with good grace, recognizing that 'however desirable the adoption of any plan may be, the time of its adoption is not less important than the scheme itself'.

Improvements had been urged by Rockefeller and his New York associates even before Mackenzie King had been called in, but the Colorado management had been firm in its resistance. They wished to postpone any reform programme until the strikers caved in. Mackenzie King noted in his diary:

> I believe I could have saved Mr. Rockefeller most of the trouble that has grown out of this position, and possibly the lives in Colorado as well had I been here to advise him earlier, within a

month or two of the inception of the strike. I certainly would
have prevented many of the false steps that I think have been
taken.

Obviously, however, the timing had not been right for a visit in
September. Aside from the matter of the continuing strike, Mackenzie King recognized that the minds of the Colorado management had to be prepared for changes more drastic than their own
patching-up programme. Welborn wrote that they were considering the advisability of at some time inaugurating 'a plan ... by
which our men could ... reach the higher officers of the company'.
Mackenzie King had seen that he must make personal contact with
Welborn. He had his first opportunity for this later on when
Welborn came to New York. The two men took to each other
at once and, before many months had passed, relations of personal
friendship were established. That had been a good beginning, and
Welborn was to come later to the point of approving Mackenzie
King's plan of industrial representation, and even of inviting him
to come to Colorado.

II

The strike had been settled early in December — that removed
one obstacle to a personal visit to Colorado; the Walsh commission
hearings in New York ended late in January — that removed another. In the meantime King had learned much about conditions in
the coal-mining industry; he had been shocked more and more by
the stories of political intrigue, petty and major tyranny of senior
and junior bosses, disgraceful housing conditions, closed company
towns, frequent armed clashes between strikers and mine guards,
lack of provision for collective bargaining or redress of grievances.

While there were signs that the Colorado managers were coming
around to a more conciliatory point of view, Mackenzie King was
still critical of their attitude. It was not, he felt, in the best interests
even of the corporation: 'While the managers talked a good deal
about union recognition they were doing so as a means of conceal-

ing their own methods of dealing with employees and of permitting themselves to persist in these methods which were wholly against the interests of the men who were making the investment.'

In long talks with Welborn in New York in February, Mackenzie King was able to induce a substantial change in his attitude, but Welborn was slow to commit himself; he 'thought the company should go slow in introducing new features, lest it might appear that they had been forced into this position by the United Mine Workers'. King had a strong ally in Rockefeller, however, who agreed that this line of argument 'was a good reason for delaying while the strike was on, but was no reason for not introducing any features that would be helpful in restoring the best relations possible at the present time'.

An article by John A. Fitch in the *Survey* on 'Law and Order in Colorado' impressed King as excellent, 'impartial, well balanced, comprehensive and fair. It reveals a cruel situation, at the bottom of which lies hatred between classes bred of arbitrary power and its use to fetter men.' It rekindled in him a desire to do something about it, and he wrote on:

> How I wish I had been sent out to Colorado in June. I could have ended the strike easily, and it would have made a fine beginning to the work on Industrial Relations. The effort must now be to change the scene of industrial strife into a valley of contentment & happiness if that be possible.

While he felt under no obligation to consult the trustees of the foundation about his plan to make Colorado his first area of investigation, he thought it desirable to win their support by informing them of his intentions. A letter to the foundation would be useful, he told himself, 'partly as a means of protecting myself against misunderstanding or misrepresentation later, with all parties, including the public'. Accordingly he wrote a letter to the secretary, in which he said in part:

> Now that the strike is over, it would appear that, were I to visit Colorado in the immediate future rather than at some later time, my doing so might enhance such opportunity as my present

studies may afford of ascertaining the root causes of disturbances in Colorado, and of possibly furthering, in the manner indicated, an improvement in the relations between capital and labor and the maintenance of harmonious relations.

He knew that the trustees of the foundation were meeting on the following day. By good fortune, or by design, he was invited to attend. After his letter was read he amplified his case. Two members questioned the wisdom of his going: one 'thought it would be better in some ways for me to go to Europe'; another 'that it would be wiser to take up a field like Pennsylvania as a beginning'. Another trustee took the opposite view and said that 'if he were in my position he would probably feel as I did: that I should not want to miss the hot spots'. Mackenzie King argued in effect that the right place to begin was in an industry in which the foundation had a responsibility because of its investments, that the beam in Colorado should first be cast out before attempting to pull out the mote in some other area. One member concurred in this by saying 'that I ought to take Colorado first; that a physician would go to the spot in which there was disease; that it was perfectly apparent to everyone that Colorado was the diseased spot in America to-day'. Even though the foundation's consent was not required, Mackenzie King was pleased that the general sentiment was one of approval. The view prevailed that 'I should be perfectly free to use my own judgment in matters of this kind, and go wherever I thought desirable, at whatever time I thought best'.

The attitude of the trustees reassured him of the independence he desired. It was a confirmation, too, of the wisdom of his own decision to go to Colorado. By this time Ivy Lee, Rockefeller's adviser on public relations, who had earlier strongly opposed the idea of Mackenzie King's visit to Colorado, had come around to his way of thinking. He urged that two representatives of the government should be approached to see if they had any objection. One was Seth Low, chairman of the commission of three appointed by President Wilson on December 1, 1914, to inquire into conditions in Colorado; the other was Hon. W. B. Wilson, Secretary of Labor.

Mackenzie King first approached Seth Low, and learned that his commission had planned a visit to Colorado early in 1915 but had postponed it until the end of the year largely because 'substantially all of the operators, except the Colorado Fuel & Iron Co. declined to accept the good offices of the commission'. Mackenzie King had already had a long conference with Seth Low and his colleagues, but had not then discussed with them the possibility of his going to Colorado. He now told Low frankly that he hoped to get things so far under way in Colorado that by the time the commission came out 'they could not do other than report very favorably on the progress made in improved conditions'. Low agreed that it was better for King to go immediately. Mutual confidence had developed to such a point that Low read over to him the interim report he proposed to send to President Wilson and the mine operators, a report which Mackenzie King considered fair in all the circumstances.

Then came the talk with Secretary of Labor Wilson, in Washington. He had gone to Colorado himself, before the strike was called, but he had found that things had gone too far to stop it. He had had much to do, as Secretary of Labor, with the appointment of the Seth Low commission. His reaction to Mackenzie King's proposal was the same as Seth Low's, that he should go, and 'the sooner the better'. The interview went better than Mackenzie King had hoped. At first Wilson 'seemed a little sensitive and a little embarrassed. . . . As I discussed the situation with him he became more at ease and before I came away he seemed to be entirely cordial. When I said to him, at the close, not to hesitate to call on me, he said: "I would have given a good deal for someone to have said that to me when this trouble commenced or during different stages of it. If I could have got near Mr. R., I think we could have ended the whole thing in an hour or two." '

Mackenzie King's plans had been made in the hope that he and his principal should go to Colorado together, so he had been pleased when Rockefeller told the Walsh commission that it was his intention to go. Personal contact with the miners would, King knew, be a revelation — a revelation to Rockefeller as well as to the miners. President Welborn had misgivings about the proposal, said he 'would not care to take the responsibility for his life in the mining districts, considering the bitter feeling there was against him'. Mr. Rockefeller, Sr., shared Welborn's apprehensions and suggested that Mackenzie King might go out first and send back word, after he reached Colorado, 'whether it was entirely safe for Mr. R. Jr. to go to Denver'. As for Rockefeller, Jr., himself, he was not concerned. In the end, however, his departure was postponed until the autumn because of the death of his mother on March 12.

III

The postponement of Rockefeller's visit did not affect Mackenzie King's own plans for action. Before he was able to leave for Colorado, however, rapid worsening of the situation there — serious unemployment in the mining areas — was brought to his attention. During the strike hundreds of men had come in from outside points and had been put on the payrolls of the United Mine Workers to make it appear that the union was supporting a large number of men on strike, and to prevent the possibility of the places of those on strike being filled by non-union men. The result was that the supply of labour had been greater than it otherwise would have been, while the number of jobs was less and the distress greater in consequence. Further hardship was experienced when strike benefits were withdrawn by the union in February: the union's funds were running low. It was a sad community, which had not enjoyed prosperity even in the best of times. Feeling was running high, and late in February the unemployed miners, in a mass meeting in Trinidad, the chief urban centre in the southern mining district, were vehement in their demands that something be done to relieve their distress. The chairman of the meeting, Joe Rizzi, a miner, telegraphed to Rockefeller describing conditions as desperate, and telling of miners and their families facing starvation. Mackenzie King's immediate reaction had been that Mr. Rockefeller or the foundation should not hesitate in responding to the appeal. King was at his energetic best in seizing this opportunity and making the most of it. Rizzi's telegram was discussed with Rockefeller and Welborn, and it was decided to ask for further information from the Chamber of Commerce of Trinidad and from the general manager of the Colorado Fuel and Iron Company. From the company came the answer that it was already doing everything it should for the men who had been in its employ, an opinion which Welborn had already expressed. From the Chamber of Commerce came an entirely different reply: 'There is great distress among the working classes, caused by the recent trouble. We suggest that you could do a great deal for mankind by helping relieve the distress in this community among other than your former employees.' Mackenzie King made up his mind at once that these circumstances provided a most fortunate opportunity for paving the way for the restoration of good conditions in Colorado and placing Rockefeller in his true light before the miners and the public:

> I decided that I would urge him to take a bold course, and offer assistance for relief generally, confining it, however, in the first instance, to miners and their families, no matter by whom they might have previously been employed. I foresaw, also, a further possibility that, namely, of myself undertaking the work of ascertaining the extent of the need and advising the Foundation. This, it seems to me, would pave the way very naturally and splendidly towards looking into conditions of the Fuel Company.

He had, however, still to convince Rockefeller and Welborn. Rockefeller held back:

> He thought it would open the door to every municipality in the country where there was unemployment. He feared that miners would regard it as a means of trying to purchase their friendship; also that it would lead to all kinds of impositions as there was no guarantee as to the nature or extent of the need.

Mr. Welborn, while reluctant, was more easily persuaded. Mackenzie King had prepared a draft telegram in reply to the Chamber of Commerce. Rockefeller, after giving it overnight consideration, was prepared to send something along the lines it suggested, but thought it should include certain safeguards and limitations. The two men discussed the final draft:

> I advised against making the message too cautious ... the spirit was all important, and it was well to shew a free and cordial disposition. He replied to this that, while it might be true, I had to remember that other demands might come to him in consequence of a loosely drafted message. He added further 'You do not know how hard it is going to be to get this through the Foundation. ... Besides ... I doubt very much if Father would agree to this at all.' Then he added, 'Perhaps I should not say that. He would be satisfied with it, though his judgment might differ.'

Before the discussion was over, they had prepared together, by drafting and re-drafting, the final message which it seemed desirable to send.

It was decided to defer sending the message until after the meeting of the trustees of the foundation which had been called for the following day. Mackenzie King was invited to attend the meeting, made a strong presentation, and persuaded the trustees to agree unanimously to an appropriation of $100,000, the amount he had recommended. It was a personal triumph:

> I have the satisfaction of feeling that I have succeeded at least in having the offer made to them and the Foundation and Mr. R. put in a position where they can be no longer justly criticized for helping others while unwilling to do for their own.

Later he wrote that more had been done to allay bitterness in Colorado and to put Rockefeller in his true light than could have been possible by any other stroke. He was aware, too, of the usefulness of the offer as a gesture of goodwill to the miners and as paving the way for Rockefeller's proposed visit to Colorado, as well as for his own investigation of industrial relations in that field.

The telegram containing the offer was sent before the meeting of the foundation was over. It included the suggestion that 'official representations' should be made to the foundation. This was in the hope that the Governor of Colorado would make the formal application. Negotiations were carried on in Colorado on this point and on matters of organization, but before they were concluded Mackenzie King had arrived in Denver. In the language of the football field, he was speedy enough to get to Colorado in time to catch the ball which he himself had kicked in New York.

On the day he arrived, March 19, instead of going at once to the offices of the Colorado Fuel and Iron Company, he had an interview with Governor Carlson. He told him that 'Mr. R. was only too ready to assist if there were actual need but he did not wish to appear to be butting in, or to be appearing to try to square himself or his company with the people of the State; that for this reason he had taken particular care to see that anything the Foundation might be asked to do should be at the instance of the public authorities.' The governor was much impressed by the possibilities of the programme and invited King's assistance.

The next day, Mackenzie King, with the assistance of the attorney for the Colorado Fuel and Iron Company, began drafting a message which it was thought the governor might send to the foundation. They also drafted a telegram to be sent by the Trinidad Chamber of Commerce. At the same time the governor appointed a committee of three citizens to act as a Committee on Unemployment and Relief. The name had been suggested by Mackenzie King; presumably the personnel had been chosen by the governor. In the end it was this committee, rather than the governor, who made the application to the foundation, but in this, too, Mackenzie King had his part — he drafted their telegram. He sat in with the members of the committee at their organization meeting and took an active part in their deliberations. He records an interesting incident at the first meeting: 'It was somewhat amusing to me to find myself sitting in the Governor's chair when he left the room, telling the members of the Committee what they should do.' Wisely, he left it entirely to the committee to supervise the distribution of the funds provided by the foundation, and his relations with them continued on a cordial basis. The members of the committee welcomed him as a wise counsellor. When they made their report several months later, they expressed their deep appreciation of the value of his assistance and added: 'His suggestions were always timely, and his counsel wise and helpful. We take pleasure in giving this public recognition of his most substantial contribution to the success of the undertaking.'

IV

His work with the Committee on Unemployment and Relief had absorbed his attention for several days after his arrival in Colorado. Having finished his part in that project, he now turned to the real purpose of his visit. In the East he had completed the preparatory work of study, conference, and consultation. He had set out with the goodwill of the company management in the West, of his associates in New York, and of important representatives of government. His way had been made easier by the wide publicity which had been given to the trouble in Colorado. The activities of the investigating agencies and the continued activity of the union, even after the strike settlement, had applied pressure on owners and management to give him, now, a freer hand than he otherwise would have had.

Once in Colorado, Mackenzie King found confirmation of many of the bad impressions he had received in the East. But there were evidences, too, of a new spirit developing. To Starr Murphy he wrote:

> The leaven is beginning to work in the right direction, but many old methods are so deep-rooted and reactionary forces are so strong, it is going to take time to bring about a change that is even more in the Company's interests than in the interests of the employees.

Interference with political and judicial processes had been one of the bad features practised by the coal companies, who had employed their own attorneys to assist in the prosecution of strikers. Under pressure from Rockefeller in the East these activities had been curtailed, but to an astonishing degree businessmen and politicians were still playing into each other's hands to the detriment of labour and the public. King could observe, however, some signs of change for the better:

> The parties most interested are by degrees quietly admitting to me the mistake it has been, and by degrees they are shaking off a terrible incubus that political manipulations through years past have placed upon the industry. . . . I am glad to say that the President of the Company is determined to have a complete severance of this relationship, but he cannot be held too firmly to the effective carrying out of his determination.

And in his diary two days later he noted:

> Welborn spoke to me about his desire to change the whole policy of the Fuel Company from the old lines to new ones. He admitted that there had been little attention paid to Welfare work, and that the old policy of controlling legislatures, etc. was bad.

There were other signs, too, that improvements were on the way. James Dalrymple, the State Inspector of Mines, a union man who had worked in every capacity in the coal mines from labourer to superintendent, told Mackenzie King: 'There is a great improvement in conditions in Colorado in the last four years. There is nothing like the same amount of political interference.' Mackenzie King saw that the heads of the companies were now striving to improve conditions and would no longer sanction unfair dealings; but some of the superintendents and other underlings had not caught the new spirit. 'Some of them are too arbitrary,' Dalrymple said, and then went on to give a colourful example of the reaction of a superintendent to a circular letter from the president of one of the fuel companies protesting against the miners being cheated by false recording of the weight of the coal they mined. In his letter the president had declared that any superintendent would be dismissed who allowed any employee to be cheated out of a pound of coal. When this superintendent opened the letter he was completely taken aback; he exploded: 'Some God-damned son-of-a-bitch has either got religion or gone crazy.' It was a sad commentary on the attitude of some bosses to the rights of the employees under them. Dalrymple referred to the incident as showing 'how bad the system had been in some of the mines'.

It was obvious that the important thing at this stage was to convert many superintendents and pit bosses to new ways of thinking and acting. The directors and managers had already, for the most part, changed their attitude. The ultimate aim was, of course, to establish the right of employees to a voice in the determination of their own working- and living-conditions. To this end Mackenzie King's efforts were at once directed. A beginning had been made by Welborn after the strike was called off in December. Representatives of the company's employees, chosen by ballot at each of the camps — one representative to every 250 employees, had been invited to Denver to a joint meeting with the executive officers of the company. The meeting was called 'for the purpose of discussing matters of mutual concern and of considering means of more effective co-operation in maintaining fair and friendly relations'. Welborn had been highly pleased with his plan, which he said embodied 'Mr. King's suggestions as far as seemed practicable'. Rockefeller had been pleased too. He had told the Walsh commission that the company had

> ... already taken steps to initiate a plan of representation of its employees. It is my hope and belief that from this will develop some permanent machinery which will ensure to the employees of the Company, through representatives of their own selection, quick and easy access to the officers with reference to wages or other conditions of employment.

This was an example of the changing attitude of the owners and managers, but Mackenzie King was far from satisfied with what had been done. He wrote to Rockefeller:

> Mr. Welborn's plan is not at all the plan outlined in my letter [of August 6]. I think Mr. Welborn's plan is a mere beginning, which may come to be viewed as little more than a formality, which would be worse than nothing, or which may develop into some-

thing real and substantial and of permanent value. It all depends
on how the scheme of representation it purports to make is
developed in practice. . . . Should the attitude of 'sufficiency' be
maintained, there will be accorded the [Seth Low] Commission
the surest opportunity for finding and stating that the directors,
in leaving it to the management in Colorado to deal with the situation, have failed to realize a responsibility for conditions, and
should continue to be held responsible for them.

To make it something of 'real and substantial and of permanent
value' Mackenzie King's idea was that there should be an 'industrial
constitution', some form of representative govenment in which the
company's twelve thousand employees would have a recognized
standing when it came to decisions affecting working- and living-
conditions. The Industrial Representation Plan which was to em-
body these principles was taking shape in his mind.

His first step, however, was to make a first-hand survey of existing conditions. He visited every community in which the company
had interests. It was not a 'conducted' tour. He talked freely with
everyone he came across from president to mule-drivers, and, outside the company, from governor to merchants and school teach-
ers. Most of them in turn talked freely with him. He had a knack
of establishing friendly relations with and winning the confidence
of the men and women he talked to. In going about from camp to
camp Mackenzie King sought information about housing and rents,
fencing and gardens, water supply, sanitation facilities, wash
houses, industrial accidents and workmen's compensation, hospitals
and doctors and nurses, recreation and social centres, social
workers, churches, schools, company stores, saloons, and the administration of justice. He went into the mines and steel mills,
workers' homes and schools, and even into at least one saloon.
Always he had in mind, not so much recommendations to the company for improvements it might finance (though he did make some
such suggestions), as ways and means whereby the employees
themselves could participate in the shaping of policies affecting
their interests and in carrying them out. The whole emphasis was

upon the human element; the whole objective was a framework within which ideas of joint control and partnership, a limited form of representative and responsible government, could be developed.

At the managerial level, too, he was successful. It was not long before the friendship with Welborn, begun in their short meeting in New York in September, had ripened into affection. He was soon on first-name terms with both him and his wife, and their talks together were not limited to 'industrial relations'. Mrs. Welborn was a gifted woman with a wide range of interests in the world of art and music, as well as in poetry and religion. It was in the latter field that Mackenzie King was more at home, but he enjoyed it all. Welborn's chief interest apart from his business affairs was in his farm, on which he raised pure-bred cattle. Mackenzie King told a delightful story of a week-end visit to the farm. Welborn pointed proudly to three young bulls he had recently added to his herd, and broke it to him that the names he had given them were Mackenzie, Macdougall, and McGregor, in honour, first, of King, and then of his brother and his secretary. Mackenzie King was pleased: 'Some chance now,' he commented gaily, 'of descendants bearing my name.' But a social week-end was not merely social. 'After dinner,' he entered in his diary, 'I finished drafting the memorandum on social and industrial betterment, and read through the whole of it to Mr. and Mrs. Welborn. We all three discussed very freely and fully the points raised in its several divisions. Welborn seemed particularly pleased to have this outline as a guide.' The evening was a nice example of one of Mackenzie King's techniques, an intermingling of seriousness and fun, of purposeful discussion and discursive talk. More was accomplished in that week-end of friendly intercourse than could have been achieved in a week of board meetings.

CHAPTER 8

Mackenzie King on the
Witness Stand

Mackenzie King had made a good beginning in establishing cordial personal relations with the management, and had won the confidence of the miners he had visited. This useful work was cut short in May by another subpoena from the Walsh commission, this time to appear as a witness in Washington. The first subpoena had been served in October, for hearings in New York in January, but his appearance had been postponed. Now, in May, Rockefeller and Ivy Lee were being recalled to the stand, and the reactionary L. M. Bowers was to appear for the first time. In view of the constructive work then under way in Colorado, Mackenzie King regarded Walsh's decision to reopen the old controversy as 'certain to prove prejudicial to present and future situations'. He felt that the trials of the strikers in Colorado, and particularly the trial on a murder charge of John R. Lawson, the western U.M.W.A. officer who had been a strike leader, were responsible for the reopening of the inquiry. He had his secretary write to Rockefeller's secretary:

> I happen to know that Mr. King is strongly of the opinion that from the very outset the actions of the Walsh Commission have related themselves in the most intimate way with the trial of

Lawson and others; and he thinks Mr. Rockefeller should expect that the questions directed to him by the Walsh Commission will all be for the purpose of raising in the public mind a suspicion that the attitude of the interests which he represents afforded from the outset justification for extreme measures by Lawson and his friends, and that their attitude ever since, including their present attitude, affords reason why a new trial should be granted to Lawson, and his conviction if possible annulled. . . . His [Walsh's] whole purpose, as Mr. King sees it, is to help Lawson, by setting over against his conviction the prejudice that he hopes to arouse, and which there may be grounds for, that Mr. Rockefeller knows nothing about.

Lawson's trial was in progress when Mackenzie King was notified of the Washington hearings. On May 3 he was convicted of murder and the jury recommended life imprisonment. Mackenzie King got this information from Welborn and made the following entry in his diary:

Apparently there were eleven for hanging and one for life imprisonment. Hardly less surprising than the verdict is the report that the judge had allowed the prisoner out on his own bail and that of his counsel pending an appeal to the Supreme Court. This verdict will be a surprise to everyone. At the same time, having seen conditions as we have, one cannot but feel that it will prove a wholesome thing for this community. It shows that at last lawlessness has to reckon on the possibility of condemnation in the courts, and that the courts are not wholly delivered over to the fear of popular clamor. The jury in this case was composed of six farmers . . . a couple of garage men, one bus driver, and a commercial traveller.*

One ground for the appeal was that the judge had at one time acted for the Colorado Fuel and Iron Company in certain cases against

---

* Lawson was acquitted ultimately. He had not been in custody long. He ran for the presidency of District 15 in 1916 and was elected by a large majority, but the international executive suspended District 15 as no longer self-supporting. When the District was re-established in 1917 Lawson was defeated for the presidency, and then organized an Independent Miners' Union, which did not last. He and Doyle were both expelled later from the U.M.W.A.

the miners; another was that two detectives who gave important evidence were at the time of the trial still in the employ of the coal companies. After Lawson's trial some union officials sought to make it appear that the Colorado Fuel and Iron Company had assisted in the prosecution. This time, however, the company's record was clear; in line with the new policy it had refrained, at the insistence of Rockefeller and King, from any interference with the courts or any participation in the proceedings. It was Welborn's hope, and Rockefeller's, that Lawson would get a new trial and be acquitted, but they did not feel free to advocate this because it might seem like endeavouring to influence the courts. Welborn stated that he thought it would be in Rockefeller's interest and in the interests of the industrial peace of Colorado to have the indictments put out of the way.

When the hearings of the Walsh commission opened in Washington Mackenzie King was confirmed in his view that they were

> . . . brought on at this time as a means of influencing the course of justice in Colorado. . . . It was clear that Walsh intended to make Mr. R. commit himself either in favour of the conviction [of Lawson] for murder, in which event he knew the most frightful prejudice would be raised against him, or have him express sympathy with Lawson, in which event he intended to force him into a position of a man who, while professing a sympathy, was seeking to destroy another. I think I rendered Mr. R. one of the greatest services possible to render another by drafting on the evening of the day his examination commenced a statement for him to read on the day following, which made it impossible for Walsh to pursue these tactics by pointing out that it was improper for anyone to express publicly opinions on criminal proceedings before the courts. For Walsh to have persisted in the course he started out upon would have made it necessary for the administration at Washington to take some action. Indeed the administration was alive to the situation, for during the session on the day following the President's Secretary, Mr. Tumulty, was present as a listener with one of the members of the cabinet, for a considerable part of the day, and Mrs. Harriman and one of

the Commissioners told me that she had had a talk with the President and that he had expressed approval of Mr. Weinstock [also a commissioner] and herself publicly protesting and if necessary withdrawing from the Commission on the day following should the Chairman proceed with the inquiry in the persecuting manner in which he had begun it. Walsh's tone changed considerably on the following day, as the Commissioners had a meeting before the session opened and both Weinstock and Mrs. Harriman registered their protest and gave him to understand what the nature of their action would be in the event of his continuing as he had begun.

II

In spite of the temporary change in the chairman's attitude, Mackenzie King felt that the examination of Rockefeller was anything but fair, that it was one constant effort on the chairman's part to have him appear as a criminal in the eyes of the public.

With reactions such as these, Mackenzie King was not in any complacent frame of mind when it came to his own examination two days later. There were many angry exchanges between chairman and witness. In his diary he confessed:

I found it impossible when on the stand to restrain myself in the matter of taking direct issue with Walsh, the minute he began his contemptible insinuations and perversions of truths with me. All week I had considered quietly and thoughtfully the attitude I should take towards him. I knew that I could ... by adopting a quiet and conciliatory manner, get through with an examination in half an hour and escape untouched as far as public criticism might be concerned. I knew too that I would be considerably at a disadvantage in a controversy with Walsh, being a citizen of another country appearing to find fault with the institutions of a country that had taken me for work over the heads of its own citizens, and above all else I realized that any attempt to find fault with the Commission or to appear to be defending Mr. Rockefeller would be construed as subserviency on my part to wealth and be used later to my disadvantage in public life. At the same time, I felt I would be a moral coward if I would let any or all of these considerations combined prevent me from speaking out boldly, if the occasion should demand, in protesting against the gross unfairness of all of Mr. Walsh's procedure. . . . I did speak out, as a perusal of my evidence will show, and what I did in this connection I did deliberately. At the same time, I felt a little annoyed at myself for not exercising a greater measure of self-control at the time of speaking. . . .

On the whole, the reporters did justice to my point of view at the first day's hearing. On the second day, when I felt on the whole well satisfied with the day's examination and all that was said, and when I was not in the least flustered at any point, I found to my chagrin that the press had omitted all of the evidence that was of any value and focussed attention on one sensational feature.

What he specifically resented was Walsh's attempt to make it appear that he had 'boasted while giving his testimony, that the will and conscience of John D. Rockefeller, Jr., were more potent in Colorado than all of the public opinion of all of the people of the United States, and that the American people must look to that one man for an improvement of conditions, conceded by all to be un-American and intolerable.'

Mackenzie King had had much to say in his political career about the efficacy of enlightened public opinion in the redressing of public wrongs. In this instance he was not questioning its potency; he was taking exception to a government agency misguiding public opinion by deliberate misrepresentation of facts and motives. He felt so strongly about Walsh's statement being a 'complete perversion' of his testimony that he wrote to several newspapers quoting extracts from the official record. He had this letter, along with some editorial comment on it, printed and fairly widely distributed. These extracts, and others included in the following quotation, show the ground there was for his resentment, and show also the unmasked animosity of chairman and witness towards each other:

Q. We must have the facts?
A. Certainly.

Q. And the people must have the facts?

A. Who do you mean by the people?

Q. Well, there are a great crowd of them here, the people of the United States?

A. Yes, sir. Well, do you mean that everyone in the United States wants to know exactly?

Q. If it is possible to get it into everyone's mind?

A. That otherwise it is impossible to remedy the situation?

Q. No, but they must know, in order to get behind it, — the one most powerful public opinion that it is possible to get, so that these deplorable conditions will never occur again?

A. I hope they will never occur again.

Q. Is that not the way to do it, to put it into the minds of the people, before the people?

A. I don't know that that is the way to do it, and I don't know that you honestly think it is. The way to do it is to get hold of the forces controlling the situation, and if they are wrong, to remedy it.

Q. Is there any force in the American people . . .

A. We are playing in words.

Q. No, I am not. Is there any force to control the Rockefeller interests in Colorado, to do the right thing if they are not doing the right thing, except the ordinary people in America?

A. If you are speaking of the immediate force and immediate influence, I think that the conscience of Mr. John D. Rockefeller, Junior, is more powerful on that, and will affect social justice in Colorado quicker than any other single force that you could bring to bear. I think he realizes there is a great work to do there, and he intends to have it done.

Q. You think that the will and conscience of Mr. Rockefeller in bringing proper conditions and enduring conditions in Colorado is more powerful than the will and conscience of all the balance of the people of the United States, directed in that field?

A. No, Mr. Chairman, I don't put it that way at all. I am speaking now of the particular question of the conditions in Colorado at the present time. You asked me what factors can do the most in Colorado?

Q. Pardon me, I didn't ask you that. I asked you if it was not necessary for all of the people of the country to get a knowledge of what was taking place, and had taken place in 1903 and '04, and in '13, right down to the present time?

A. I don't think if every man in the United States knew what took place in 1903, that that would be a factor to influence the present situation one way or the other, if you had not along with it the will and intention on the part of the man that has great influence and power there . . .

Q. That is Mr. Rockefeller?

A. (continuing) . . . to use his influence in that direction.

Q. That is Mr. Rockefeller?

A. Yes, sir.

Q. If the heart and will of the whole country was at work toward bringing decent and just conditions in Colorado, —

A. That is a different question.

Q. Well, put it yourself, put it any way you want to.

A. I assume that the purpose of the Commission is to get the truth, not to distort or pervert evidence that is given.

Q. Will you please answer my question? There is nothing that you can say that is going to irritate me.

A. We are talking today to the American people, and it cannot be made too plain that we are, and I don't intend to allow you to distort or pervert anything that I may say.

Q. And I don't care how insulting your attitude may be toward me, I am going to pursue the same course that I did in my examination of your employer, Mr. John D. Rockefeller, Junior. I am going to insist on your answers. You have given your opinion of me here, but I have not given my opinion of you.

A. I have no doubt you will do it.

Q. Indeed, I will. But I would like to have you answer my questions, without any further comment, if you will, with regard to how I am doing my work, or my personal characteristics. They have nothing to do with it. . . .

Q. . . . Now, if you will answer my question. I understood you to say, I will put it again, that if the hearts and wills of the entire population of America were concentrated upon the desire to establish just relationships in Colorado, between the employees of the Colorado Fuel & Iron Company and that corporation, that the result thus desired could not be obtained unless it had the heart and will of Mr. John D. Rockefeller, Junior, with it. Do I state that correctly?

A. You want to know if it could be done without that?

Q. Is that your statement?

A. No, sir, certainly it was not.

Q. Then tell me what your statement was with respect to the necessity of having Mr. John D. Rockefeller, Junior's, will and conscience, with all the rest of the people, before proper results could be obtained?

A. This is a practical world, Mr. Chairman, and we are trying to get practical results. If the heart and conscience and interest of every citizen of the United States could be directed to that Colorado situation, certainly there would be no need for any other force to be exerted. But it will be a long time, and you and I are going to pass off the scene before that time comes. . . .

Q. Before what time comes?

A. Before the heart and interest and conscience of every citizen is directed on Colorado, so that these questions that you ask, I must feel it is a waste of time to discuss them, because we are discussing absurdities.

Q. Say a majority of the people then?

A. What my statement came to is this, if I wanted to improve conditions in Colorado to-morrow, and was looking for a force to do it, I would go after Mr. John D. Rockefeller, Junior, and I would say if he would put his energy and time into that situation, and get men to put their time and energy into it, and let his support and purpose be known, that more will come about in Colorado than in a number of years spent in efforts trying to focus opinion on the conditions that took place in 1903.

Q. 1903 and '04 and 1913 and '14? That is your belief, that it could come from Mr. Rockefeller more readily than any other force?

A. I think at the moment that he is a very strong factor. But mark you this, I would be entirely wrong if I assumed that he could do it, or go beyond his own company. In the company that he is interested in, he can do a very great good. There are industrial conditions, in Colorado outside of that company altogether, and what I would like to see, and expect to see, is the co-operation of public opinion and Mr. Rockefeller on conditions in Colorado. An example set by Mr. Rockefeller, which will be so marked that every other concern will have to follow it. I don't think there is any antagonism of necessity between the two. I don't think it is helpful to industrial conditions to try to raise a gulf between them. . . .

Q. Now, as to the necessity of having something from Mr. Rockefeller in bringing about just conditions as distinguished possibly from what might be brought about by popular opinion, you are aware, of course, when a sufficient number of people in this country get of one mind, they can take over the mines and run them themselves?

A. I don't see the necessity of drawing that distinction. Mr. Rockefeller is not desirous of opposing public opinion; I think he is distinctly anxious to fall in line with it.

Q. But you stated, as I understand it, the way this line of questioning began was, that you did not give accord to the proposition that these facts that you were developing ought to be laid out and given to the American people, all of them; all of the facts?

A. Our discussion had reference to what could be accomplished within a certain time, practical men dealing with practical questions; nothing more than that.

The New York *Times* commented on the incident in an editorial which concluded:

It is obvious that Mr. King's words did not justify the interpretation that was placed on them — the interpretation that he thought young Rockefeller more powerful than the American people. His intention, of course, was to emphasize the efficiency of one man whom he credited with high and sincere conscientiousness to do a particular thing at a particular time and place.

The New York *Tribune*, in an editorial under the heading

'Walsh at His Old Tricks', referred to 'the unbearable conduct of the man in whose hands the control of the investigation was unfortunately placed'. Another paragraph in the editorial read:

> Mr. Walsh has conducted the whole inquiry with which he and his associates have been charged in a spirit of the meanest and cheapest demagogy. He has browbeaten witnesses and taken every unfair means to color and falsify their testimony. He has made extravagant charges against the great humanitarian and public service agencies of the country, before ever acquainting himself with their work. He has been an accuser, not an investigator, and his methods of terrorism have led to a revolt within the commission itself against his rabid partisanship.

III

The Walsh commission completed its hearings and studies soon after these sessions, but no report representing the views of the commission as a whole was ever presented to Congress. Basil M. Manly, the commission's director of research and investigation, prepared a lengthy statement embodying 'the findings of fact, conclusions and recommendations of the staff, based upon their investigations and the testimony of public hearings'. This statement was endorsed by the chairman and the three labour members of the commission, but was repudiated by the other five members, who found themselves unable to agree to any of its findings or recommendations. They objected to their being made part of the commission's records without the endorsation of the commission; they were 'so manifestly partisan and unfair that we cannot give them our endorsation'. John R. Commons and Mrs. Harriman were unable to agree with the findings 'because they are directed to making a few individuals scapegoats when what is needed is serious attention to the system that produces the demand for scapegoats, and, with it, the breakdown of labor legislation in this country'.

Printed as an 'addendum' was a 'Report on the Colorado Strike' by George P. West, one of the commission's investigators. This report reflected a strong bias against John D. Rockefeller, Jr., and sought to show that the ultimate responsibility for the strike rested on him. It contained no reference to the Industrial Representation Plan of the Colorado Fuel and Iron Company which was, as he knew then, being drafted, but criticized sharply the tentative precursor of the plan: 'It embodies none of the principles of effectual collective bargaining and instead is a hypocritical pretense of granting what in reality is withheld. . . . Mr. King speaks of the "shadow of recognition" indicating that he sees the labor problem as merely one of securing for the workers a decent degree of physical welfare, and in no sense as a problem of democratizing industry and freeing the wage earners from arbitrary economic control.' Such a charge was, of course, ridiculous, in view of the provisions for self-government which were embodied in the Industrial Representation Plan. These were essentially democratic, and gave to the workers a voice in the determination of their own working- and living-conditions which was more effective than anything they could have dreamed of in the earlier days when economic control was indeed arbitrary and undemocratic. The improvements in their 'physical welfare' which resulted from this new relationship were all but revolutionary. At the same time it was unquestionably true that the Colorado Fuel and Iron Company had gone much further in both directions than it would have if pressures had not been applied by the Walsh commission, unfair though much of its propaganda appeared to be at the time.

IV

The term of the Walsh commission expired on August 23, 1915, but in the following January Walsh and several of those who had been associated with him (including the three labour members and Manly and West) established themselves as a Committee on Industrial Relations. They planned an educational or publicity campaign to further the interests of trade unionism through legislation and otherwise. One of their first objectives was to secure the printing by Congress, for free distribution, of 10,000 copies of the testimony and 200,000 copies of the 'final report' of the commission, which included majority and minority reports as well as staff reports which the commission had not endorsed. When Mackenzie King learned of this proposal he wrote to Rockefeller suggesting that some members of Congress should be 'informed' of certain facts with respect to the commission's report: that the so-called final report had not received the endorsation of the commission, that none of the testimony had been taken under oath, and that none of the witnesses had been permitted to be represented by counsel. He thought it would be unfortunate if, at the very time the Seth Low commission was planning to go to Colorado on a constructive mission, encouragement were given to 'persons who are desirous of perpetuating trouble rather than helping to maintain industrial peace'. He took pains to emphasize that he meant only to 'transmit information', not to exercise influence. 'There is a big difference,' he wrote, 'between *informing* individuals as to facts, and attempting to *influence* them in a course of conduct.' The aim would be, not to suppress the report, which had already been made public, or the evidence, which had been taken in open hearings, but to discourage the very wide distribution which the Walsh group were anxious to secure. Mackenzie King's advice was not taken in this instance. John D. Rockefeller, Jr., replied that his advisers in New York felt most strongly that nothing could be more unwise than for them to make the slightest effort to affect in one way or another the publication of these reports. They did not feel that their publication could do them any particular harm, and even if it did, they believed that the harm would be trifling in comparison with what would be done by following the course suggested. Mackenzie King doubtless had convinced himself that it was right to suppress untruth and distortion, but it is strange that he had not realized what capital Walsh and his friends would have been able to make of any effort on Rockefeller's part to limit the distribution of a government document. No surer way could have been found to stimulate demand for the report; 400,000 copies might well have become the target!

Mackenzie King's judgment on this issue was not unaffected, perhaps, by his dislike and distrust of Walsh. He felt, too, that the low opinion he held of the chairman was shared by the American public. He was confirmed in his judgment by something Harris Weinstock had told him, that he had gathered all the editorial opinion that it was possible to obtain on the commission's reports, and that over ninety per cent of it was unfavourable to Walsh. When King mentioned this in a letter to Rockefeller he added: 'The truth is, his association with any labor movement is going to help to discredit rather than further it.'

Another and quite different appraisal of Walsh and the results of the work of his commission is given by Selig Perlman in *A History of Trade Unionism in the United States*. He refers to Walsh as an able and versatile chairman, with a particular eye for publicity, whose work served to popularize the trade union cause from one end of the country to the other:

> For the first time in the history of the United States the employing class seemed to be arrayed as a defendant before the bar of public opinion. Also, it was for the first time that a commission representing the government not only unhesitatingly pronounced the trade union movement harmless to the country's best interests but went to the length of raising it to the dignity of a fundamental and indispensable institution.

CHAPTER 9

The Industrial
Representation Plan

Although the call to Washington to appear before the Walsh commission had interrupted Mackenzie King's survey in Colorado, he had gathered enough data to enable him to prepare the kind of industrial 'constitution' he had in mind. He spent most of July working on the draft at Kingsmere and sent it to New York early in August. Rockefeller was immensely impressed and wrote immediately, expressing appreciation of 'the statesmanlike, constructive, carefully worked out plan which you have submitted'.

But the Colorado management was far from enthusiastic. President Welborn came to New York early in September and the group of five, consisting of Welborn, Rockefeller, Starr Murphy, Ivy Lee, and King, discussed the draft in detail. The first thing Welborn said was that although it was a fine piece of work he did not see how it could work in their business. They discussed it clause by clause. Welborn, who had been inclined to pronounce against it *in toto*, was asked to state his objections to each clause as it was considered. He found it difficult to criticize any particular clause, and was obliged to admit and allow to pass in principle all of the sections it included, but he did this with the reservation that some of them would be subject to reconsideration. In the end, the tentative draft, with no amendments of consequence, was approved by the group. It was decided then that Rockefeller should go to Colorado immediately and present the plan to the representatives of the company's employees; if they approved it, all the employees in the mining camps would be given opportunity by secret ballot to accept or reject it.

As Mackenzie King knew better than any of them, it was one thing to draft a bill and have it approved by Cabinet, quite another to convince many of the affected interests of the wisdom of the proposed legislation. The Industrial Representation Plan would very seriously affect the western organizers of the United Mine Workers of America. Mackenzie King knew he could get nowhere with them; his previous talks with them had already satisfied him that their reputation for irresponsibility was warranted, that their one objective was power for themselves. They were not interested in any improvement of conditions not dictated by them, nor in any development of harmonious relations between management and men. They were committed to the method of the clash of opposing forces, a continuance of the futile clashes for which both parties in the past had been responsible.

If Mackenzie King was distrustful of the western group of union leaders, so were the responsible heads of the U.M.W.A. in the East. John P. White and William Green, president and secretary of the international organization, had long opposed the violent tactics of their western colleagues; so had John Mitchell and Secretary of Labor W. B. Wilson, both former officers of the union. For these union leaders Mackenzie King entertained a very high regard; he had established good relations with them when he was Deputy Minister and Minister of Labour in Canada, though he had not always agreed with them. It was a wise move on his part to arrange for Rockefeller to have talks with them. Unfortunately a meeting with Samuel Gompers, president of the American Federation of Labor, could not be arranged because of his absence from the city. Interviews were arranged, however, with White, Green, and Mitchell, all of whom had been favourably impressed by many evidences of Rockefeller's sincerity. Their good wishes and suggestions were beyond anything Rockefeller and King had hoped for. Specifically, White and Green advised: (1) that Mr. Rockefeller himself should go to Colorado; (2) that he should have the company make an agreement with its own employees, not with the union; (3) that the agreement should be for a term of years; and (4) that the agreement should provide that there would be no discrimination against employees because of their joining a union. It was an immense satisfaction to King that everything they asked for had already been decided upon and the agreement actually drawn up.

One other preliminary step was necessary: he must 'sell' his product to Welborn's chief lieutenants in Colorado — vice-presidents, managers, and other senior officials, some of whom had been frightened by rumours, many of them well founded, of revolutionary changes. Lack of understanding on their part, or reluctance to carry out the programme in the spirit in which it was conceived, could wreck it before it got well started. For this purpose Mackenzie King went out to Colorado a week ahead of Rockefeller. He continued where he had left off — conducted a short course of indoctrination, listened to objections, invited suggestions, and agreed to changes which would meet objections without altering any basic principles. It was all highly successful and before the week was over the complete support and goodwill of the company's key men had been won.

As for employee reactions, Mackenzie King had talked at length on his earlier visit in the spring with hundreds of miners, including the representatives they had chosen in December. He was to meet them again with Rockefeller, in the tour of the mining camps planned for late September and in the joint conference that was immediately to follow that tour. As a result of these contacts he was convinced that the employees would welcome action to end the hostility and prevent the recurrence of the conflicts that had bedevilled their existence for years.

II

When Rockefeller arrived in Colorado, late in September, he set out immediately, accompanied by Mackenzie King, to visit every mine and mining camp of the Colorado Fuel and Iron Company in the southern coal area. He was accompanied also by a group of un-invited newspaper correspondents, some of them friendly, some, at least for the first day or two, less than friendly. Mackenzie King had already covered the same ground and was therefore qualified to act as guide, pointing out the good spots as well as the bad ones, recent improvements as well as still-existing primitive conditions. In one place the visit might be something in the nature of a slum-ming expedition; the next camp could show evidence of slum clear-ance, houses newly painted, vegetables and flowers growing behind new picket fences. Here were mining camps at their worst and al-most at their best. But even at best a mining camp is a dismal place in which to live and bring up a family. It was not what could be des-cribed as a triumphal tour; neither was it a disappointing one. It did achieve its purpose in giving Rockefeller opportunity to meet and talk privately with coal miners and their wives and to observe the conditions under which they worked and lived. For many of the miners the visit merely gave an opportunity to satisfy natural curiosity; in their midst was a celebrity as well known, if perhaps not so exciting, as a movie actor. There were many signs of warm welcome, born of hopes for better things, but there were also in-dications of indifference and resentment reflecting suspicions it would take years to eradicate. There were no hostile demonstra-tions such as Rockefeller Senior had feared, fears which had led him to advise against the trip altogether and to suggest that if his son did go his secretary should carry a revolver. Mr. Heydt, the secretary, went out unarmed; there was no body-guard, and no incident occurred which remotely suggested the need of one. Day after day Rockefeller was his genuine unassuming self. He put questions to individuals and to small groups and won their confidence by his frank answering of their questions to him. Usually it was a man-to-man talk; occasionally Mackenzie King joined in, but company officials and newspapermen were excluded by design. The two principals donned miners' overalls and caps, complete with headlamps, and went far into the slope mines and down the deep shafts. At one camp the visiting party was surrounded by a hundred or more miners eager to shake hands with Rockefeller. The crowd became an audience when an elderly Negro miner, distinguished-looking with long grey hair and walrus moustache, stepped forward and delivered an apostrophe to the guest of honour. Evidently he was a local character, and the camp orator. Holding out his long coal-blackened arm and hand in a dramatic gesture he exclaimed: 'Yo' see that hand, gentlemen, that hand has just shook hands with John D. Rockefeller.' (It was reported later that 'that hand' was unwashed for weeks after.) He went on: 'Mr. Rockefeller, yo' are not great in stature, but yo' are surely great in fame.' The harangue lasted for fully ten minutes, interspersed with much laughter and applause from the miners, and was received with genuine if embarrassed appreciation by its subject.

It was a strenuous fortnight for both travellers, with serious talks together while going from camp to camp. Long evenings were spent in comparing notes of interviews and incidents and discussing details of the plan to make sure that provision was made for redress of every justifiable grievance and for every possible improvement of physical conditions and personal relations.

On the last evening of the tour Rockefeller was guest of honour at a social gathering in the schoolhouse at the Cameron camp. He gave a short talk to the miners and their wives and then suggested that the floor be cleared for a dance. When the orchestra struck up for a foxtrot, he was the first to respond. His first dance was with the superintendent's wife; before the evening was over he had danced, so the exaggerated report ran, with every miner's wife, daughter, and sweetheart on the floor. When he stepped on the floor himself the newspapermen in the entourage were thrilled by this raw material for a 'story'; they rushed from the dance hall to the telegraph office to tell the world what at that moment seemed to be an incident of national importance.

III

All this was in preparation for the joint meeting of representatives of employees and management at which the Industrial Representation Plan was to be presented. The stage was all set for the conference at Pueblo that was to mark the beginning of a new era. This day, October 2, 1915, was a red-letter day, as he himself described it, in the life of John D. Rockefeller, Jr.; a red-letter day, too, for the company management and the company employees. The steelworks club-house was filled to capacity: nearly two hundred miners' representatives were there; they had come from every Colorado Fuel and Iron camp in the state. President Welborn and his entourage of managers and superintendents were there, and two others — guest artists they might have been called — John D. Rockefeller, Jr., and W. L. Mackenzie King. In many respects it could have been likened to the opening of a new Parliament, but the ceremonial element was absent; the occasion was one of complete informality. As the men gathered outside the building, there was no immediate intermingling of officials and miners, but before they settled down for the meeting inside, the dividing line had disappeared and they were all part of one audience, with Welborn on a slightly raised platform flanked by his two special guests. Rockefeller had already met most of the employees' representatives during his tour of the camps and he remembered many of them. They had not forgotten him, this modest, approachable young man, just turned forty, with a wisp of a smile, and an unforced friendliness that was so unlike what they had expected. They were even more convinced of his genuineness when he began to speak.*

---

* Most of this address was reproduced in his book, *The Personal Relation in Industry*, Boni and Liveright, New York, 1923, pp. 90-106.

Those who listened to him will never forget the human qualities of his approach. Earnestness and honesty could be expected, but there was an occasional unexpected touch of humour that induced an atmosphere of relaxation. He spoke of his two-week tour of the mining camps with Mackenzie King, his visits to scores of homes and talks with hundreds of miners and their wives and children, his inquiries about water supply and facilities for education and recreation. 'I went into your wash-houses and talked with the men before and after bathing. As you know we have pretty nearly slept together — it has been reported that I slept in one of your night-shirts — I would have been proud had this report been true.' When one of the miners remarked, 'I think we are getting somewhere', Rockefeller's sense of fun led him to tell the story of a man in a theatre who had sat on his neighbour's hat; he rose quickly and apologized, 'I think I have sat on your hat.' 'You think you did,' retorted the irate owner of the hat. 'You know damn well you did.' The audience, to whom the word 'damn' hardly qualified as an oath, enjoyed Rockefeller's unaccustomed and self-conscious use of it and applauded vigorously when he repeated it with the obvious application, 'You think we are getting somewhere, you know damn well we are.'

More serious, but hardly less entertaining, was Rockefeller's ob-ject-lesson in economics when he illustrated, by heaping a pile of coins on a table, how the earnings of the Colorado Fuel and Iron Company were distributed. He introduced it by recalling the ti-rades shouted across the country against 'those Rockefeller men in New York, the biggest scoundrels that ever lived, who have taken millions of dollars out of this company on account of their stock ownership, have oppressed you men, have cheated you out of your wages and "done" you in every way they could.' Then, turning to the pile of coins, he removed some to represent the share of the wage-earners, 'the first to put a hand into the pile'. More coins were removed to represent the share of the officers and superintend-ents. 'Then come the directors and they get their directors' fees', and with that he removed the few coins that were left. 'And, hello!

there is nothing left! This must be the C. F. and I. Company! for never, since my father and I became interested in this company as stockholders, some fourteen years ago, has there been one cent for the common stock.' The common stockholders had put $34 million into the company without getting one cent in dividends: 'I just want you to put that in your pipes and smoke it and see if it tallies with what you have heard about the stockholders oppressing you and trying to get the better of you.' Rockefeller's speech was simple and homely; his object-lesson, using coins and table as concrete illustrations, was more impressive and certainly more entertaining than many a lecture by learned economists on the distribution of wealth.

All this was merely introductory to the presentation of Mackenzie King's plan of industrial representation. Mr. King had primed his chief on every vital point, but kept himself in the background, for this was something in the nature of a family gathering. Representatives of the press had not been invited to attend. It fell to Mackenzie King to tell them that this was a closed meeting. There was no demur on their part. He assured them, in a jocular way, that if anything untoward should happen — if, for example, any shots were aimed at Rockefeller — he would rush out to let them know.

What was offered to the employees at this meeting was a plan whereby all the company's employees would elect their own representatives by secret ballot, one representative to every 150 men, who would serve with representatives of management on joint committees in determining working- and living-conditions. In each of five districts joint committees would be established to deal with such matters as industrial co-operation and conciliation (including prevention and settlement of disputes, maintenance of order, company stores, etc.); safety and accidents; sanitation, health, and housing; and recreation and education. District conferences would be held at least every four months. Elaborate provision was made for the adjustment of grievances, including the appointment of a travelling representative of the president, whose job was to look for trouble and prevent it. The company undertook also to reimburse employee representatives for time lost and expenses incurred in the performance of their duties. Employee representatives were protected against discrimination through appeal to senior officers including the president and, if necessary, to the Colorado Industrial Commission.

A memorandum of agreement attached to the plan committed the company to continue wage rates for over two years, these rates to be increased, however, to match any increases granted in competitive areas; to fix moderate charges for house rent, light, and water; to build fences around all houses; to erect bath- and club-houses. In addition, employees were given the right to caution or suspension before discharge, to hold meetings on company property, and to purchase where they pleased — not, as formerly, only at company stores.

Of great significance at the time was the provision that there would be no discrimination by the company on account of membership in a labour union. In earlier years membership meant dismissal, and union organizers were not permitted to enter the camps. In the face of management opposition Mackenzie King had insisted on this provision. Company officials feared it would encourage organizers of the U.M.W.A. to canvass in the camps for members, which might open the way to irresistible demands for recognition of the union.

The presentation of the plan to the meeting was followed by thorough discussions in which managers, superintendents, and miners expressed themselves freely. Unanimous approval was the end result and the decision was made to submit the plan to every coal miner in the company's employ. So many different nationalities were to be found amongst the workers that the document was printed in thirteen different languages, so that it might be understood by all.

The taking of such a referendum vote was a new experience for company officials; but the electoral machinery was set up with great care to ensure that the individual miners could cast their ballots in secret and without pressure. It took three weeks, from October 4 to October 25, to cover the whole territory and to complete the vote in all the camps. Seventy-three per cent of the average working-force at the mines and coke ovens actually voted, a suprisingly large percentage, and of the votes cast 84.47 per cent were in favour of both the plan and the agreement.

IV

This enthusiastic acceptance of the plan by the miners was a personal satisfaction to Rockefeller, and even more so to Mackenzie King, who had devoted weeks to its preparation and had convinced board members, company officials, government representatives, and the responsible labour leaders of its merits. More than anyone else he had been responsible for Rockefeller's coming to Colorado and for the success of his tour of the mining camps and the equally successful inauguration of the plan. Together they had seen with their own eyes the beginning of a new and happier relationship between management and men.

Reactions to the Industrial Representation Plan were not all favourable. They varied all the way from enthusiastic acceptance to questioning, suspicion, and outright condemnation; but on the whole the response was distinctly favourable. Shareholders, managers, and employees (three of the four parties to industry) endorsed it. Public sentiment in Colorado, expressed in newspaper editorials and reports of interviews, was overwhelmingly in favour of the new order, which promised an end to the industrial strife which had been the plague of the state for years. Unanimous approval could not, of course, be expected so long as the demands of the Colorado union organizers for recognition of their leadership were not met. Their denunciation of the Industrial Representation Plan, as a substitute for trade unionism, was bitter and was echoed by the radical press in many parts of the country. It was not generally known then that the heads of the United Mine Workers of America in the East had virtually disowned their Colorado colleagues and had encouraged Mackenzie King to go ahead with a scheme which they felt would lead in the end to union recognition. Presumably Samuel Gompers, president of the American Federation of Labor, was also unaware of the attitude of the U.M.W.A. heads. It was a pity Rockefeller and King had been unable, when they talked with other labour leaders before going out to Colorado, to arrange a meeting with him. They might have persuaded him, as they had the others, that the Industrial Representation Plan was not a device designed to by-pass his organization. John Mitchell, ex-president of the U.M.W.A., had told them he thought that Gompers would be satisfied with Mr. Rockefeller's position if he understood it as it had been explained. If it had been explained to him, his outburst in a statement to the press, after the plan had been introduced, might have been less vehement:

> So Mr. Rockefeller has formed a union — a union of his employees of the Colorado Fuel and Iron Company, and perhaps imagines he has solved the problem of just relations between himself and his employees. But with all his wealth and all his brains and the brains he could buy and suborn he has missed his mark.
>
> Imagine an organization of miners formed by the richest man in the world, who employs its members. What influence can such a pseudo union have to insist upon the remedying of a grievous wrong or the attainment of a real right? ... These miners have been formed into a union by Mr. Rockefeller's benevolent altruism. But he *has* organized them, and for that, at any rate, Labor is truly grateful, for when men come together to discuss even in the most cursory way their rights and interests and welfare there is afforded a splendid field for development and opportunity ...

In spite of the sarcasm of the earlier part of this attack, Gompers' closing remarks left the way open for future friendly relations.

v

The Seth Low commission took a very favourable view of the plan. It had visited Colorado in December 1915 and made an intensive study, and when its report was published two months later it commented that the plan was a new departure in the United States. They knew of nothing just like it in force anywhere. They could say little about the success of the experiment, for it had been in effect less than three months, but its success would almost certainly influence other Colorado operators to follow its example. The plan had been conceived, the commission was satisfied, as something more than a means of escaping from dealing with the union, as basically a bill of rights, relations between the parties being defined by contract; it was a first step in the direction of democratic control of industry and corresponded with the beginnings of political development leading to representative and responsible government.

The commission was impressed by the protection afforded representatives against abuse by the company, and noted with approval that if they thought they had been discriminated against they could appeal to the Industrial Commission of the state, whose finding must be accepted as final by the company. They found that the further safeguard of appeal for redress of grievances, from one authority to another until the president of the company was reached, was having the effect of modifying and making less arbitrary the attitudes of mine foremen and mine superintendents and other subordinate officials; already the company was finding that an increasing number of complaints were being adjusted locally.

The joint committees which had been set up to provide co-operation between the employees as a body and the company also met with their warm approval as being a very promising experiment in co-operation, and they discounted entirely the suggestions of the western officials of the U.M.W.A. that the plan had not been set up in good faith. They believed that, while a certain amount of distrust might still exist on the side of the company's employees in view of some of the events of the recent past, time would tend to dissipate this distrust.

To John D. Rockefeller, Jr., the successful inauguration of the Industrial Representation Plan was an occasion for great rejoicing, and his advocacy of its principles was to continue throughout the years. While the plan has often been referred to as 'the Rocke-feller Plan' he always gave full credit to Mackenzie King as its author and as his guide in his efforts to induce management and men, fellow directors, and the public to accept its principles.

VI

Mackenzie King realized, before he left Colorado, that adaptation of the plan to the needs of the steelworkers in the company's employ was the inevitable next move in view of the promising beginnings that had been made in the coal-mining areas. He discussed with Welborn its extension to the Minnequa Steel Works at Pueblo. In Ottawa he re-drafted the plan for this purpose. In the midst of its preparation he conferred with company officials in Chicago (as a meeting-place half-way between Ottawa and Denver), as well as with Rockefeller and others in New York, and with all of them he carried on an extensive and detailed correspondence. The new plan was finally agreed upon, and was first presented to representatives of the steelworkers and then submitted to all the company's employees in Pueblo. The employees voted by secret ballot early in May 1916: of the total votes cast, 73 per cent were in favour of the proposed plan and agreement. Indicative of the interest of the steelworkers was the fact that over 80 per cent of the working-force had cast their ballots.

The plan at the steel-works at Pueblo was off to a good start, and was soon extended to cover employees of the company's iron mines at Sunrise, Wyoming, and the company's newly acquired Colorado and Wyoming Railway. In the latter instance agreement was made with representatives of two labour unions, a significant departure from company policy.

Management, once it got over its initial scepticism and found itself committed to sharing control with employees, carried on with all the fervour of a new convert. Fear of the union helped. Backslidings did occur at times during the next few years, and it was not always easy to restrain superintendents and petty bosses from the arbitrary conduct they had been used to. But on the whole the heads and the subalterns were faithful to the new creed. In so-called social welfare or social betterment work, the beginning which had been made even before the adoption of the plan developed into an elaborate programme. Company funds were spent on a large scale, on house improvements, fencing, wash-houses, schools, buildings for recreation centres, and additions to hospital and medical services.

VII

The plan of industrial representation which Mackenzie King had devised was the first important experiment in the United States in establishing representation for employees, and was a forerunner of the shop committees, or work councils, which were to multiply rapidly in a variety of industries during and after the war. Several of these later schemes were modelled on the Colorado plan.

Employees, at first as sceptical as management but not for the same reasons, came to realize that the reform at the top was genuine, and on the whole they entered into the spirit of the new venture. If the enterprise had been more of their own making they would without doubt have been even more enthusiastic about it. But they did make use of the new facilities for adjusting grievances. They were human enough to show little enthusiasm about attending meetings of the various committees, and even when it came to voting for representatives they were apathetic. When the men would not take the trouble to cast their ballots at the club-house the management decided to have the ballot-box brought to them at the pit-head or in the mine. Without training in self-government they showed no keenness to achieve it; to a degree self-government had to be imposed upon them. Their indifference might be interpreted as in some measure an evidence of confidence in a reformed management. The record of the next few years shows a wholesome growth of good relations between management and men, a complete contrast with earlier conditions. Notable, however, was the extent to which these activities were inspired by management rather than by the employees themselves, and the extent to which the company financed the various projects. Such expenditure was money well spent (improved relations meant increased production) even though owners and managers were thereby exposed to the charge of paternalism. This was a word that Rockefeller had come to regard with positive dislike, yet there had to be a certain element of paternalism, especially in the early stages. Full partnership had not been achieved under the plan. The workers were very junior partners in the early stages, but they were not silent partners. They had a voice in discussion of their working- and living-conditions and, to a marked degree, in the determination of these conditions. In 1915 Mackenzie King thought of the Colorado plan as an experiment. Rockefeller described it as 'a comprehensive industrial constitution' and thought of the new relationship as one of partnership. Both of them regarded it then as a mere beginning, only a framework.

VIII

Even though the Colorado plan was merely an experiment in 1915 and was considered by some in 1921 as a still incomplete experiment, even though the company did provide the funds and most of the initiative, even though the employees did not achieve full partnership or complete self-government, even though the company persisted in its policy of refusing to recognize the trade union, the thing worked, and worked successfully for twenty years. Mackenzie King had been called in to find a remedy for a condition of conflict which, in his opinion, was 'one of the worst, if not the worst, labor struggle America has known'. He made a thorough diagnosis, performed a major operation, and the patient enjoyed a life of normal health for more than two decades under the treatment prescribed.

CHAPTER 10

'A Friendship for Life'

The experiences they shared in Colorado made both Mackenzie King and John D. Rockefeller, Jr., realize that the warm personal relationship established through their first contacts little more than a year before was destined to become a lifelong friendship. For three weeks and more they had lived together in Colorado under conditions more like those of a camping expedition than of a series of business conferences. Although normally reticent in his expressions of personal feeling, and cautious about accepting at face value friendly gestures from men whose motives might be open to question, Rockefeller spoke and wrote generously of his appreciation of all that Mackenzie King had done, and all that as a man he was. It was a gracious impulse that led him to write to Mackenzie King's parents in Toronto, at the end of the Colorado tour, to express his 'deep regard for the mother and father of the man whom so unreservedly I respect and admire, and for whom I entertain feelings akin to those of a brother'. It was not the first time he had so expressed himself. In the trying ordeal of the Walsh commission hearings they had worked together more as close friends than as client and counsel. As they parted on that last day, King was embarrassed by his sincere tribute: 'I feel that I have found in you the brother I have never had and have always wished to have.' Seldom, Rockefeller declared to a friend, had he been so impressed by a man at first appearance. And subsequent meetings confirmed and enhanced his first impressions. If he felt this strong personal attachment to the Canadian who had come into his life, Mackenzie King was equally impressed by the discovery that this man, concerning whom many could say no word too bitter, was a person of singular charm, of deep moral purpose, inspired by ideals of life similar to his own.

That day of their first meeting in June 1914 was one that would always be remembered by both men. Rockefeller had heard of King only the week before, through one of his associates who had suggested he invite him to his home. While Mackenzie King had, of course, heard of his host, he had heard much more of his host's father, and newspaper stories, headlines, and cartoons had usually shown him in a rather unfavourable light. John D. Rockefeller, Sr., had been described and caricatured for years as a hard man who had reaped where he had not sown and gathered where he had not strawed. Popular prejudice is a penalty most men of great wealth must pay, at least until they prove themselves worthy of public approval. Mackenzie King was one who had shared this prejudice against the rich, and against the Rockefellers because they were very rich, and he admitted as much to John D. Rockefeller, Jr., before they had known each other long. The two men were of the same age, both born in 1874. They were both deeply religious. Simplicity in early home life had marked the upbringing of both, even though the Rockefellers were fabulously rich while the Kings had never been more than comfortably off. In his own country Mackenzie King was known as a man of deep social sympathies inherited from a revolutionary grandfather and intensified by personal involvement in many industrial conflicts. He had always included labour leaders among his friends, had drafted legislation which had proved to be the greatest boon to Canadian workingmen, and in a thousand and one ways had shown the direction of his sympathies. The views of Rockefeller on social questions were not widely known; in the public mind his name was associated with Big Business, with Standard Oil, and, in the months immediately preceding the meeting of the two men, with the conflict between the management of the Colorado Fuel and Iron Company and the western leaders of the United Mine Workers of America. Many labour leaders and the general public too thought of him as anti-labour.

As for politics, had Mackenzie King been brought up in the United States he doubtless would have been a Democrat, perhaps a Democratic leader. Rockefeller never engaged in political contro-versy, though he was, at least nominally, a Republican. Had he been a Canadian his natural political alignment would have been with the Conservative Party; but a Mackenzie King, if given the oppor-tunity, might have found ways of projecting the man of wealth through the eye of a needle into the kingdom of Liberalism. The realm of politics, however, was one into which their conversations seldom drifted. Rockefeller could not understand his friend's pre-ference for public life as against social reform work, for which he had shown such unique talent and aptitude. Mackenzie King never lost his interest in establishing better human relations within in-dustry, but he was convinced that the problem was one, and only one, of many that could be more effectively solved by the right kind of government policies. Neither man ever persuaded the other to his own point of view.

When their talks turned to more personal matters they found themselves in closer sympathy. One evening, as they walked home from the office at 26 Broadway, Mackenzie King broached the subject of religion for the first time: his interest in social problems, he said, sprang from his belief in the life of Christ and the rightness of His teachings. Rockefeller's response was one of complete ac-cord: 'He said he was glad I said this, that that was his motive, and that I could be a moral support to him in carrying through measures with this aim.' At the end of the day Mackenzie King wrote:

> I feel a perfect sympathy in all things as we talk together and
> have felt it since we first met, it is the more extraordinary as it
> is the last thing I should have expected to experience. Clearly

there is a spiritual or psychic power that has attracted and that attracts and holds.

There were times when Mackenzie King ventured a certain criticism of Rockefeller's way of life:

> I spoke to him about his own method of living and the degree to which he was becoming immersed in a multitude of obligations, which left him no time for mental rest or spiritual growth. I said I thought he ought to be in the country a good part of the time, and have his office so organized that he could leave to others a multitude of things he was now undertaking; otherwise he would break down.

The course of this true friendship did not always run smooth. On one occasion King referred to Rockefeller in his diary as 'a dominating type, though he seeks not to be'. There were times, too, when he could criticize him for 'being a little petulant when his wishes were not quickly met'.

To his friend Violet Markham, who had at first doubted the wisdom of the association, he wrote:

> I have found in Mr. John D. Rockefeller, Jr. one of the best of men and most welcome of friends. . . . Whatever his father may have done or is, that man I have found to be almost without exception the truest follower of Christ. . . . His humility, his sincerity, his fearlessness, his simple faith, his fidelity to principle — so far as he has horizon at all his one purpose is to serve his fellowmen.

II

Mackenzie King may have continued for some time to have reservations about Rockefeller Senior, but no man could be a trusted friend of John D. Rockefeller, Jr., who lacked faith in his father. He was proud of his father, as proud of him as Mackenzie King was of his parents and of his grandfather. 'You will see,' he said at the time of their first meeting, 'that he is not the kind of man he is represented to be. You will see, too, how great is my responsibility having a father such as I have.' King came to be deeply impressed by the relationship between father and son: 'It could not be more intimate or affectionate and it is an intimacy and affection founded on mutual respect and regard.' His first impression had been wholly favourable:

> Far from being the kind of man he is pictured to be by the press, he seemed to be the very opposite. In appearance, he is not unlike pictures one sees of the old popes. In manner he is singularly simple and natural and genuinely kindly. He spoke in the most natural way of his boyhood and life on a farm and of some of his early experiences. He reminded me very much of Sir Wilfrid in the way in which the phrases he used seemed to be expressive of opinions reached as the result of long experience. I thought too, he had the same charitable point of view towards men.

After one of their later conversations he wrote:

> I had the feeling I was talking with a man of exceptionally alert mind and great discernment of character. He is a good deal of a mimic, and in telling of people and of his own feelings is apt to imitate the expression of the person or the attitude he is representing. He is full of humor, particularly in conveying a shrewd knowledge of situations and men. His whole nature is a gentle one and a sweet one. I still feel about him what I did the first time I met him, that in some respects it is almost a benign nature.

This conception of his personality might have been more generally accepted had the senior Rockefeller permitted himself freer contact with the public. It was too late now to alter a policy and practice of secretiveness as far as the father was concerned, but it was one of Mackenzie King's resolves to do his part in preventing this particular mistake being repeated by the son. A wrong beginning had been made because the young man had inherited a distrust of modern public relations. With the advent of his new and more liberal-minded adviser, he welcomed a change in policy and his father seemed to acquiesce in its desirability. At least he made no demur when Mackenzie King told him what his advice would be:

> I told Mr. Rockefeller, Sr. that I thought his son should come

more in touch with people who were interested in social problems
... that once men came to know him, they would appreciate his
spirit and purpose, but that not knowing him, many false impressions would make headway which would never arise if he were
really understood aright.

Rockefeller was touched by these words and commented: 'I wish
I had had you the thirty or forty years I was in business to advise
me on policies.' Mackenzie King long remembered this remark and
his son's rejoinder: 'I am glad you didn't, because I would be prevented then from having Mr. King for the next thirty or forty
years.'

III

The two friends talked freely of personal matters, and it was
almost inevitable that Mackenzie King's unmarried state should
become the subject of discussion and advice. It was a subject in
which he was still very much interested, a condition he was still
anxious to remedy. Mrs. Rockefeller shared her husband's sympathetic interest in this. Just as Sir Wilfrid and Lady Laurier had
counselled marriage when he was in his thirties, so now, when he
was nearing his mid-forties, did Mr. and Mrs. Rockefeller. They
even went so far as to suggest the person they thought would be
suitable, and urged him, as Sir Wilfrid had done, to take some positive steps. He listened with interest each time they spoke of the
matter. He was in a better position financially now, with the old
fear of future penury removed. He decided to make some tentative
approaches. These were not given any actual encouragement, but
then neither were they definitely discouraged. The new object of
his devotion was 'all that I most wish to find in a woman'. In subsequent entries in his diary, for weeks, all her fine qualities were
dwelt upon in detail and in superlatives. He wrote letters, sent
books and flowers, made personal calls, then more letters. Unfortunately her replies, waited for with eager impatience, were few, and
those brief and unrevealing.

It was at this time, early in 1918, that Rockefeller was pressing

Mackenzie King to establish himself in New York. He may have realized – though there was no such ulterior motive in his suggestion – that the matrimonial alliance he had proposed would have more drawing-power than all the bright business or professional prospects he could hold out. With political prospects in Canada dimmed at the time by the indifferent attitude of Laurier and his Quebec colleagues, and with new opportunities opening up in the United States, it was no wonder that a move to the south was an enticing possibility. 'Much, though,' King wrote in his diary, 'will depend on Miss "X". With her help I would feel I could accomplish most either there or here, & of this I feel quite satisfied in my own mind that to win her love would be better than all else in the way of position or power either here or across the border. It would mean the realization of my highest & noblest self, and the homelife for which my soul longs.'

Two attractive possibilities were thus linked together in his mind: achievement of success in the United States as an industrial consultant and the winning of a wife to share that success with him. 'The chance is so great,' he wrote with enthusiasm and hope, 'that if Miss "X" will "fall in line" I am strongly tempted to plan to leave for New York & open an office there & commence a life work of practical reforms in industry in a big way.' When he discussed things with Rockefeller in Ottawa a week later he spoke of the feelings he had about leaving Ottawa and its associations and friends. The contrast of 'the loneliness of New York' was painful, but 'if the marriage question were settled it would make a difference'. Rockefeller had no encouragement to offer: 'He seemed to think she had no thoughts of marriage.' She had told him, he said, of 'her feeling being I was rushing things a little hard'. Perhaps she felt that the saintliness which he had attributed to her could not be lived up to, that she would find it difficult to live a natural life in such a rarefied atmosphere, or it could have been simply that she did not care, or care enough, for him, yet did not wish to offend by saying so. Rockefeller hinted at this when he observed that 'women preferred to be pleasant and agreeable'. He advised, the diary entry concluded, 'my going slowly, treating her only as a friend and await developments'. Mackenzie King did go slowly thereafter, but there were no developments. In the end — and the end was not many weeks in coming — he had to realize that this latest venture, too, had failed: Miss 'X' disappeared from his life. It was a genuine regret to Rockefeller that he had been able to do so little to help solve such a vital personal problem for his friend, for whom he coveted the kind of domestic happiness he had found for himself.

How far-reaching might have been the effects on Canada's future, and on King's own, if the decision of one American citizen had been different! Her acceptance of him would have meant, or so he thought at the time, living in the United States. But there might have been an alternative possibility of life in Canada if suitable political opportunities opened up, although in the latter event an American wife would be less of a political asset than a Canadian. As things turned out, such international considerations did not have to be taken into account. Whether as industrial counsellor in the United States or as prime minister in Canada, Mackenzie King was to carry on his work alone.

Rockefeller realized how much he owed to Mackenzie King and was grateful for all he had accomplished. The wish he had expressed to his father that he might have him 'for the next thirty or forty years' had been a fine tribute in itself. He did 'have' him for another thirty-five years, but as a personal friend, not, as he had hoped, as a business associate. King had been invited into an inner circle. As an adviser on labour policies he had proved himself in dealing with a series of worrying problems: 'I was merely King's mouthpiece,' Rockefeller generously conceded. 'I needed education. No man did as much for me. He had vast experience in industrial relations and I had none.' But he was more, much more, than an industrial counsellor. Even after their paths diverged in 1919, his visits to the family home on West 54th Street, and to the summer retreat, The Eyrie, at Seal Harbor in Maine, continued to be frequent, and there was a constant flow of correspondence between them. Mackenzie King had proved to be, as Rockefeller's biographer Raymond B. Fosdick wrote years later, 'not only an indispensable guide but probably the closest friend JDR Jr. would ever have. He had influenced the thinking of the younger Rockefeller perhaps more than any man except his father.'

CHAPTER 11

The Plan and Trade Unionism

If there was one criticism of the Industrial Representation Plan that troubled Mackenzie King more than any other, it was the suggestion that the plan was designed as a substitute for trade unionism. That question had arisen even before the plan had been introduced, and he was on the defensive for years, charged with sponsoring 'company unions'. One answer to the charge is to be found in the record of his whole career: his sympathies had always been strongly with labour unions, even though he had not given them undeviating support. Something of his philosophy had been put on record when he testified before the Walsh commission:

> I have a very strong feeling — I may be wrong in this — that Labor makes a mistake some times in these long strikes for union recognition ... I think, if emphasis were laid upon conditions and injustice that Labor is trying to remedy, rather than upon that abstract term 'union recognition', the unions would receive more support and understanding support from the general public than they sometimes do. I think to carry a fight for four or five years simply on the question of recognition, and leave the actual conditions out of account altogether, is leaving the substance while you are chasing the shadow. ... My feeling is that true unionism is not an end in itself; it is a means to an end. It is a means of obtaining and improving standards for the working classes.

Until Mackenzie King came into his life, John D. Rockefeller, Jr., had not felt, as a director, any positive sense of responsibility for labour policies, and was opposed to union recognition. Such opposition was in accord with the Rockefeller tradition in the Standard Oil companies. He was much impressed by the argument that since most of the Colorado employees were content without any such outside intervention (he had only the word of the managers that they were content) they should not be compelled, as they would be under a union agreement, to pay dues to a union organization. His impressions of the western union leaders, based also largely on reports from the company managers, were distinctly unfavourable. Mackenzie King had little hope of altering his opinion of them, but he did induce a more sympathetic attitude toward the trade union movement through the personal contact he arranged with the more responsible leaders of the U.M.W.A.

II

Rockefeller's attitude toward the possibility of union recognition some time in the future was changing, and so, to a lesser degree, was that of the president of the Colorado Fuel and Iron Company. Welborn attended the conference with the Seth Low commission and went further than Mackenzie King anticipated he would go, when he said that while his company did not recognize the United Mine Workers today, he was not saying what they might not be prepared to do at some future time; but, he added, 'certainly with the present management he could have no dealings'. Other company officials would not have gone this far: if they had had their way they would have refused to employ union men, and would not have permitted union organizers to enter the camps. One man who, in September 1915, was being considered for an important post in the administration of the Industrial Representation Plan had expressed himself in favour of this policy of exclusion. It drew down upon him a well-deserved rebuke from Mackenzie King and it almost cost him the job. Mackenzie King told him, among other

things, that 'if Mr. R. took a position against unionism and the
right of men to join the Union, I myself would get out and fight
against him; that it was fundamentally wrong that a man of his
wealth should be placed in antagonism towards organization of
labor; that Mr. R. Sr. himself had admitted the right of labor to
organization'. Ivy Lee, one of the Rockefeller advisers of that day,
agreed absolutely with Mackenzie King and went so far as to say
that 'even should it be necessary before long for the Colorado
Company to make an agreement with the United Mine Workers,
he would prefer to see this to a continuation of the fight.... The
men should have the right to do as they please about joining an
organization.' Mackenzie King added that he intended to fight very
hard for this position and to make no compromise on it.

While he was convinced from the first of the 'wrongness' of the
union men in the extremes to which they had gone, he recognized
that they had been provoked to anger by the attitude of the operators. In 1915 Rockefeller and Welborn *feared* that union recognition was inevitable; the union men *hoped* that it was; Mackenzie
King was sure that it would come about eventually and that both
sides in the end would be satisfied. Before the plan was introduced
in Colorado, White and Green of the U.M.W.A. had been impressed, in talking with Rockefeller and King, by the company's
changed attitude, its readiness to adopt principles of employee representation and collective bargaining even though the union for
the time being had no part in the bargaining process. To them, as to
Mackenzie King, this was a temporary expedient: it meant that the
arbitrary controls of the past would be relinquished and that the
still-existing tensions would to a large extent be alleviated. The
provision in the plan that employees would be free to join the
union or not, and that union organizers could carry on their
membership campaigns even within the camps, had come as an unexpected concession. To them this was an exceedingly valuable
concession, for it gave promise of opening the way ultimately to
union recognition. They had discussed, first, ways and means of
allaying the hatred and suspicion that still existed in Colorado. Then

came the discussion of the company's future relations with its employees. Mackenzie King thought it important enough to give in his diary a full account of this part of their conversation:

> [They] urged that Mr. R. should have the Company make an agreement for a term of years with its own employees. I noted particularly his emphasis of the words 'its own employees', seeing thereby that clearly the head organization knew the matter of union recognition to be out of the question *at present*.
>
> They preceded this statement by saying that in labor unions much education was necessary and speaking of the difficulties they had in dealing with the masses of uneducated labor of which the mining classes were composed. They said many things had been done in Colorado which were wrong, many things on both sides, that must never happen again if they can be prevented. They did not try to put blame on one side or the other, but seemed entirely to take the point of view that they would help to further industrial peace and could be helpful in getting their men to agree to an agreement which might be made between the company and its employees.
>
> Mr. R. wanted to know why for a term of years. Why not for an agreement to be continued indefinitely. They thought a definite period was better. It lent definiteness to the agreement. I agreed with this. They said not perhaps too long a period, and spoke of three years or thereabouts. I said that what was really important was getting things into writing where there could be no misunderstanding as to what the rights of superintendents, pit bosses or the men themselves were. Both Green and White appreciated this and emphasized that that was the significance of the agreement.

Another point which was developed by Mr. Green was that

> ... such an agreement should contain a clause which would provide that there would be no discrimination against employees because of their joining a union. Mr. R. gave them his position on unionism, reading them the statement made before the Industrial Relations Commission. They said that that statement was liberal, generous and entirely satisfactory, and that position would satisfy

them. Mr. R. said he thought an agreement should have a clause to that effect in it, putting union organization on the same basis as race and religion. They thought that would be very satisfactory.

This was all that was suggested. Later, when we were about to say Goodbye, Mr. White said to me himself about the agreement that they could not expect anything in the way of an agreement with the union, that it was an agreement with the Company's own employees, leaving them free to join the union or not. *It would be sufficient at this time.* He and Green would go a long way and their union would go a long way in helping to right Mr. R. with Labor and the people if this much were done.*

III

In expressing approval of the new measures proposed for Colorado the union leaders thought more of the use they could make later on of the new machinery and of the new freedom to campaign for membership than they did of the merits of the plan itself. Rockefeller and King knew what they were thinking, and were ready to let things take their course, even if union recognition was at the end of the course. 'When we left Mitchell,' Mackenzie King wrote, 'the thought that seemed to be in Mr. R.'s mind was that the agreement was the thing, but that it meant unionism in the long run.' He went so far as to say that 'if under this arrangement every man did become a member of a union so that at the end of the period there were none but union men to deal with, there could be no objection to dealing with a union'. The entry in the diary continued:

> I said to him I thought the important thing was to let Time take care of that feature. Four or five years hence personnel would have changed materially, a new condition would be met in the light of the then circumstances, that this meant peace in the interval and opportunity for the Company to make matters so satisfactory with its own employees that if at the end of five years

* The words in italics, such as 'at present', in these extracts from the diary were not underlined in the original entries.

they were faced with a position of having to vote in favour of an agreement with the Union or a continuing of their own agreement with the Company, they would vote for the latter; just as the employees had done in the case of the Rapid Transit Company of Philadelphia. Mr. R. said we might as well go into this thing with our eyes open, and not blind them to the possible development of unionism, and that in discussing matters with the Colorado officials it would be as well to take that position, leaving it to them to work out the agreement in a manner which would best serve the interests of the Company, when the time for its change came. I agreed with him and said that there was a difference between dealing with the U.M.W.A. in Colorado as at present constituted, and stating that unionism would never be considered. The latter position I told him he could never afford to take. The former position he could take consistently, provided he held to the non-discrimination feature as already agreed upon.

It is obvious that ultimate unionization was not an objective Rockefeller hoped for; it would be a just retribution if employees were not content under the new dispensation.

When the plan was made public early in October, William Green, secretary of the U.M.W.A., gave a statement to the press:

Mr. Rockefeller seems to have taken a step in the right direction, but he does not go far enough. The only way to establish a lasting industrial peace is by the employees being organized through the miners' organization and being permitted to select their own representatives to speak for them.

Green's attitude was in no way inconsistent with the position he had taken when he and White had talked earlier with Rockefeller and King. They had honestly welcomed the promise of the first step, but it was obvious then that as union leaders they intended to press for the second and third. Criticism of the representation plan was a necessary part of a membership campaign, and nothing would be more natural than that union officers should take a swing at an organization which many of them professed to think was designed as a substitute for trade unionism; it was, in any case, a good talking-point. They welcomed the plan at its inception because it removed restrictions which hampered their union activity, but their welcome was not accompanied by any good wishes for a long life. Indeed they did all they could to shorten its life. 'A substitute for trade unionism' was to become the union's battle-cry. The cry was taken up by many who had no realization of the reasons why in 1915 union recognition was out of the question — and admitted by union leaders themselves to be out of the question. Such criticism showed little or no awareness of the first step having been a stride, and a long one, toward unionism.

Under the plan, employees could learn at least the rudiments of collective bargaining and co-operative effort on their own behalf. Most important of all, at that time, was the establishment of harmonious relations in an industry which had experienced constant turmoil, bitterness, and armed conflict. Yet, just as the joint councils in Great Britain had found it possible to work in harmony with trade unions, so it seemed to Mackenzie King distinctly possible that the plan and trade unionism would enjoy a peaceful co-existence.

IV

In 1915 Mackenzie King was unduly optimistic in insisting that there must not be another strike of Colorado Fuel and Iron employees. In later years, however, looking back over the company's record, he could view it with some satisfaction. Five strikes did occur between 1918 and 1922, but with one exception they were of very short duration. In one of them, in 1918, the employees of the Colorado and Wyoming Railway, a subsidiary of the Colorado Fuel and Iron Company, were involved, but the strike was settled within twenty-four hours when the company entered into agreements with the railway unions. This was the first time the management had ever negotiated a trade agreement with any union officials. The longest strike, that of the steelworkers in 1919, lasted for over three months. It had had its origin, not in Colorado, but in the East, and was part of a nation-wide movement to organize the steel and iron workers of the country. The Colorado Fuel and Iron Company was less seriously affected than most of the other steel companies, for a back-to-work organization was formed by the employees in Pueblo about two weeks after the strike was called and normal operations were resumed long before it was officially terminated. The three other strikes, all quickly settled, occurred in the coal-mining industry, two of them affecting all the coal mines in the United States; the other, in 1921, affected only the employees of the Colorado Fuel and Iron Company. The company had appealed to the workers to accept a reduction of wages because of the loss of markets after the steel-works had closed down. Employees in several mines agreed to accept the reduction, but the United Mine Workers opposed it and called on the miners to cease work. The dispute was referred to the Colorado Industrial Commission, which approved of the reduction on the ground that the higher rates were 'far in excess of any wage rate paid to employees in any other craft requiring like skill, apprenticeship and ability'.

In these developments Mackenzie King had had no part, but it was a satisfaction to him to know that management and men had learned to treat each other with respect and that, even in times of stress, the relations between them were not marked by the violence and bitterness of the early years. The strike in 1919 was the first large coal strike, as one impartial observer put it, to be carried through without violence in the history of Colorado. The new labor policy of the company was showing results in a new spirit in the company's relations with the miners.

v

The years ahead were to present Mackenzie King with many opportunities to advise Rockefeller on labour policies and in particular to strengthen his faltering faith in trade unionism. Early in 1919, when Rockefeller hesitated to accept an invitation to participate in a joint conference lest his acceptance be interpreted as a recognition of organized labour, Mackenzie King was aroused to the point of exasperation. He saw in this invitation an opportunity for Rockefeller to put himself clearly on record on the question of union recognition. 'I determined,' he wrote in his diary, 'to write him in a strong way with a view to having him come to the point where he will cease to question, each time a matter comes up, whether it means recognition of Organized Labor or not, and come at once to the attitude of being prepared to deal with Organized Labor wherever Organized Labor is prepared to deal squarely and honestly and honorably with him.' In Chicago, where he was working on problems affecting the Standard Oil Company of Indiana, using the company's board-room as a temporary office, he dictated what he referred to as 'a pretty strong letter. . . . Indeed, I imagine that no such letter was ever written to a Rockefeller from any of the precincts of the Standard Oil as this one which went out from the Board of Directors' room of the Indiana Company.'

On the day he wrote this letter he had spent half an hour with Robert W. Stewart, president of the Standard Oil Company of Indiana, and had given him his point of view as being against welfare work and primarily for contractual relations between capital and labour. . . . 'I told him Mr. R. and I had never seen eye to eye on this Y.M.C.A. work, that it was better that business and religion should be kept apart.'

VI

Mackenzie King had always seen the Colorado plan as something that would solve, at least for the time being, only the particular problem in Colorado — not as a device that could be applied to every industry and every area. Rockefeller, on the contrary, continued to think of it, though perhaps only subconsciously, as something that could become a substitute for unionization generally. Some managers of the Colorado Fuel and Iron Company, and of other companies in which similar plans had been introduced, were even more of this mind and were inclined to use the plan as a definite block to 'the entering wedge of unionization'. Mackenzie King was unceasing in his efforts to counteract this tendency. An extract from one of his letters to Rockefeller is typical:

> I think it cannot be too clearly seen that this is a period of transition in which Organized Labor is bound to come in for an ever increasing measure of recognition. The path of wisdom on the part of management seems to me to be that of bringing about the necessary adjustments in the most natural way and the one least liable to friction.

Another opportunity to advise presented itself when Rockefeller consulted him on the stand he should take as a participant in another conference. He was preparing to present his views on the representation idea and Mackenzie King feared that the only collective bargaining he would endorse would be that between a company and its own employees, ignoring, if not opposing, the idea of employees being represented in the bargaining process by trade unionists not in the employ of the company. He had a long talk with Rockefeller and Starr J. Murphy at Pocantico Hills, and again the theme was the plan and trade unionism:

> I tried hard to impress on Mr. R. not to let the representation plan be construed as a device for a company union, and to avoid conflict and contrast between the plan and unionism ... I think I did much for Labor in helping Mr. R. & in part Mr. Murphy over to the point of view of realizing Unionism is here to stay & desirability of working out a plan to change its militant attitude into one of co-operation.

In thus advising on the trade union question Mackenzie King was aided by Raymond B. Fosdick, who, in New York, had firsthand contacts with Rockefeller, while King, in Ottawa, except for the single-day visit to New York, had to rely on correspondence. They corresponded with each other and Fosdick wrote to King:

> I think you will agree with me that the right of collective bargaining is now an established fact beyond all controversy. Even efficiency in management and production must take a secondary

place to this great desire of the workingman to determine, through his own machinery, the conditions of his life. It seems to me that Mr. Rockefeller should be in a mood not only where he will agree to this principle, but where he will fight for it. He should fight for it not only because it is the right end to be achieved, but because it is only through such a spirit of liberalism that revolution can be avoided — if indeed it can be avoided.

Mackenzie King agreed that the principle was worth fighting for and wrote to Rockefeller before the conference opened. It was a forceful letter urging that he should give up seeking to avoid any expression of opinion on unionism, and come out fairly and squarely either for it or against it.

> To come out against it [he warned] is to put yourself, and the industries with which your name is associated, in the path of certain destruction. To come out in favor of it, surrounding your position with all the safeguards that may be necessary to prevent any misunderstanding, is to put you where you may help to change what is at the moment a great militant force arrayed against Capital, to the detriment of society, into a great co-operative force which will work with Capital for the good of human society.

Rockefeller's stand may not have been the forthright encouragement of trade unionism which Mackenzie King and Fosdick had advised. He did, however, win the approval of the labour group at the conference and incurred the displeasure of many of the employers' group by voting for the following resolution:

> The right of wage-earners to organize without discrimination, to bargain collectively, to be represented by representatives of their own choosing in negotiations and adjustments with employers in respect to wages, hours of labor, and relations and conditions of employment is recognized.

In a letter which was warm in its commendation of the stand he took, Mackenzie King stressed again the undesirability of the individual contract as making 'the individual workingman a helpless unit against a corporation which he realizes to be all-powerful'. Labour should have the same right as capital, he insisted, to retain as negotiators the persons in whom they had the greatest trust. That would be an essential in any fair system of collective bargaining:

> The Colorado Plan, it seems to me, is half-way along the road toward the goal of real justice in the matter of collective bargaining for which Labor is contending. That struggle Labor will never give up until the goal is reached, no matter how serious its losses in the interval may be.

VII

In Canada, in the late years of the war, several companies had introduced a system of joint councils, as they were called, patterned after the joint councils which were operating successfully in Great Britain, and the joint committees which were a basic feature of the Colorado plan. Examination of the method of joint councils was made an important feature of the work of a Royal Commission on Industrial Relations, which the Canadian government appointed in April 1919 to study the causes of post-war industrial unrest and to suggest means for permanent improvement in the relations between employers and employees. The commission was composed of seven members: Chief Justice T. G. Mathers and six others representing employers, employees, and the public. Tom Moore, then president of the Trades and Labour Congress of Canada, and J. W. Bruce, were the labour representatives. Seventy sessions were held across Canada and nearly five hundred witnesses were examined. Special attention was given to the Whitley Councils in England and to the so-called 'Colorado Plan' in the United States. When the commission reported in June it recommended, unanimously, that the government 'establish a bureau for promoting Industrial Councils'. 'The general principle,' the commission said, 'can with advantage be adopted in Canada.' Mackenzie King had reason to be delighted with the result. If he himself had drafted the section of the report which dealt with joint councils, he could not have given warmer endorsation of the general principles, more honest admission of inherent defects, or more pointed warning of

the danger of regarding joint councils as a panacea or as a substitute for unionism.

A National Industrial Relations Conference was appointed in
September, as had been recommended by the Royal Commission,
to give further study to the same problems. Participating were
over two hundred persons — a veritable parliament of industry, as
Mackenzie King described it: about eighty representatives of employees, eighty representatives of employers, and about fifty other
persons, including several federal and provincial Cabinet ministers
and government officials. Mackenzie King was a member of the
latter group. Each one of a dozen or more subjects was assigned to
a joint committee. No over-all report was made by the conference,
but a verbatim account of the proceedings and the findings of the
several committees was published. The Committee on Joint Industrial Councils (composed of three employers, three trade unionists,
and two representatives of the public) brought in the following
unanimous report:

> Your Committee is of the opinion that there is urgent necessity
> for greater co-operation between employer and employee. We
> believe that this co-operation can be furthered by the establish-
> ment of Joint Industrial Councils. Your Committee does not be-
> lieve it is wise or expedient to recommend any set plan for such
> councils.

The conference met in plenary session in the Senate Chamber
for six days and discussed every phase of the problem of industrial
relations, including the committee recommendation in favour of
joint councils. It was a shock to Mackenzie King when Tom
Moore, who had signed the report of the Royal Commission, rose
to assail with vigour the Colorado plan and all its works. He claimed
to see in it an attempt to by-pass the legitimate trade unions, and an
attack on unionism:

> The base of the Rockefeller plan is the non-recognition of unions.
> ... There are many ways of destroying trade unions, and they
> have nearly all been tried except the one of agreeing to them but
> seeing that they do not operate and function; and this is the design
> of the plans which are based on the Rockefeller plan.

Such an attitude was utterly out of keeping with the report of the Royal Commission which Tom Moore had signed, and in direct conflict with the unanimous report of the joint committee which had included three trade unionists. Mackenzie King replied with an equally spirited denial of the charge, assertion of his own belief in trade unions, and an appeal to the conference to endorse an honest effort to bring management and men closer together without curtailing any of the rights of organized labour. He explained the particular circumstances in Colorado in 1915 which had made union recognition impossible, and gave details of his talks with senior officers of the U.M.W.A. who had agreed that such recognition, under existing conditions, was out of the question. He paid sincere tribute to the unions for their most important part in improving labour conditions:

> I would have had no part in the concern one way or the other if it had been even remotely intended for the purpose of fighting the unions. I believe in labor unions. I believe that the progress which has been made in improving labor's condition has been made in a larger measure through unions than any other institution that I know of. But I do not believe, for that reason, that everything the unions have done is right, or that their methods, on all occasions, are right.

Mackenzie King was fortunate in having such a forum in Canada for the presentation of his case for the Industrial Representation Plan in its relation to the trade union movement and for the declaration of his own faith in both. It was a case that was convincing to fair-minded listeners. He could hardly hope that it would silence for all time the criticism of those who, for personal or political reasons, would choose to misrepresent him as an enemy of trade unionism.

In the United States a year later a similar body, the President's Industrial Conference, reached similar conclusions on joint councils, and reported that, for some time, in industries in which employees' representation and trade unions operated side by side, they had been functioning harmoniously.

VIII

In assessing the rightness or wrongness of attitudes towards trade unionism in the early years of the century, care should be taken to examine them in the light of conditions then existing. Trade unionism in the United States was not then the accepted institution that it is today. 'The thing to do' nowadays is for workers to belong to a union and, provided the union leaders are deserving of confidence, for employers to recognize the union. In 1915 the local union organizers in Colorado did not have and did not deserve the confidence of their own leaders in the East, or the Governor of the state, or the employers, or for that matter a majority of the workers themselves. In terms of membership the trade union movement as a whole was then at a low ebb. Total union membership in the United States in 1915 was 2,582,600, or only 6.4 per cent of the civilian labour force. In 1958, membership was reported as 16,899,000, or approximately 25 per cent of the civilian labour force.

The United Mine Workers of America reported 600,000 members in the United States in 1958. They had 311,600 members in 1915. The intervening period was one of ups and downs even under the militant leadership of John L. Lewis, who was president from 1919 to 1935. In 1932, for example, the U.M.W.A. 'was virtually moribund, its membership dwindling from 432,000 to a twenty-year low of 150,000. But within a year, revived by the N.R.A.,* the Union's enrolment had reached 400,000 and was growing at the rate of 75 a day. And this cyclic character of the United Mine Workers Union merely reflects the spectacular ups and downs of the industry itself.'

One of the policies of the National Recovery Administration was to insist on collective bargaining through labour unions. This led many companies all over the country to establish unions of their own, company unions, thus fulfilling the letter of the law but frustrating its spirit. The counter-move of N.R.A. was to condemn

---

* The National Recovery Administration, established by President Roosevelt early in 1933.

all such unions and to make it an offence for any company 'to dominate or interfere with the formation or administration of any labor organization or contribute financial or other support to it', or 'to refuse to bargain collectively with the duly chosen representatives of employees'. However great a boon the Colorado plan had been to the miners and steelworkers (its benefits to them had really been enormous) it could not be argued that it was not company-dominated. N.R.A. ruled that it was not an independent labour union and that it depended upon the company for financial support. Passage of the N.R.A. legislation in 1933 marked the beginning of a phenomenal increase in union membership and, as far as the Colorado Fuel and Iron Company miners and steelworkers were concerned, the end of the Colorado plan and the beginning of contractual relations with the U.M.W.A.

Measured by present-day standards, the Industrial Representation Plan does not appear a revolutionary measure. Appraised in the light of conditions existing half a century ago, however, it stands out as a step of first importance in a movement in the direction of industrial self-government. In 1918, Mackenzie King had thought progress had been made half-way along the road to unionism and he had prophesied that the industrial representation plan would serve as a possible bridge to an agreement with the unions. It did. It had served its day and generation — or almost a generation. Militant trade unionism had failed sadly in Colorado because of its extreme and offensive militancy. A saner trade unionism, no longer thwarted by managerial obstinacy, had ultimately come into its own. Company policy and union policy, in the two decades after the introduction of the Industrial Representation Plan, had both undergone modification — controversy had had its stimulating and leavening effect. Each side had had to reckon with the other, and out of the reckoning had come a relationship, if not an institution, that was better than either.

CHAPTER 12

The Writing of a Book

In attempting to solve the Colorado problem, Mackenzie King had felt that he could at the same time gather material — indeed he could make material — for his far-reaching study of industrial relations. He soon began to envisage the results of this study as taking the form of a book. Some of the ideas which he thought should be developed in such a book could be tried out in the coal-fields and steel-works where he would have a relatively free hand to experiment. He could turn all his observations to good account and he planned to make notes for future use in the chapters which were already taking shape in his mind.

At the end of 1915, after he had completed his mission in Colorado, he presented to the trustees of the foundation an interim report on the results of his first fifteen months' work. The report related almost entirely to what had been accomplished in Colorado. That work, he explained, had interfered with the progress he had hoped to make on the studies for which he was engaged. But it was an integral part of those studies — he had used the Colorado Fuel and Iron Company as a kind of laboratory in which to test the practical bearing of some of his ideas on joint control of industry. More than that, it was essential that labour relations within the company (in which the Rockefellers and the foundation itself had large investments) be transformed and placed on a basis beyond reproach.

Until their own house was set in order they would not be justified
in trying to convert others to more liberal principles and policies.
With this the trustees agreed, and one of them declared that in his
judgment the work that had been done in Colorado was one of
the really constructive contributions which had been made toward
bettering relations between labour and capital, that it had served a
great public purpose.

II

The discussion about the 1915 report marked the beginning of a
debate, carried on chiefly by correspondence, on the methods of
further inquiry and the ultimate results that might be expected.
Mackenzie King was free to continue his inquiries in his own way,
but he felt an obligation to keep his sponsors informed of his plans.
He told Jerome Greene in January 1916 that he had at last begun
to draft, in the form of tentative propositions, some of the conclusions he had been formulating. He thought he should apply himself exclusively in this way until he was ready for a series of interviews with individuals for the purpose of obtaining their comments
and criticisms upon the accuracy of deductions made. He had in
mind particularly the charts in which he was so much absorbed.

    Jerome Greene reflected the opinion of at least some of the
trustees when he wrote to Rockefeller in April of his misgivings
about the progress of Mackenzie King's studies in Ottawa and about
the evident changes from the original conception of his task. He
had no misgivings whatever about the value of his services in Colorado: 'Such a conciliatory and what may be called statesman-like
activity I believe to be his forte.' In his opinion 'Mr. King's strong
point is not that he is a profound scholar. His strong point is that
he has had a wonderfully illuminating experience in the actual
adjustment of labour difficulties.' His book, Greene thought,
should be related closely to this remarkable experience, but if it
were to be the mere enunciation of certain sound and helpful
doctrines suggested by this experience, the trustees of the founda-

tion would probably take less interest in it. It was most desirable, he felt, 'that Mr. King should not get away from our original conception of his task, which was to assemble the experience of the world in different aspects of the industrial problem and set forth the facts of any particularly illuminating or helpful experience as a guide to general efforts in similar directions'. Rockefeller did not share Greene's misgivings but agreed that it would be wise to have King present to the trustees a full statement of his plans and ideas. When the trustees met in New York on May 23, Mackenzie King had ready for them a memorandum of twenty-seven pages in which he gave his conception of the exact nature of his studies and a brief summary of what he proposed to include in each chapter. What deviation there had been from the course originally planned, he explained, had been largely forced upon him by three factors: the war, the opportunity in Colorado, and the investigation of the Walsh commission. 'It would indeed be difficult,' he commented, 'to imagine circumstances more unfavourable to the inauguration of any work than those which surrounded the inception of these preliminary studies.'

Industry and Humanity had already been decided upon as the title of his book. He told the trustees it would be a volume which would bring out features of the problem as they had resolved themselves in his own mind. It would not be a profound economic treatise, but he hoped it would possess some practical value in suggesting 'lines of procedure which if applied will assist in affording to labour "the protection it needs against oppression and exploitation, while at the same time promoting its efficiency as an instrument of economic production." ' The problem of labour and capital would be presented as an international problem, not merely one of national or local concern. He thought of industrial relations as essentially human relations, and the underlying thought of the book would be that 'the ends of industry must be made subservient to the ends of humanity, not humanity made subservient to industry'. The volume, he said, was about half complete, but he hoped to have it ready for publication 'not later than the termination of the present European War, if, as is generally supposed, the War continues on into 1917'.

Mackenzie King was not happy about his presentation to the trustees. There was not the enthusiastic response he had hoped for. The questioning attitude of some of them was discouraging, but he was not utterly cast down. He still had faith in himself and in his book. The next year and a half was, however, to be a period of painful attempts to concentrate on his writing in the face of many long and frustrating interruptions. He had counted on making headway with his book at Kingsmere that summer, but family responsibilities interfered. June was interrupted by his visit to Toronto for ten days to assist his mother and father in moving from 4 Grange Road (where they had lived for many years as next-door neighbours of Goldwin Smith) to an apartment at 236 Avenue Road.

III

On his return to Kingsmere, still troubled by his interview with the trustees and its interruption of the course of his work and thought, he resumed the writing of his diary. This had been neglected for months, and one of his first entries was to record that he had 'fretted' and 'worried' because he felt the impression he had made at the meeting was a poor one: 'On no side did I do myself justice.' 'How hopelessly ignorant I am,' he lamented, 'how incompetent to discharge the task I have in hand save as to the vision of it.'

To avoid interruption in his work he had his telephone taken out and for a while he lived like a hermit. At the same time he was keeping up his political connections with Laurier and his colleagues, and was beginning to fear that in seeking to keep two avenues open he might fail to get very far on either and might lose both. It was a period of abnormal introspection: 'I can well see wherein I have become almost morbid.' He consulted his Ottawa physician, who reported him to be in perfect physical health but 'nervously overwrought' and advised him to knock off work and get his mind occupied with other things. He found it hard to act on advice of this kind because his worry came mostly from not making headway with his work. Some respite he did plan, however. He arranged to have his father and mother join him at Kingsmere and he laid aside his writing for a time to prepare for their visit. An extension to his cottage was to be built and his supervision of that project took much of his time. But even the reunion with his parents was interrupted for ten days by a call from Rockefeller to come to New York. Altogether, circumstances were not conducive to progress in writing, and at the end of the summer he was faced with a new ordeal. His father, who had been in ill health and virtually blind for several years, died on August 30, a few days after returning to Toronto. The responsibility was now Mackenzie King's to deal with new domestic problems, including the winding up of his father's estate and plans for his mother's immediate future. It was decided that the apartment on Avenue Road should be closed and that his mother, for the time being, should go with her daughter Jennie (Mrs. H. M. Lay) to live in Walkerton.

For weeks again the diary was neglected, an indication in itself of a troubled mind, and when it was resumed, in mid-October, references to *Industry and Humanity* were few. He was occupying himself with other things, not because his doctor had so advised, but because his highly nervous state made concentration all but impossible. It was for him a dark and difficult time. A new sense of loneliness overwhelmed him: 'Last night I wandered about alone in Toronto, sat alone for a while in Queen's Park, realizing that for the first time in life I had no home to go to.' His wandering had taken him past the old home on Beverley Street, to Grange Road, and the apartment on Avenue Road; he took the walk round the University which he and his father had often taken together. As he walked he reflected with mingled sadness and satisfaction on all the 'sacred associations of bygone days'.

Concern about his own nervous condition continued throughout the autumn months. When he visited New York before the end

of October he told Rockefeller of his intention to consult a specialist. Rockefeller advised him to talk with Dr. Simon Flexner, head
of the Rockefeller Institute for Medical Research. Dr. Flexner
recommended Dr. Llewellys Barker of Johns Hopkins Hospital in
Baltimore, and within two days Mackenzie King was a patient
under Dr. Barker's care. For two weeks the treatment continued,
the most thoroughgoing examination imaginable, by as many as a
dozen specialists. It was a satisfying experience, which gave needed
rest and a chance for good counsel.

It was early in December before work on his book was resumed.
He had been giving attention to many other things, including Canadian political affairs, the reading of the manuscript of his brother's
book, *The Battle with Tuberculosis and How To Win It*, and
other matters of personal concern. The year 1916 had indeed been a
disappointing one; with the return of health, however, he was approaching his task with renewed vigour. The year ended on a note
of thanksgiving and with a prayer for forgiveness. He might well
have uttered another prayer, the prayer of Job, 'Oh that my words
were now written! Oh that they were printed in a book!'

IV

The new year, 1917, was to bring new tribulations. It was another
year of frustration as far as 'the book' was concerned. My own
illness left him without the aid of his one assistant for the first six
months of the year. The second half was disrupted completely by
the political crisis that culminated in the wartime election. And
throughout the year he was tortured by anxiety about his mother.
He had set his heart on having her live with him in Ottawa and after
Christmas 1916 he took on the responsibility of her care in his own
small apartment in the Roxborough. She was by then seriously ill,
but, with the nurses he engaged, he took his part in the sick-room, a
model of patient and affectionate devotion. At one time her life
was despaired of by her physician, a man who had long been an
intimate friend. Mackenzie King so strongly resented the doctor's

pessimism that he dismissed him in anger and thereby lost a friend. His mother's life was saved — by his own faith that Providence would spare her to him, as he always proudly claimed, and by the love that he lavished upon her. She was the centre of his life throughout that summer and autumn, but the end was near. It came in December. The day she died was for Mackenzie King the saddest day he was ever to know — he felt he had indeed lost the centre of his life.

It was little wonder that by the end of 1917 he was still far from the end of his book. Indeed it was remarkable that he had achieved as much as he had. Until he entered the election campaign he lived the kind of secluded life he had so often envisaged as the perfect life for him. Yet when the opportunity came he chafed at the confinement and longed for a change that would restore human contacts but still permit withdrawal into a private world of his own. 'The active life of politics suits my temperament better,' he wrote at one stage. 'I can do more and better work under its pressure than being left alone this way.' 'The truth is I am not suited to theoretical work, but to practical, and need the active touch with men and affairs to give vitality to what I write.' He concluded the entry: 'However I am glad to be again "on the job" and will stick at it.'

v

While he did not lack facility with words in speeches that might run an hour or two, or more, when it came to the writing of *Industry and Humanity* he found it a painful process. He was more fluent with his tongue than with his pen. There were times when he could write without pause just as when he wrote or delivered a political speech. More often it was an ordeal, a struggle to find the right word, a more telling turn of phrase, the better construction of a paragraph. Words and sentences seemed to conspire so often to prevent lucidity. It vexed him to realize that 'a trained mind' should find such difficulty in expressing simple thoughts in simple language. With him it was always a struggle to achieve a perfect mating of words and ideas. Every paragraph of the book, like his entries in the diary at this stage, was written by hand, usually with a steel stub-pen (never a fountain pen), sometimes with one of his short unsharpened pencils, resulting in something to be deciphered rather than read easily. In this type of work, as he remarked playfully one day, he was no dictator — a modern dictaphone machine would have been an abhorrence to him. From his study came, not a steady stream of finished manuscript, but spasmodic instalments which bore on every page the marks of vigorous editing — changes made, it sometimes seemed, before the first ink was dry. Finally he would produce a first draft — the first, perhaps, of as many as a dozen or more drafts. Revision after revision made slow going. He subjected everything, as he put it, to 'a sort of microscopic treatment'. In the process he was not averse to suggestions of change. Many an author would resent a secretary's questioning of his handiwork as a reflection on his ability to write. Mackenzie King was a patient and considerate listener. There was a nice bit of fun over one incident. He had just completed the last paragraph of the book: it was a peroration he was proud of and he handed the sheets over to me with a triumphant remark that no fault could be found with *that*. He was a trifle discomfited, however, when I informed him, ever so politely, that the first sentence was not without flaw, that it was introduced by what the grammarians call a dangling participle. 'Dangling participle,' he protested, 'I never heard of such a thing.' He made the appropriate change, however; the participial phrase was retained, but in the final printing it no longer 'dangled'. Revisions continued, of course, even into the stage of galley and page proofs; the bill for 'author's corrections' was a substantial one.

VI

He had his moments of 'great cheer' but they would have been more frequent had he received more encouragement from his sponsors. Even Rockefeller was showing some signs of impatience.

The engagement with the foundation had been extended to the end of 1917 and he expressed the hope that, by that time, King's studies would be in such shape as to enable the board to decide what future policy should be. What he evidently hoped for was to have the book out of the way, either completed or given up, so that Mackenzie King could be free to devote his talents to what he (Rockefeller) regarded as a much more appropriate use, advising other corporations as well as his own how to improve their industrial relations.

When Mackenzie King was talking with him on the significance of the book, he was shocked and hurt by Rockefeller's very apparent lack of enthusiasm and by his slighting reference to it in his question: 'Did I honestly feel or certainly believe that I would be rendering a larger service by going on with the book ['a mere book', he seemed to imply] than I could by taking this chance in the industries?' An emphatic 'yes' was the immediate, and probably the expected, reply. Mackenzie King told him that he felt the book would have a far-reaching influence, that it would lay down important principles, and that his subsequent work could be the application of those principles in a practical way. In this he was referring to his possible future work as an industrial counsellor, work which Rockefeller was anxious that he should go ahead with.

VII

During the whole of the 1917 election period Mackenzie King's time and attention were naturally concentrated on things political: the bitter question whether Canada was or was not to conscript men for military service, the prospect of a Union government, and the Tory enactment of an 'iniquitous franchise law', became more important after September than self-government in industry, the winning of an election more exciting than the publication of a book, loyalty to Sir Wilfrid more compelling than any other claim. Once the die was cast and the political campaign became a certainty, all thought of the book was set aside. After spending three or four days on further revision of the early part, he went to New York and arranged that his salary should be suspended as of November 1. With some trepidation he left the first few chapters with Rockefeller. 'I wonder what he will think of it,' he wrote. 'I cannot but feel how impossible it is to write the truth as one sees it, and not appear to be reflecting on him and his methods.' Indeed he had been critical of nothing Rockefeller had done or left undone, but he could not agree, of course, with the suggestion that he give up Canadian politics for a career in the United States as an industrial-relations counsellor. His talk with Rockefeller had left them both with a clear understanding that when the book was finished his work with the foundation would be at an end. Rockefeller had suggested the possibility of a personal retainer if King were not returned to Parliament, but they agreed that it was well to leave the matter open until after the election.

VIII

Mackenzie King was defeated in North York on December 17, and this seemed to mean the closing of a door to the glorious political future on which both he and his mother had for so many years set their hearts. But he did not abandon hope — other doors might be opened later on. In the meantime he returned to the immediate task, that of completing his book. He wrote to Rockefeller on the day of the elections, after the result was known, that he would immediately resume work on his book. He thought a couple of months would be sufficient to complete it, but it was February before he was able to get down to serious work on it, and September before he turned over his last pages of 'copy' to his publishers.

He had had in mind having a preliminary edition printed for private circulation amongst a few friends whose criticism he would welcome. He had thought, too, of arranging for a series of conferences with informed persons whose opinion would be of value. Nothing came of either proposal, but he did send typewritten copies of several chapters to his brother in Colorado and to Rockefeller, who in turn showed them to Dr. George E. Vincent, president of the Rockefeller Foundation. Dr. Vincent had already discussed with Mackenzie King, in Ottawa, the winding up of his work with the foundation and the completion of his book. When now he read the first five chapters he thought it would not be fair 'to express a judgment of a fragment of an essay of this kind' but he did make a few comments. In his opinion, he wrote to Rockefeller, 'the practical people who want concrete programs and definite suggestions as to social policy will be disappointed because the book deals in general and abstract statements'. On the other hand, Vincent continued, 'the persons who are interested in theory, the economists, sociologists and social philosophers, will be likely to question the validity of Mr. King's method and the nature of his reasoning'. He gave an example: 'He speaks of the "law of peace, work and health" as though it were almost, if not quite, identical with a physical law like that of gravitation. Of course these are two very different ideas and the term "law" cannot be applied to both in the same way.'

Further candid comments came from Dr. Vincent in a conversation when Mackenzie King visited New York a couple of months later. Vincent gave what was described in the diary as 'a very fair criticism' of the plan of the book. He doubted if by philosophers it would be regarded as profound enough, or by extreme labour men as radical enough. As for the large class in between, they would read it appreciatively. He thought it would 'receive much notice and occasion considerable discussion'. This was followed by Dr. Vincent's less than flattering assurance that 'the Foundation would accept the report and keep it intact in case of it being called for'. It was not Vincent's idea that the foundation would sponsor publication of the book, but he assured Mackenzie King that they would give him full liberty to publish. 'This is just what I want,' he wrote in his diary. 'Altogether I cannot help feeling how very fortunate I am & have been, the way is now cleared to a completion along lines I have all along hoped for.'

During his visit to New York, which lasted a week, he had talks

with many other important people, including the heads of three
publishing firms, (Macmillan, Century, and Fleming H. Revell)
and with several personal friends. The interview of most importance, as far as his book was concerned, was with Rockefeller. Mr.
and Mrs. Rockefeller had invited him to sit in their pew on the
Sunday morning in the 'unpretentious looking' Fifth Avenue
Baptist Church and to come home to dinner with them afterwards.
In the library they discussed, first, the main lines of the new personal relationship they were considering, and then turned to the
forthcoming *Industry and Humanity*. Evidently Rockefeller
shared Dr. Vincent's 'disappointment that it was not more practical
— that it was too philosophical'. His first question was worded unfortunately: 'Who do you expect will read it?' Instead of taking
umbrage, the author patiently pointed out that criticism of the first
part of his book, as being too philosophical, was natural — it dealt
with basic principles — but the last part, which they had not seen,
had to do with concrete advice. Rockefeller may or may not have
been convinced, but his last word was one of admonition rather
than of encouragement, and again he was thoughtless in the language he used: 'He said I owed it to myself and the Foundation to
see that a good piece of work was accomplished in view of the
amount of money and time spent.' With this Mackenzie King
agreed: he had always intended to see that the work was well done,
and he returned to his writing and revising with redoubled energy.
Again, however, his work was seriously interrupted by a visit the
Rockefellers asked him to make with them to Colorado. This
robbed him of the better part of a month in May and June.

IX

In May he had had discussions in Boston with Ferris Greenslet
of the Houghton Mifflin Company, who were to publish his book,
and as a result of Greenslet's advice he added some personal references to his work on Oriental problems. It was 'as important as any
service I have rendered in a public way, and it has an historic interest and place'.

The end of the long road was in sight in August, when the publishers sent out their notices of the forthcoming volume. 'It frightens me rather,' he wrote, 'to see myself announced as a leading authority in America.' But he believed the book would have a wide circulation and would be of real service at this juncture in the world's affairs.

His publishers had given him a deadline of September 15. If he could have had till Christmas he was sure he could make it 'a real work'. (It was the kind of comment he was accustomed to make before important political speeches — 'If we only had another day this could be a masterpiece.') But to him there was something propitious about September 15 — it was his father's birthday. When the day came he wrote: 'I strove to finish the book today that I might make the date of the preface coincide with it'. This he was not able to do, but he wrote on the following day, 'Today I have finished the book.' Even this was hardly true, for he had to add a characteristically Kingsian qualification, 'that is to say the preliminary writing'. Still to be completed was the final revision of the preface and of the last four chapters, 'a simple and pleasurable task compared to the laborious work of composition'. He felt at any rate that he had completed the last of 'the book proper'.

He was reflecting that this meant a dividing line in his life when, as he recounted, 'I looked up to the little clock on the cottage shelf and to my surprise saw both hands over the hour twelve. I exclaimed aloud at the significance of the fact.' Equal significance might have been discerned if the hands of the clock had been opposite each other, or at right angles. What the significance was is not clear from the context, nor was it ever made clear in the many references to the position of the hands of the clock which appear in the diaries of later years. 'It may be,' MacGregor Dawson observes, 'that he interpreted such coincidences as confirmation of the rightness of the decision reached or the action taken at the particular moment. Or he may have taken them, for reasons which he only could understand but never explained, as a grand indication that he was in tune with the infinite. They comforted him.'

X

Industry and Humanity was not finished on his father's birthday
nor on the day after. In the end the prefatory note bore the date of
October 3, 1918. All that was left to do was the final reading of
galley and page proofs. Rockefeller had been reading with care the
galley proofs as they were sent to him. 'His comments make the
galleys well worth preserving. They reveal a very noble & fine
nature, & just.' With one of the last batches of proof, however,
Rockefeller sent a letter which Mackenzie King described as disappointing and disheartening. He expressed regret that, being
pressed for time, he could not read the manuscript as thoughtfully
as he would have liked. 'In reading the galley sheets I have not
gotten the impression of the book which one would get in a bound
volume.' He was impressed by the work as 'full of value', containing a great mass of information that not one man in a thousand is
familiar with; 'the original presentation of your views is striking
and forceful'. He did think that a shorter volume might be a little
easier to read and might claim a much wider circle of readers. He
offered congratulations on having finished the task ('What a relief
it must be to have it off your mind.'); he believed the book would
render a real service to industry.

'I suppose I was expecting too much,' Mackenzie King wrote in
his diary when he received the letter, 'but I felt deeply disappointed; I had hoped for some recognition of the generous attitude
I had taken towards the Colorado Plan, what I had done to take
opprobrium away from the situation and to give the Plan historic
significance.' He was unhappy about the general nature of its commendation — 'full of value', 'mass of information'; even the reference to originality was confined to 'presentation'. 'Mr. Rockefeller,' he wrote in the privacy of his diary, 'will live to see that in
the bold conceptions of the book and its fundamental disclosures
there is true originality. . . . These ideas will have more influence
in the course of time than all his wealth.' He appreciated the comment that he had rendered real service to industry, but he felt it
would have been more to the point if he had said service to human-

ity. 'However,' he concluded, 'I am grateful that he has read the book through before it appears, both for his own sake and mine, for it is not a volume that is likely to pass "unnoticed" in these times. The public at best will see that there is no subserviency or fear, so far as I am concerned, of interests or influence or classes.' The final word in the entry for the day was a footnote: 'I continued work of revision, but with a heavy heart till after 6.'

Mackenzie King's strong feelings were never made known to Rockefeller. He did say in his diary that he had written pretty frankly 'so that he may see wherein I think his appreciation has been inadequate'. But even reading between the lines of the letter, Rockefeller could not have perceived how much his friend had been hurt by his direct and implied criticism.

CHAPTER 13

'Industry and Humanity'

Industry and Humanity – a Study in the Principles Underlying Industrial Reconstruction was finally published in December 1918. Whatever Rockefeller or others might think of its worth, Mackenzie King was convinced that it was 'a good piece of work'. It was a contribution to a world-wide problem, and he had good reason to be proud of it. Its publication coincided with the ending of the First World War. Designed as it was to assist in the work of post-war industrial reconstruction, it came at the right moment, at a crisis in world affairs when it was most needed.

In many respects the proposals in it were radical, if not revolutionary, for this continent and that generation. In Great Britain and on the Continent, long before 1918, much had been written about co-partnership, profit-sharing, and various measures of social security, and some of the ideas were being translated into action. The British National Insurance Act of 1911, for example, provided for both health insurance and unemployment insurance. Joint councils were being established in England during the war years. These ideas did not originate with Mackenzie King. His own thinking about them, based upon long experience and wide reading, was closely akin to that of the more progressive writers in England. He had been favourably impressed by much, but not all, of what the socialists of the day were writing. In Canada and the United States the public mind was not yet prepared for such a drastic reversal of attitudes. It was Mackenzie King's part to assist in the necessary educational programme. In this, as Bruce Hutchison observed shortly after King's death in 1950, he was a generation ahead of his contemporaries. There were few who recognized this in 1918 and the years immediately afterwards. To many it was but another preachment against the sins of industrialists, an appeal to them to take a kindlier attitude toward the men whose lives they dominated.

The politicians of the day, or at least those who paid any attention to them, failed to recognize that the proposals in *Industry and Humanity* had political as well as industrial implications and a strong leftward tendency. Indeed, Hutchison went so far as to say that 'had the managers of the Liberal Party read it, or believed it, they probably would not have made him their leader'. One might question the political wisdom of Mackenzie King in espousing such heresies less than a year before the convention which he hoped would elect him to succeed Sir Wilfrid Laurier. His advocacy of a programme, for example, which would give to workers in industry a voice in the determination of their own working- and living-conditions, even though not a decisive voice at the beginning, was an act of courage and far-sightedness. It was courageous because it was flying in the face of the traditional view, still widely held in Canada and the United States in the early decades of the century, that the parties to industry were masters and men, that masters were masters and men were men. A socialist demagogue might have preached such doctrine as part of his trade, but for a man aspiring to leadership of a reasonably orthodox political party, it required courage, and understanding that changes then in the making would some day lead to a substantial measure of self-government on the part of workers, a system of representative and responsible self-government in industry, a development which would parallel the evolution of democracy in the world of politics.

II

The central theme of *Industry and Humanity* – it runs through all its 539 pages – is that industry must be made to serve humanity rather than humanity be made subservient to industry. The title was well chosen. The preacher and prophet – he was both – could not refrain from crying out against the crass materialism of an age in which too much emphasis was placed upon property rather than people, upon wealth rather than life. In *Industry and Humanity* he diagnosed as one of the principal causes of industrial unrest the tendency on the part of industrialists to ignore the human element, to regard labour as a commodity (they could refer to 'the labour market'), as a means to an end, a mere item in the cost of production.

In the early part of the century, before trade union activities began to keep pace with enormous industrial expansion and centralization, the workers in many industries had little to say about working conditions and, in some industries such as mining, even about their own living conditions. The inevitable result was resentment on the part of employees against employers with whom they had little or no contact – a good deal of resentment, and, frequently, open conflict. However, until contacts could be established, *Industry and Humanity* asserted, and until workers were given opportunity to express themselves freely and take part in decisions affecting their own lives, antagonism would continue. To have their views presented by their own elected representatives, sitting in joint conference with representatives of management, was one way of achieving harmonious relations. These were words of sound advice, and the advice was given complete with illustrations, showing not only what could be done, and how, but how it *had* been done and with what beneficial results. The Industrial Representation Plan in Colorado had been constructed as a model: every clause in the written constitution had been worked over as if it were to be a legislative enactment. It was not a law of the Medes and Persians, unalterable; it was a declaration of basic rights; the details of its superstructure could be revised (and they were revised) as adjustments became necessary to meet new conditions. Success of the Industrial Representation Plan would be dependent, of course, on the goodwill of the participants on both sides – no machinery, however wisely constructed, could operate without the will to make it work. Positive co-operation must be expected also from shareholders and directors; they must recognize that acceptance of dividends on capital invested imposed responsibility for labour conditions. The community, too, the fourth party to industry, must play its part, through legislation or otherwise, in assuring fairness to all the parties concerned.

Industrial disputes impossible to solve by the parties themselves are certain to occur even in the best-regulated economy, and the State must then be prepared to intervene where public interests are threatened. Mackenzie King's views on the nature of such intervention were well known; he enlarged upon them in *Industry and Humanity*. His first counsel was that 'in industrial, as in domestic relations, it is wise for people to keep their differences to themselves, and to settle their own disputes. Outside intervention and publicity are desirable only where it appears that a settlement cannot be effected without them, or where intervention is necessitated by the interest of third parties.' Much of the success of conciliation and mediation would depend upon the qualifications of the conciliator: 'Given half a chance, personality, combined with experience and resource, and with the weight of authority behind it, usually finds a way or makes it.' Where the way could not be found, any strike or lock-out should be prohibited until after full publicity had been given to the report of an investigating agency. A strong case was made in the book for compulsory investigation in such circumstances. Answering labour's objection to such a provision in the Canadian Industrial Disputes Investigation Act, which he had drafted in 1907, he insisted that it gave to labour a right which it had never before enjoyed, the right to have investigated, 'at public expense, upon Labor's own motion, and in part by its own named investigators, any adverse industrial conditions likely to involve a lockout or a strike'. His justification for the prohibition of the right to strike before the completion of investigation was the public injury that might result from hasty and ill-conceived action, and the desirability of establishing a 'cooling-off period' during which better judgments might prevail. 'Where there are tribunals with adequate powers to do justice,' he contended, 'strikes or lockouts in defiance of their existence are violations of fundamental rights. To shut off supplies of food and coal, by means of a strike, is equivalent to a forcible blockade, which may result in starvation.'

He was just as insistent on the application of publicity as a means of informing the community of the relative merits of opposing contentions. He had enormous faith in 'the power of an intelligently formed Public Opinion to remove any injustice and to redress any wrong. There is a class of evils which publicity is more effective to remedy than penalty. Most industrial wrongs belong to this class.' He was able to draw upon his own wide experience as deputy minister of labour in Canada to prove that he knew what he was talking about.

III

Mackenzie King's wholesome respect for the trade union movement is revealed in every reference to the subject in his book, and there were many. His was not an attitude of unqualified approval of every assertion of labour's rights. His experience as an impartial mediator in scores of industrial disputes had conditioned him to an open-minded approach. He was in complete sympathy with the fundamental aims of the movement as he defined them, 'the establishment and maintenance of labor standards, and the introduction into industry of an effective procedure for the settlement of all matters requiring settlement'. But many union practices did not accord with these aims; they could be obnoxious, just as many of the practices of capital and management could be obnoxious. He recognized that 'in union is strength', but he had seen too many instances of labour strength being used unwisely and for ignoble ends. Consequently he could be critical of many of their policies and some of their leaders. 'Like every other great movement,' he wrote, 'trade-unionism has had its weak apostles, and has at times adopted policies which, to say the least, have been inimical to progress.' Practices which had brought trade unionism into disfavour with many included 'delays and restrictions in output, the monopoly of the closed shop, interference by violence with the liberty and rights of non-union men and women'. These were the exceptions in a movement 'founded upon principles of voluntary association and mutual aid'. Just as much was said of the obnoxious practices of some employers and some employers' associations, such as 'cutting down wage-rates where output is increased, interfering with the right of legitimate organizations and the employment of spies'. He could have added many more to the list of undesirable practices on both sides. On the whole, he concluded that 'labour owes to the trade-union movement more than it is possible to express in words'. It would come into its own under a more democratic organization of industry, in which labour would enjoy the status of partner along with capital, management, and the community, and would share with these other parties to industry in determining policy with respect to matters in which each is vitally concerned.

IV

It would be only a first step, he emphasized in his book, to provide for representation of employees in joint councils of management and men — all employees, whether union members or not. Unless such joint control of industry could be achieved, the only alternative he could foresee would be 'a continuance of conflict of controls'. Each element had sought a monopoly of control: capital, by thwarting labour's right to collective bargaining, and by circumventing the community's right to just treatment in matters of prices and rates; management, by claiming for itself exclusive right in the employment and dismissal of workers while denying to labour the right of membership in associations for its self-protection; labour, by insisting on the exclusive right of trade unions to speak in the name of labour and to enforce its newly acquired control by the weapon of the strike, regardless of the effect upon other interests. The community, the state (an all-powerful state), might, in certain circumstances, as many were contending, own everything or dominate everything.

In *Industry and Humanity* he raised his voice against monopoly of control by any one of the four parties to industry. Instead, he favoured a joint control whereby each of the parties would be afforded a voice in the determination of the terms and conditions upon which its services to industry were rendered. 'There are four parties to be reckoned with ... each has distinct functions and individual rights which, in the interest of all, require to be safeguarded and promoted in common.'

In painting this highly idealized design of a balanced government of industry Mackenzie King realized that he was not submitting a blueprint which could be translated overnight into a new industrial order. Some headway had already been made. Joint control could be effected, and was being effected, in a variety of ways. 'Today it may be agreement upon a minimum wage, or methods of adjusting industrial differences; tomorrow, it may be the fixation of a trade agreement governing all conditions of employment, between Management and Labour, the rate of return guaranteed to Capital, and the prices at which commodities and services are to be made available to the Community.'

All this was a long-range objective. It would probably take years and perhaps generations to accomplish. The workers themselves would need training in the art of self-government, and managers and investors would have to accommodate themselves to a programme which would entitle employees to share in decisions affecting their lives, their working- and living-conditions. Also the public (the fourth party to industry) and their representatives in legislatures and cabinets must come to recognize labour's right to this new status and the obligation upon the state to contribute, to an extent hitherto undreamed of, toward a wider measure of social justice and social security.

v

Industry and Humanity makes much of the parallel which Mackenzie King saw between the evolution of representative and responsible government in the democratic state and the evolution which must develop if similar democracy is to be achieved in the government of industry. Government within the state had been widened down from autocratic authority, as in King John's day, to authority broad-based upon a people's will. Mackenzie King believed it could be shown 'that law and order within industry at the present time is just about at the stage constitutional development reached in England under the Norman and Plantagenet Kings. . . . Industry at the moment is at the threshold of another revolution as mighty in its transforming powers as the Industrial Revolution of a century ago. The change to be wrought out is the transition from centralized authority to self-government. It is likely to parallel, in all essential features, corresponding evolutions in government within the State.'

With the development of the highly centralized industrial organizations of our day, widening of the gulf between those in authority and those under it was inevitable. Owners and directors, further and further removed from workers, had less and less opportunity to know them and the conditions under which they were working, and consequently less and less inclination to do anything about them. Their responsibility was recognized more in relation to strictly financial and business aspects than with respect to determining labour policies: 'Emphasis has been upon material considerations of plant and equipment, output, prices and profits, and not sufficiently upon human considerations.' Absentee ownership was thus one factor which contributed to industrial unrest. Mackenzie King had found it so in Colorado and he spared no words in condemnation of it. It had been something new for an industrialist like John D. Rockefeller, Jr., to be told that he and other directors and shareholders must share responsibility for the deplorable conditions under which the coal miners had been working. It was a subject on which Mackenzie King had frequently lectured Rockefeller. In his book he now addressed himself to a larger audience: 'The authority of directors . . . should be fully exercised in determining working conditions and the standards of justice by which the relationships of employer and employed are to be maintained. It should reach even farther. It should embrace responsibility for the spirit in which all industrial policies are to be made to prevail.' It was a feather in Mackenzie King's cap that he had induced Rockefeller to recognize this responsibility; it was equally to Rockefeller's credit that he had risen to the occasion and had been responsible for transforming an existing autocracy into a working partnership in which three of the parties to industry participated and from which the fourth party, the community, derived enormous benefit.

VI

A strong believer in competition in industry, Mackenzie King nevertheless recognized that certain types of unfair competition operate to the serious detriment of workers by reducing standards of living. He described it as the Law of Competing Standards, and again and again he urged that the community should play a more assertive role in circumventing its ill effects. Several examples were given of workers being compelled to work under degrading conditions because unscrupulous employers in unregulated markets exploited them, through scandalously low wages or piece-rates and wretched working-conditions, in their practice of underselling and outselling similar commodities produced under better conditions — 'mean men' as he described them, 'profiting because of their meanness'. The inferior standard tended to drive out the higher or to drag it down to its own low level. The law of competing standards, he declared, 'is just as relentless in its operation in industry as Gresham's Law of the precious metals is with respect to money and the mechanism of exchange': coins made of inferior-quality metals tend to drive the better out of circulation.

Most of the illustrations of how poor working-conditions bring labour standards to low levels were drawn from his own experience. The sweating system in the garment trades in Canada had been dealt with, as far as government contracts were concerned, by publicity and by the adoption of the fair-wages resolution which Mackenzie King had himself recommended in 1900. In the manufacture of matches, white phosphorus had been used in Canada, to the serious injury of workers, but one competing company could not or would not introduce a higher-cost substitute unless its competitors in Canada and elsewhere also changed their policy. The situation had been met by prohibition in Canada of the use of this poisonous material and by international agreement to prevent its use. (Mackenzie King had introduced the bill in the Canadian Parliament and had taken part in the discussions in the International Labour Association which led to the international convention.)

Also, lower standards of Oriental labour were adversely affecting standards on the American continent. That, too, was a problem for government rather than for industry. Restriction in the number of Oriental immigrants was desirable but it should be effected, not by such means as the obnoxious poll-tax, but by negotiation at high levels of government. Since he had been singularly successful in conducting such negotiations in India, Japan, and China, on behalf of the governments of the United States and Canada, Mackenzie King could speak with confidence and some authority about the prospect of keeping Oriental immigration down to levels which would not seriously threaten labour standards on the North American continent.

VII

Mackenzie King's thinking along these lines had led him into the first stages of a qualified acceptance of the doctrines of the welfare state. His early academic training had been severe in its *laissez-faire* orthodoxy. He had started off as a fundamentalist in economics, but heretical tendencies had soon appeared; his strong social sympathies had brought him to the brink of socialism, but from that extreme he had recoiled, as he feared 'the uniform conventional mould into which a regime of Collectivism would tend to force all men and things'. 'The War,' he stated in his chapter on 'Government in Industry', 'has added to existing fears by demonstrating in the Socialist State baneful possibilities hitherto unrealized.' He added, it is 'unlikely that Socialism in the form of the omnipotent and ever-present State or Industrial Unionism controlling Industry in conjunction with a democratized State, will ever permanently succeed the present order'.

While not accepting the socialist philosophy, he recognized idealistic elements in it which could be incorporated in the kind of liberalism he believed in. He thought it altogether probable that collectivist ideals, and in particular what they represented of the community idea and improvement in the status of labour, would vastly expand their influence. His own ideas of economic liberalism were changing. He could write of 'the older conception of *laissez-faire*' as if it were hopelessly out-of-date, and he could approve of 'at least a measure of State interference'. Regulation, especially as respects a minimum of social well-being, was becoming, to him as to most of his thinking contemporaries, more and more the accepted thing.

Mackenzie King's belief in the institution of private property was unshaken. 'It is not because of inalienable and indefeasible right that property exists; it is because no other better system has been devised.' He quoted with approval William James's dictum that 'private proprietorship cannot be practically abolished until human nature is changed'. He could not foresee either possibility, but he did recognize 'inevitable limitations' in the institution of private property, injustices to which it had given and might continue to give rise. In such circumstances society might well consider ways and means whereby injustices might be remedied without abolishing the institution itself. Consideration should be given also to the distribution of wealth in a manner which would prove of service to rich and poor alike.

These ends could be attained without any revolutionary change in the social order. State assistance could and should be provided — though the author of *Industry and Humanity* could not have realized then at what enormous cost — by such social security measures as unemployment insurance, old-age pensions, workmen's compensation, sickness and disability insurance, widows' pensions, maternity and infant benefits. These were all part of the 'National Minimum' which the Labour Party of Great Britain had been advocating as a further step in the direction of the welfare state; the first step had been taken in 1911 when, as already noted, provision had been made for unemployment and health insurance in the British National Insurance Act. The National Minimum was a much more radical programme; certainly it was far in advance of any proposals then current in Canada or the United States. It was all the more significant, therefore, that Mackenzie King should give it unqualified support: 'The wisdom of a National Minimum in matters of health and well-being is not open to question.' He realized the perplexing problem that would face government, namely, how to attain this end 'without undermining qualities of initiative and self-reliance'. But in spite of this, and in spite of the fact that the Canadian mind of that day was not prepared for such advanced measures calling for enormous public expenditure, Mackenzie King came out as unequivocally as his cautious nature would permit in favour of a radical programme of social security, and gave his reasons:

> Insurance against unemployment recognizes that an isolated human being, not less than a machine, must be cared for when idle. It recognizes also that nothing is so dangerous to the standard of life, or so destructive of minimum conditions of healthy existence, as widespread or continued unemployment. Where idleness is the fault of the social order, rather than of the individual con-

cerned, it places the onus on the State to safeguard its own assets, not more in the interest of the individual than in the interest of social well-being.

Of other types of social insurance he wrote:

> Workmen's compensation, sickness and invalidity insurance, widows' pensions, maternity and infant benefits, recognize wherein personal relations in Industry have changed, and where as a consequence of new conditions permanent handicaps arise.... To save the spirit of men from being crushed is quite as important as to prevent their bodies from being broken or infected. Many a man's spirit fails, when, through no fault of his own, or of his family, efficiency is permanently impaired through accident, or savings become exhausted by unemployment or sickness, or where a new life in the home suggests an additional burden instead of a joy. Much invalidity and penury is due to lack of character and thrift; but much also is evidence of want of effective social control. What society fails effectively to prevent, society is in some measure under obligation to mend.

Provision by the state for citizens of advanced years was endorsed as another desirable measure of social security:

> Old age pensions ... are based, not on the theory that the State owes every man a living, but rather on the fact that the provision of an assured competence for old age is an easy matter for some, whilst, for others, it is most difficult, if not wholly impossible.... There is need for society to assist in the protection of its members against a condition which simultaneously places burdens upon the worker whose day's work is done, and on the worker whose day's work is just beginning. If the young are to be given a fair start in life, the care of the aged should not be their first responsibility. If life-long public service in Industry is to receive its fitting reward, years that are denied opportunity of employment should not be subjected to the humiliation of dependence on charity.

VIII

Although the ideas he was promulgating were not all strictly original — were 'in the air', as he said — credit must be given to the sensitive ear that heard them, the intelligence that recorded them, and the energy that led to their adaptation to the needs of the changing world in which he belonged. No one in those days could fail to be affected by the seething unrest which was developing during the war years and which followed in the wake of war. In Canada in 1918 and 1919 industrial disputes were to increase in number and seriousness beyond all records; most serious of all was the outbreak of violence in the Winnipeg strike in the summer of 1919. The times called for strong measures, not of suppression but of understanding and remedial action. It would be wrong to suggest that Mackenzie King's *Industry and Humanity*, published only the year before, met the needs of the hour, but it did call attention to the underlying causes of industrial unrest and pointed the way, by constructive proposals, to necessary changes of attitude in industrial relations.

These were some of the social reforms advocated in *Industry and Humanity*. The book was not received with the universal acclaim which the author had hoped for and which it deserved. In some quarters it was welcomed as prophetic and practical, positively exciting. But there were many adverse criticisms too, most of which appeared in papers politically unfriendly. In them the censure was principally of style rather than substance; they pronounced it too long, too diffuse, too laboured and rhetorical, dull and dreary, too much given to platitudes and sermonizing. Many of Mr. King's best friends would admit that his style of writing suffered in some degree from all these defects. Even the author himself was at times conscious of these shortcomings, but he never succeeded in writing the kind of crisp prose that could be read easily by the man who runs. Perhaps, in writing this book, he was too full of his subject, too anxious to record all the truth as he knew it, 'simply encumbered', as one reviewer put it, 'by the weight and copiousness of his own thoughts'. It is striking, though, that many of the adverse comments on style were followed by tributes to the book's substantial worth. An example is taken from the *North American Review* of March 1919: 'The whole treatise is indeed somewhat labored, somewhat disproportioned, somewhat heavily abstract. But these defects should blind no one to the profound and fundamental clearness of Dr. King's ideas. . . . He has written what is perhaps the most truly philosophical, and hence the most practical, of books concerning the industrial problem.'

His friend Violet Markham was naturally immensely interested in the book and agreed entirely with its point of view. She felt on reading it, however, what she had felt when she met Samuel Gompers at the Trade Union Congress, that the labour movement in America was in a different state of development from that in England, that in the book Guild Socialism had been dismissed too lightly. She wrote to him: 'Here it's a movement much to be reckoned with [she had just been defeated by a Labour Party candidate]; your appeal to moral sentiment doesn't cut much ice on this side. The workers are all in revolt against moral theories in the conduct of industry and they listen very impatiently to talk about brotherhood and goodwill. They want concrete facts — like controls, higher wages, security against unemployment. . . . Class war is the note at the moment and the more eager spirits are content with nothing less. All this is *bad*, but I am only stating facts. The appeal in your book wouldn't restrain the elements which are out of hand here because they won't listen to that view at the moment.'

Sidney Webb, with whom he talked in England a few months after the publication of the book, referred to 'the reactionary and belated position of the Labor movement in Canada'. With this Mackenzie King agreed. 'It would serve to excuse,' he wrote to Webb before leaving England, 'a tone less radical than would accord with the present trend of the advanced industrial movements on this side [i.e. in Britain].' *Industry and Humanity* had been written, he added, 'for a constituency which still requires much in the way of persuasion to an acceptance of first principles in the readjustment of human relations in industry'.

IX

It could be said that *Industry and Humanity* was also written for, or could be made to appeal to, another and very important con-

stituency — the Canadian electorate. The author could foresee, as
he wrote, the immense political possibilities of the programme he
had drafted, a programme that could be put into effect only by
stupendous effort: 'Such an effort means a political program so
radical as to be revolutionary in its nature. I believe, however, that
it is the work of Liberalism for the future, to take the emphasis
from property and place it upon life in all that affects the well-
being of the working classes.' It seemed like a new dedication of
his life to a cause in which he profoundly believed.

Although four Canadian editions and something like ten thousand copies of the book were sold within a year of its publication,
Mackenzie King heeded advice to present his views in a form which
would reach a much wider audience in Canada. He had had more
experience in public speaking than in writing; he enjoyed the one
more than he did the other, and, besides, he was not unmindful of
the political advantages which might accrue from frequent appearances on the public platform with a message made to appeal to the
popular imagination. Consequently, in the early months of 1919,
before and after Sir Wilfrid Laurier's death in February, he accepted several invitations to address Canadian Clubs and Reform
or Liberal Clubs on the subject to which he had given months and
years of study: 'The Four Parties to Industry'. One of these
speeches, bearing this title, was printed in pamphlet form and was
given wide circulation. It could have been described as a very much
condensed version of his book; he had crammed into thirty-two
pages the essence of what had appeared in the 529 pages of *Industry
and Humanity*. He believed in the gospel he was preaching, the
gospel of industrial peace, and he was determined to use every
possible agency to make it known.

He was equally determined that it should be the central theme
of his political future if the door to public life should open to him.
On the day the Armistice was signed, November 11, 1918, he impressed a group of friends gathered at his brother's home in Denver
when he talked about the significance of representative and responsible government in industry. He described it as 'a policy which

would some day be the subject of a national movement as far-reaching in every way as that of the Reform Bill in British politics, and the evolution of responsible government in our own country'. His entry in the diary was more personal: 'I believe the statement of this policy in my book *Industry and Humanity* and indeed the whole groundwork of industrial development as set forth therein will come, in time, and that possibly very quickly, to be the basis of a program of Liberalism in Canada. . . . I am recording my belief now to see if later on the reality is not even greater than the present vision.' The door to public life in Canada was still not open, but if it should open his duty was plain, as he wrote several weeks later, 'to make *Industry and Humanity* my platform and the realization of its program my life work — that seems inevitable, that seems the leading of God'.

In the end Mackenzie King had to leave it to others 'to complete the circle'. He had warned in his book that the period of preparation and transition would be a long one; but in the three decades that followed the publication of *Industry and Humanity*, some at least of his high hopes were realized in legislative enactments as well as in improved industrial relations. Certainly his plea for 'the infusion of a new spirit in industry' has not been unheeded, nor his central theme that 'wherever in social or industrial relations the claims of industry and humanity are opposed, those of industry must make way'. All this cannot be dismissed as unrealistic idealism. The ideal of joint control of industry or representative and re-sponsible government in industry has not been achieved, but *Industry and Humanity* has served a great purpose in making the ideal live and in pointing the way to its ultimate realization.

CHAPTER 14

Industrial Relations Counsellor

The tentative plans for a personal association with John D. Rocke-feller, Jr., as industrial counsellor, which had been discussed at the New York interview before Mackenzie King temporarily severed his connection with the foundation in order to take part in the Canadian election, were confirmed in the spring of 1918. His asso-ciation with the foundation had ended on January 18, and Rocke-feller immediately returned to his earlier suggestion that he should become his personal adviser. He spoke of a substantial fee, which could be easily supplemented by other retainers from industrial concerns who would welcome his services in a similar capacity. Why, he suggested, should King not give out immediately that he was in the position of an industrial counsellor . . . keep his residence in Ottawa for the present, and await developments? Rockefeller was perhaps hardly prepared for an immediate acceptance but he was delighted when Mackenzie King declared that that would suit him exactly. He re-emphasized his desire to be free to go on with politics, but if things did not work out in the Canadian political field as he hoped they would, he agreed he would then give his entire time to the work of an industrial counsellor, with Rocke-feller as his first and principal client.

This was apparently acceptable to Rockefeller. He was opti-mistic about prospects: 'Mr. King,' he said two days later, 'there

will be so much to do and so many wanting you that the difficulty
will be to get your services.' Not only did he endorse the new venture with enthusiasm, he did what he could to drum up business
by writing and speaking to several prospective clients. That approach achieved results, as he was sure it would.

As a result of these talks Mackenzie King was launched, or so
it seemed, on a new career. After he returned to Ottawa he wrote
to his brother about his new plans:

> The position of Industrial Counsellor represents my present
> status. In this connection I am open to accept engagements from
> any source to do work of the kind done in Colorado when my
> book is finished; I hope to receive retainers from different sources
> and to make work of this nature my profession. Just whether it
> will be carried on in connection with public life in Canada, or
> require subsequent removal to the United States is something
> which the trend of affairs throughout the present year will have
> to determine. . . . My association with the Foundation has termin-
> ated in every connection except my outstanding obligation to
> complete the book on which I have been engaged. I am open,
> therefore, for fresh undertakings in any field that may offer.

In spite of this avowed intention, his heart was still in Canadian
politics.

He could not bring himself to give up residence in Canada, certainly not his Canadian citizenship. At most he might open an office
in New York on a short-term lease and live in the hope that changing political conditions in Canada would soon end the temporary
exile. But 'the whole question,' he wrote in a letter to Violet
Markham in March, 'is too large to attempt to solve hurriedly.' Mr.
Rockefeller had 'agreed not to urge hasty action', and was willing
'to allow time to disclose its opportunities, that the final decision
may be made in the light of them.'

Nothing could be more characteristic of Mackenzie King than
a policy which would 'allow time to disclose its opportunities';
nothing in the end could be more convincing of the wisdom of his
policy of avoiding hasty action. It was not like him to make a

promise without a qualification, or a commitment without an escape clause. In this instance, time, and a very short time at that, played its part.

From then on, for days and weeks, there were moments when he looked with favour on the prospect of going to New York even though it should mean abandoning his political career. The pull to the south was strong. The International Harvester Company, to whose president Rockefeller had spoken, was interested; the Bethlehem Steel Company and other large industrial concerns had been making more than casual inquiries. 'This may mean,' he felt assured, 'a very wide and far-reaching development and lead to a very considerable forward movement along the lines of industrial democracy.' Suggesting a figure first of $15,000 and later of $18,000 a year, of which he would pay one-third in return for one-third of his time, Rockefeller was sure that the balance and more would easily be made up by retainers from other companies. Such companies as United States Steel, for example, could be charged a larger fee. Rockefeller told King that, if he could do for them what he had done in Colorado, it would be worth double the amount. He advised him strongly to get into this work, which he thought afforded greater opportunity than politics. King's resistance to leaving Canada was expressed less vigorously than it had been. He protested mildly, but their detailed discussion of terms and Mackenzie King's acceptance of them gave Rockefeller reason to believe that the decision had been made to embark on this new career.

II

His first opportunity to establish himself as an industrial consultant at large came in April, from the Consolidation Coal Company, which operated mines in Maryland and several other eastern states. The invitation came at a time when he was struggling to complete his book, but he welcomed it as the first opportunity in his new career. The Davis Coal and Coke Company, operating in the same areas, also sought his services. In both companies the Rockefellers held substantial blocks of shares. Rockefeller was unhappy about the reputation the Consolidation company had acquired for ruthlessness and autocratic dealings with its employees, and about the political manoeuvring which J. H. Wheelwright, president of the company, and his close associate, Senator Watson, had used to get results. The men had gone on strike in April and the United States Fuel Administrator, Dr. Garfield, was keen to get them back into production, indeed had ordered them back. At that stage Mackenzie King was called in. He drafted an agreement which marked a complete change in the labour policy of the Consolidation Coal Company. With some minor amendments, and after discussion with union representatives, it was adopted by Dr. Garfield and made applicable to all the mines on the eastern seaboard. One of Dr. Garfield's close advisers at the time was John. P. White, president of the United Mine Workers. The agreement was also endorsed by all the other operators in the area. Wheelwright was enthusiastic: in all his life, he told his own counsel, he had not met anyone who had been so helpful to him. To Mackenzie King himself he remarked that they had done at least ten times better than they would have done if he had not come. Most of the mines in the area were not unionized, and at this stage union recognition was not the issue. The solution for the moment was an agreement whereby grievances could be settled amicably without undue delay. It had some of the features of the Colorado plan but none of its elaborate machinery. The Consolidation company had been bitterly opposed to union recognition, but before these discussions were concluded there were evidences of a changing attitude. C. U. Calloway, president of the Davis Coal and Coke Company — a non-union operation — and also an adviser to the Fuel Administrator, thought that 'unionization had to come — might come in six months, might come in two years, but it would be all the better for coming by degrees'. Calloway made another comment, several weeks later, that 'there was every probability of the [Consolidation] plan being adopted by other operators in other states as a consequence of the action of the Consolidation company; that we must expect a very wide development'. Rockefeller agreed with Calloway that it would be better to have union recognition come by degrees. He told Wheelwright that he was not opposed to unions but believed they were necessary, a statement that must have been gratifying to the man who had been steering him in this direction. He doubted, however — and Mackenzie King would take no exception to this — 'the wisdom of going too far in the way of recognition at the start, until it became apparent what class of men the company was to deal with'. He had not forgotten the Colorado experience.

A beginning had been made in the direction of a representation plan and also in the direction of union recognition. Within less than a year a representation plan was introduced, though reluctantly and half-heartedly, by the management. Within a few months, in August 1918, a union agreement was signed, but it applied to only a few of the areas in which the company operated. To Mackenzie King's mind this had all the earmarks of a political deal: 'My belief is that . . . to win the vote of the miners of the State as a Democratic candidate for U.S. Senate, Watson had manoeuvred an agreement with the mineworkers. . . . It is apparent that this company buys, directly or indirectly, its support from Labor where it cannot exert its influence by force. It is apparent too that officers of the U.M.W.A. are prepared to make deals of one kind or another.'

All this was but an interim solution of Consolidation's many-sided labour problem. In the spring of 1919 he returned to make a more thoroughgoing survey of conditions in the company's mines in several states and to prescribe remedies.

III

In June an inquiry of lesser importance came from the Western Union Telegraph Company in New York. The company had found itself in difficulties with its employees and with the National

War Labor Board. The board had recommended that the company should concede the right of its employees to join the union and the company was disposed to disregard the order. The president, Newcomb Carlton, had telegraphed to Rockefeller in Denver asking him to arrange to have Mackenzie King come to New York immediately for consultation. Mackenzie King, who was accompanying Mr. and Mrs. Rockefeller on a tour of the Colorado mines, declined. He did not approve of the company's resistance to the War Labor Board and feared that it might appear that he had gone at Rockefeller's request to help to frame machinery intended to defeat trade unionism. He favoured a representation plan, but it was vital in his opinion that any plan devised should not be framed in opposition to trade unionism but should leave membership in union organizations optional, while at the same time rendering it obviously unnecessary as a means of securing justice in the adjustment of grievances.

IV

No sooner had Mackenzie King returned to Ottawa from Colorado than he received a telegram from the Bethlehem Shipbuilding Corporation asking him to come to Bethlehem, Pennsylvania, for a conference. It worried him to have another interruption in his writing: 'This may mean drafting an important plan for that industry. If I only had my book complete how happy I should be, but the call is one of duty and opportunity combined and must be obeyed.'

The mission to Bethlehem turned out to be an exceedingly important one. A representation plan for the 70,000 employees was prepared after much discussion; it was completed and printed before the middle of July and was put into effect with the goodwill of the trade union organizations, although the company was not prepared at that time to give full recognition to the unions. The diary entry at this stage, written at Kingsmere, indicates the excitement he was experiencing: 'I felt in shaping the plan for the Bethlehem Corporation I was helping to lay part of the foundations of parliamentary government in industry. That is the field to which I intend to give much of my thought and life.' It was a satisfaction to learn, many months later, that the Bethlehem Shipbuilding Corporation had crossed the bridge to trade unionism within months of his negotiations with its officers. Agreements were reached with thirteen unions representing workers in the company's plants on both the Atlantic and Pacific seaboards.

His next call was from the Bethlehem Steel Company, a separate but related concern. This came early in August, when he was engaged in discussions with the management of the General Electric Company at Lynn, Massachusetts. Again he deplored the inroads on his time but he had to recognize this as part of the practical work of reconstruction. 'Besides,' he assured himself, 'it is important war work and the concrete example in industry is worth perhaps more than anything that can be written. These industrial concerns are the most important in the United States, which I think means the most important in the world. To get them to introduce the principle of representation and elements of self-government is the biggest service that can be rendered industrial progress today. It is difficult to say how far it may go in averting what might be very serious industrial situations in the future.'

Industrial unrest in the steel industry had developed from the same conditions that had prevailed in the shipbuilding industry. There was no adequate provision for collective bargaining, and more than one strike had interrupted wartime production. Trade unions were not countenanced. Anything that even 'savored of organization' (the phrase used by the vice-president of the Shipbuilding Corporation was much quoted) was anathema to management. 'The steel industry,' as an editorial in the *New Republic* put it at the time, 'has been like a great island fortified against the rising flood of trade unionism.' Both of the Bethlehem companies operated on the open-shop principle, union and non-union men working together.

At this stage the National War Labor Board intervened by

issuing a decree which made 'an end of the old dispensation', and gave to the workers the right to organize and bargain collectively. The board did not insist upon recognition of the unions. Mackenzie King's contribution did not include the settlement of the strike (that was effected by the board) but it did provide for a method of collective bargaining through elected representatives which vastly improved working-conditions and relations between management and men. The head of Bethlehem Steel told Mackenzie King that in introducing the principle of representation his company felt it would be regarded as 'the real pioneer in this movement, that while Colorado had set an example, it was so remote from eastern industrial centres that an eastern concern the size of Bethlehem Steel taking this thing up in a big way would make a very great impression. They had learned that the War Department would welcome this departure in the steel works as they were having difficulty in handling their own labor and that the Navy Department would also be sympathetic.'

Bethlehem Steel's adoption of the plan created widespread interest throughout the country. Within the next few months the company received hundreds of inquiries from various sources. The company had gone far in accepting a form of collective bargaining and employee representation. It should have gone further by abandoning the twelve-hour shift which, to the disgrace of the entire industry, had always prevailed. The Colorado Fuel and Iron Company had set an example in this respect: after discussions between management and employee representatives, it had established an actual eight-hour day with a ten-per-cent increase in the hourly wage rate. The eastern steel companies held to what was known as the basic eight-hour day, which usually meant four hours more at an increased rate of pay.

There was no yielding to 'the rising flood of unionism' on the part of United States Steel, the largest of the steel companies, and most of its competitors followed its example. They followed the lead of Elbert H. Gary of United States Steel, the most reactionary of all American industrialists. Rockefeller found Gary completely unyielding in 1919 when the nation-wide steel strike was impending. He told Mackenzie King that Gary was 'opposed to collective bargaining or representation of any kind, believing that it is only the entering wedge to the closed shop, which he feels is fatal to business'.

v

In between his surveys for the shipbuilding and steel companies, Mackenzie King received an urgent request from the General Electric Company at Lynn, Massachusetts, to assist in dealing with its labour problems. Strikes had occurred at Lynn, Schenectady, and Pittsfield, and the National War Labor Board and the state board had sent in conciliators. The General Electric Company had no formal dealings with labour unions. It operated on the open-shop principle, but it did enter into agreements with its employees who were members of unions affiliated with the American Federation of Labor. The strikes were settled, without reference to any question of union recognition, through the intervention of the State Board of Arbitration and Conciliation and the National Labor Board. Mackenzie King appeared on the scene a few days before the strike at Lynn was settled, but had no part in the negotiations which led to its settlement. His role was to advise on methods whereby grievances could be readily discovered and adjusted and harmonious relations established between management and men. The plan of representation of employees which he worked out proved to be eminently satisfactory. The company expressed its appreciation in a letter he received a year later:

> We have been greatly indebted to your sound, intelligent, progressive and humanitarian advice; and profiting by this advice we have established at our Lynn works a system of industrial relations which gives our employees a large voice in the determination of working conditions and conditions of employment. This,

in my opinion, puts us in the forefront among organizations of industry in dealing with the human problem.

VI

Mackenzie King's first ventures in the new field of industrial counselling had been a satisfying experience. Before accepting other commitments of the same kind he spent most of September and October in Kingsmere and Ottawa, where he concentrated on his book — writing, revising, proof-reading. He also took time for discussions on party policy with Sir Wilfrid Laurier and others. He wanted to clear the slate before sallying forth on another series of surveys, this time for western companies which had already spoken for his services.

By the end of October he was off to Colorado. The appointment there with the Great Western Sugar Company had been made in June. On the way west he took time for conversations with representatives of the International Harvester Company in Chicago and the Youngstown Sheet and Tube Company in Youngstown, Ohio. Both companies had been drafting representation plans on the lines of the Bethlehem model. No survey of the properties of either company was entailed. His part was to revise what had been drafted and to advise generally on the new labour policies which both companies were ready to inaugurate. A few days in Youngstown, and the same in Chicago, was all the time he could give them, although he did manage to do some paper work for them in Denver and in Ottawa before the winter was over. The outcome in each instance was the establishment of an industrial representation plan. Neither company was prepared at that time to concede recognition of the respective unions. The Youngstown management in particular seemed to be hostile. Mackenzie King advised strongly against one or two of their suggestions which indicated an intention to combat labour unions (they would not, for example, allow employees' representatives to hold office in a union). As always, he urged 'the necessity of the democratization of industry and the giving of labor a larger voice in the matter of control'.

VII

Conferences with directors and officers of the International Harvester Company in Chicago had been matters of only a day or two, in November 1918 and again in January and March 1919. They were principally discussions of a representation plan which officers of the company had worked out themselves when they found it impossible to enlist Mackenzie King's services. The heads of the company, including Harold F. McCormick, a brother-in-law of Rockefeller, had been watching developments in Colorado. Along with many other American industrialists they feared the growing power of the trade unions. Mackenzie King was impressed, however, by his new clients as men of a liberal point of view, anxious to do what was right and fair by labour. They were perfectly conscious that a new attitude must be taken — a little doubtful as to experiments of democracy in industry, but willing to make some attempt to reconstruct on democratic lines. Union organizers had already started a membership drive and the directors wondered what effect a representation plan would have upon organization by the unions. Mackenzie King told them that the plan he recommended would not necessarily stop organization, but without it the organizers would have the strongest argument in their appeals to the men to join up. Whatever else it provided, 'any plan should state specifically that nothing in it would prevent the men joining labor organizations'.

In the draft the company officers had prepared there were many shortcomings to criticize: no attempt had been made to enlist the co-operation of the employees in the drafting of the plan; representation of employees was inadequate — only nine representatives to each 4,000 employees; emphasis was placed on the adjustment of grievances, whereas it should have been on the development of good personal relations in joint committees, which would remove the cause of most grievances; resort to outside arbitration was too much relied upon, whereas differences might better be settled as far as possible 'within the family'. There was grave danger, too, in anything that savoured much, as this plan did, of legal process; no adequate provision was made for the protection of employees' representatives against the possibility of unjust treatment because of action they might take on behalf of fellow-employees; the administration of the plan was too much controlled by company officials and not enough by the employees themselves.

Mackenzie King criticized these and many other important details, and in the end, as one member of the group declared, they felt that 'they had been given a completely different point of view'. As finally consummated, the International Harvester plan was a much more democratic document than the one originally submitted to him. It was made applicable to the 35,000 employees of the company, in its plants in Canada as well as the United States. The joint councils were of great assistance, so McCormick told King several months later, in 'bringing our recent labor disturbances to a speedy and satisfactory conclusion'. Apparently its usefulness continued, for Mackenzie King was informed in 1922 by a friend who had had a chat with McCormick that 'his faith in your plan seems as strong as ever. Evidently it is working well under very adverse conditions.'

VIII

The main object of the western tour in 1918 was to make a survey of conditions under which men and women worked for the Great Western Sugar Company (a Havemeyer corporation), and to recommend changes in the company's labour policies. The head offices of the company were in Denver; the sugar-beet fields and refineries were located in Northern Colorado, Montana, and Nebraska. This geographical separation reduced the possibilities of human contact between management and operating forces, a condition which in itself was partly responsible for the lack of understanding each group had of the other's problems. Labour turnover was excessively high, a condition directly attributable to deplorable working- and living-conditions. The company had made a beginning in its so-called 'welfare work', but Mackenzie King was

appalled by what he found in the factories and in the sugar-beet
fields. Everything was done under extreme pressure during the
three months of the 'campaign', when seventy per cent of the
working-force was recruited to harvest the beets and make them
into sugar. When he asked why the work had to be done under
such pressure he was told that the beets would deteriorate, would
lose in sugar content, if left out in the open much over three
months. 'Obviously,' he concluded, 'the choice is between beets
losing in sugar content and men and women losing in vitality and
strength.'

He was revolted by the conditions he saw in the first plants he
visited (they proved to be the worst) and in his diary he gave vent
to his strong feelings in vivid language:

> I felt today that these workers were in a position of veritable
> servitude: a condition of slavery of as bad a kind as almost any
> conceivable. They have no home life whatever, spend the day
> amid excessive toil, no Sunday, no chance for reading, no oppor-
> tunity for bringing up their families. All this is demoralizing to
> the nation's present and future, and should be made absolutely
> impossible by the state. Clearly, the community as a party to in-
> dustry should preserve its future assets and make its chief func-
> tion the preservation of essential standards. As a stockholder, I
> would feel that to derive profits from an investment in this in-
> dustry under these conditions would be to live on blood money.
> A condition which permits men and women to work as we saw
> them working today, and on the other hand enables individuals to
> accumulate millions, is absolutely and wholly wrong. I never felt
> more the justice of the program of the British Labor Party than
> I did in what we saw today. Moreover, as a consumer of sugar, I
> felt that I should infinitely prefer to pay double or treble what I
> was paying and see that the product was made under proper con-
> ditions, instead of obtaining sugar at a lesser rate, and even in
> this remote way be a party to subjecting human beings to the
> slavery we witnessed. Clearly, the community as a consumer has
> another serious obligation to discharge, an obligation related also
> to the maintenance of adequate standards.

Conditions so fundamentally wrong called for immediate and direct action without waiting to have machinery set up for joint committees and representation plans:

> My summing up of today's observations is that improvement will not lie in the direction of any machinery which it is going to be possible for us to construct, but necessarily lies in the elimination of conditions which are fundamentally wrong. First of all, the working of three months at a stretch, with no holidays, is wrong. Working seven days in the week is wrong. Twelve hours a day is wrong; even eight hours without an hour for meals is wrong. Working amid humid atmosphere, without opportunities of bathing and cleaning before going out is wrong. The absence of any home accommodation of an adequate sort is wrong. Men need hours to work, hours to rest, and hours of recreation, campaign or no campaign. Human nature cannot be expected to endure such conditions without degradation of the standards of life. It seemed to me that most of the employees we saw at work had anything but a responsive look in their faces. I imagine that at the end of the season they must become deadened in feeling and appearance alike.

It was no wonder that all his socialistic impulses were aroused:

> The men at the top of this concern are mostly very wealthy men, living lives of social ease amid luxurious surroundings. As I went through the factory I felt, were I compelled to share the work of those I saw, I should certainly become an advocate of the Guild system of having labor take over the entire industry, I should certainly become a Socialist in the hope of having the state regulate conditions.

Before the end of his survey Mackenzie King found that the conditions he had seen the first day or two were hardly typical; he had been shown the worst. The impression formed in going through the factory at Brighton, for example, was as favourable as the first impressions of the other factories were unfavourable. In a few instances management and men were holding monthly joint meetings, called 'efficiency meetings', outside the harvesting period, but generally little attention was given to working- and living-conditions. One district manager put it bluntly: 'Technically we have been reaching out for new processes, improvements in machinery, etc.; socially we have only done the things we have been kicked into doing.' Wages for the temporary workers were appallingly low, 35 cents an hour in the 1918 season, while machinists were getting only 55 cents an hour. Labour cost was only six or seven per cent of the total cost of production; machinery and equipment accounted for something like eighty per cent.

It was Mackenzie King's mission to make directors and managers aware of their shortcomings in these respects, to induce a more active interest on their part in their employees' working- and living-conditions. His appeal to the heads of the company, almost evangelistic in tone, met with ready response. They were shocked into action by his vigorous indictment of such things as inadequate housing, excessive hours, deplorably low wages, wretched toilet and shower facilities, and the absence of any provision for the presentation and adjustment of grievances. His basic solution was a written statement of principles and policies governing industrial relations, the establishment of a department of industrial relations, and the election of employees' representatives who would act on joint committees for the shaping and carrying out of policies affecting the workers. On all these points agreement was reached by the company and its employees.

He had made a 'vigorous and thorough examination' of conditions in the sugar-beet fields and plants, and his services, as W. L. Petrikin, president of the company, told him, had contributed not only to smooth operations in an industry in which strikes and violence had restricted production, but to a very substantial increase in output. This at a time when 'an adequate supply of sugar for the military forces as well as for the civilian population was generally recognized as one of the serious problems of the War.' Petrikin was one of many who testified that 'the service he had rendered American industry during the War was a distinct contribution to the Allied cause'.

IX

Up to this point Mackenzie King had had relatively little to do with labour problems in the various Standard Oil companies. Rockefeller was anxious that all of them should take up this new policy of employee representation and collective bargaining. But even a Rockefeller could not — or at any rate this one would not — dictate to Standard Oil presidents. He explained that it was necessary to use judgment with regard to the order in which they were approached. He pointed out, in connection with the Standard Oil Company of New York, that all the officers were simply salaried men, but that, notwithstanding his father's very large interest in the company as a stockholder, they often treated with indifference suggestions he made. When Mackenzie King reminded him that 'the attitude of the managers did not relieve him or his father as stockholders from their responsibility', he countered with the remark that it was desirable that the managers too should feel their responsibility. Apparently, however, he was impressed by Mackenzie King's advice, for he did approach the president of Socony in June 1918, by interview and by letter, and urged upon him the 'desirability of providing an industrial representation plan for that company'. Nothing came of these overtures as far as Mackenzie King's services were concerned. Rockefeller had also approached the president of the Standard Oil Company of New Jersey in 1917, but at that time, as already noted, King could not do more than offer advice through Rockefeller. His advice, however, was acted upon, and the New Jersey company established a system of employee representation very similar to the Colorado plan.

X

The one Standard Oil company in which Mackenzie King did make a comprehensive survey was the Standard Oil Company of Indiana. The invitation came to him during the Christmas season of 1918 from Colonel Robert W. Stewart, chairman of the board. To take on the survey for the Indiana company would mean a further post-ponement of the trip to England which had been planned. He re-called his disappointment, and his resentment, when Rockefeller had questioned in October whether he could 'be spared from this country'. Rockefeller had given what might be interpreted as a grudging consent when he wrote to him in Denver: 'So long as you feel the advantages of your studying at first hand the developments along labor lines in England outweigh the probable service which you could render by staying in this country during the next six months, I am fully in accord with our original idea that you should go abroad as soon as you can so arrange after finishing your work in the West.'

In mid-January Mackenzie King set off for Chicago where the headquarters of the Indiana company were located. His survey was not completed until well on in March. There were interruptions in that period, some of them political, some of them having to do with certain mopping-up operations for International Harvester, and for Youngstown Sheet and Tube.

He visited the several refineries of the Indiana company and its one coal-mining plant. Good beginnings had been made, some of them quite recently, in providing first-aid hospitals, visiting nurses, rest-rooms, shower and locker equipment, safety devices, and the like. The eight-hour day had been introduced as early as 1914. The safety director reported that since his department was established in July 1918 a couple of thousand suggestions had been made through employees' representatives and most of them had been acted on by the company at the company's expense. Mackenzie King found some conditions which he roundly condemned; for example, the inhuman conditions under which men worked in cleaning out the tar stills in the paraffin works. The men were obliged to enter the stills when the temperature was 300 degrees or over and to work in the thick of fumes and smoke. The situation could have been relieved by the installation of additional stills (thus giving more time for each still to cool after the sediment had hardened) and by provision for adequate shower or rest-room facilities. In the company's failure to make the necessary outlay Mackenzie King saw 'the contrast between the estimate put upon the value of materials and the estimate put upon the value of human life. A man's life and health is set over against the use of so much idle capital.'

Mackenzie King's interest was not, however, in correcting specific abuses or in developing so-called welfare work; these things would be looked after if machinery for self-government were provided and definite contractual relations were established between management and men. He so expressed himself to Colonel Stewart, urging that social centres should be established on self-governing lines, run by the employees themselves; that the weekly meetings of heads of departments should be attended by representatives of employees; and that much that was being done from above should be effected by joint action.

A bigger problem was to induce the company to enter into satisfactory contractual relations with the unions. Throughout the years no Standard Oil company had signed a formal union contract. The Indiana company had come close to it. In some of its plants practically all the workers were organized and worked under conditions negotiated by the union. But the agreements were not embodied in formal contracts, though they were expressed, in some instances, in letters from company managers to union officers which set forth the points of agreement which had been reached in conference. More than this Standard Oil was not willing to concede – anything more would have been interpreted as union recognition. Some of the managers who favoured formal contracts with the unions thought the joint-committee idea could be worked out along lines satisfactory to the unions; such committees could deal with many questions of mutual concern, including personal relationships which would not be covered by the union contracts; they would have been willing, indeed, to allow the unions to name the employees' representatives.

Standard Oil adopted a similar policy of no union recognition when in 1917 it purchased coal-mining properties at Carlinville,

Illinois. The mines had been operated by the former owners under a contract with the United Mine Workers, and Standard Oil carried on under the conditions which had prevailed, meeting the representatives of the union pit-committees and checking off the dues, paying them into union funds and obliging men who applied for employment to become members of the union. But the company balked at the signing of any formal contract. The miners suspected that this was due either to the policy of Standard Oil not to recognize unions or to 'some controlling interest opposed to unionism'. To them, that interest could only mean the Rockefeller influence. To Mackenzie King it seemed that Standard Oil was framing up for itself a fight with unionism and that the brunt would have to be borne, as in Colorado, by John D. Rockefeller, Jr.

If an industrial representation plan were introduced here, the miners would regard it as an attempted substitute for unionism. Mackenzie King's conclusion was that what was needed at Carlinville was 'open and straight dealings with the union.... Mr. R. could wish for nothing better than to be able to point to the only coal mining property owned by the Standard Oil as being under an agreement, as evidence that the plan in Colorado was not intended to be a substitute for unionism, but rather a means of leading up to it where circumstances justified such a course.' If such a step were not taken, heads of the United Mine Workers would be 'justified in believing that they must doubt and watch the Rockefellers at every turn. The right course adopted at Carlinville would do more than anything else to remove a very bitter and still latent antagonism.'

Talks with Standard Oil managers had convinced Mackenzie King that they were divided in opinion: some were wholly willing to make formal contracts, while others were not. To him it seemed clear that the company itself must take a strong stand: subterfuge of any kind could only have damaging effects. 'It is really teaching the men to adopt underhand methods. Clearly, the United Mine Workers are more straightforward in their dealings than the

Standard Oil Company is in its dealings.' There was no question in Mackenzie King's mind as to the right course: 'In view of the world situation today my own feeling is that the Standard Oil Company had better abandon, once and forever, its policy of no dealings with the unions, and come out and make contracts where it is obviously in its interests so to do, refraining from contracts where conditions do not warrant or justify it.'

Mackenzie King had already written to Rockefeller, a fortnight before, a very forceful letter forecasting the calamity that would ensue if labour's approach to capital were ignored: 'The open hand that today is extended from a genuine desire to avert impending calamity may close, and become the closed fist resolved in nothing but to destroy.' What he now saw in his survey confirmed his judgment and inspired him to write again on the same theme. Again he counselled acceptance of 'the obvious wisdom of frank, open and aboveboard dealing with labor organizations'. Certainly, he said, there should be an end to the kind of evasion and subterfuge that marked the Indiana company's refusal to take the formal step of a contract when recognition in every other particular had been conceded.

Although Mackenzie King knew that he could secure Rockefeller's support (it would have weight even though he held less than five per cent of the company's stock) he felt it desirable to stress to the directors that his recommendation of a formal contract with the union was wholly a personal one, his own honest conviction. He wanted the directors to make the decision on their own responsibility rather than place the onus on Rockefeller, whose policy had always been to interfere as little as possible with boards of directors and managers. But the larger significance was what Mackenzie King had in mind. 'I believe,' he wrote in his diary on the day he submitted his report and discussed it with the directors and managers, '... that if I succeed in bringing about a contract between the Standard Oil Company [of Indiana] and the United Mine Workers in a natural way, and in a manner which will avoid even bargaining, to say nothing of conflict, I will have done more to bring together Organized Capital and Organized Labor in America than can be done by all the speeches that all the speakers in the country are making at the present time. . . . It is wholly because of the vision I have of the inevitable consequences, should Organized Capital represented by the Standard Oil and Organized Labor, represented by the Federation, be brought into positions of open hostility . . . that I felt I should take the step regardless wholly of the consequences in the minds of directors, managers or stockholders of the Standard Oil Company. It is an actual condition which industry is facing today, not any theoretical situation, and action must be taken in the light of the forces to be reckoned with.'

In this discussion Mackenzie King felt that he had won the confidence of both directors and managers: 'I felt that there was little or no hostility, but that the attitude of everyone was cordial and sympathetic, though there was a recognition that the point of view I was presenting was an advanced one.' He was more certain of the support of the managers; all of them had spoken to Colonel Stewart very favourably after the meeting, and had said in particular 'that I had no theories but was thoroughly practical and understood the problems'. Colonel Stewart and his fellow directors were perhaps less enthusiastic, more cautious than the managers, but then, as King observed, 'a board of directors, acting only for stockholders, is apt to take the point of view simply of the capital investors'. They were ready enough to accept an industrial representation plan, but with that modest advance Mackenzie King was not content. Some headway, he felt, had been made in the right direction, for in assessing the results of the meeting he wrote: 'Compared with what I have done today in breaking down a hitherto unalterable position built up over many years by the most powerful combination of capital in the United States, the actual work of making a survey of industrial conditions and proposing a plan of representation for the industry is insignificant.'

Colonel Stewart was the key man in this situation and Mackenzie King pressed his case again the next day. On one important point Colonel Stewart said he agreed absolutely, 'though he confessed he hated like the mischief to have to make a contract with an organization which would not permit men to work who did not belong to its ranks'. Mackenzie King had heard this argument before and he knew the answer: 'I then spoke to him of Labor's point of view toward the non-union man, who was ready to take all the advantages which came from the sacrifice involved to effect organization, but was unwilling to contribute to the collective strength by membership and payment of dues.' Colonel Stewart's way of expressing disagreement was merely to say that he 'agreed that there was something to be said for this point of view'. If the decision could have been made by Mackenzie King, contractual relations with the unions would have been approved forthwith. He made a strong case for immediate action, but after all he was merely an adviser. It may have been some consolation to him then to realize that the directors had been almost persuaded and that in some instances agreements were signed between the union and the company. And it was an ultimate satisfaction to him later on to learn that they had acted, though reluctantly, on his advice. In the meantime, however, a representation plan was established which met the approval of the 22,000 employees and the management, one which, as Stewart told him later that year, was 'daily strengthening the bonds of goodwill, confidence and understanding in our entire organization'.

XI

After completing his work for Standard Oil of Indiana, Mackenzie King still had some winding-up to do for the Youngstown Sheet and Tube, General Electric, Colorado Fuel and Iron, and International Harvester; also a more time-consuming assignment with Consolidation Coal. He had to decline a proposal in February for a survey of industrial conditions in the Hawaiian Islands for the Sugar Planters' Association. Certain packing companies in Chicago (Swift, Armour, and others) sought his advice in March, but they, and he, had to be content with a single conference.

His engagement with the Consolidation Coal Company called for a survey of the company's coal-mining properties in several states: West Virginia, Pennsylvania, Maryland, and Kentucky. He approached this task enthusiastically. He visited all the camps and found that the conditions in which the miners lived were not unlike those he had first seen in Colorado. There were signs of recent improvements (one manager commented that many of the improvements had been inspired by the Colorado example). There was great need for new buildings (wash-houses, club-houses, and recreation or social centres) and also for qualified persons who would encourage the employees to organize their own community life. These needs were not met by the union, in the few areas where the union was a factor, because its interest was primarily in such matters as wages, hours, working conditions and, of course, recognition. Mackenzie King encouraged the development of close working-arrangements with the union, and indeed union recognition, but he advised that the union's work should be supplemented by joint committees which would have to do with such questions as housing, sanitation and health, company stores, education, and social and recreational activities.

In every community he visited, the union question was a subject of major interest. In some regions managers and superintendents favoured complete recognition. In others, bosses who had been brought up in 'the old school' preferred no union because without them they had a free hand; it had been 'drilled into them in the past that they must forever frown down every appearance of unionism'. At times, when frowning was not effective, they had resorted to more forceful methods of persuasion. They were learning, however, like the rest, and the results were beneficial. In some sections, notably in Maryland and West Virginia, unionization was accepted but not to the point of union contracts. Mackenzie King came to the conclusion that full recognition, and in all areas, was the right course. His working notes included the striking comment: 'My feeling is that the day of fighting unions is done, and that companies in this region in any event [Somerset County in Pennsylvania] had better make their peace with them and come to a full recognition and agreement.'

Weeks before, in his preliminary talks with Rockefeller, he had advised him 'not to take a stand against the unions at that time, or at any time hereafter'. He was pleased with Rockefeller's response which indicated that he 'was not opposing unions and is taking no exception to my strong pronouncement in their favour'. What Rockefeller was pressing for was an instrument to bring about closer relations between employers and employees; 'the thing he was interested in was the representative idea, if not effected by unions, then effected in some other way.' In any event, 'collective bargaining was to be a factor, and constant contacts as well'.

Union recognition, then, was the course Mackenzie King advised when he completed his survey for the Consolidation Company: full recognition of the union plus the adoption of a scheme which would bring management and men into close and friendly relations in dealing with matters not covered by union contracts. To such matters he had been giving special attention as he moved from camp to camp. The other men in the party (there were usually three or four) devoted their time to inspection of machinery, buildings, stores, equipment, stock, etc., concentrating exclusively on these; 'the human side of things escapes notice'. One of them had noticed that Rockefeller, in an earlier inspection, 'did not seem to be the least bit interested in the coal deposits or the equipment, but spent all his time being interested in the sort of thing I was interested in: namely, the conditions of the people and their homes'.

Mackenzie King's experience in these communities served to confirm the social philosophy he had just expounded in *Industry and Humanity*, for he wrote in his diary, as a Woodsworth or a Coldwell might have written: 'As one goes about these camps, so numerous that one can scarcely remember them, and sees the enormous wealth controlled by a handful of capitalists, one cannot but feel that the system which permits this sort of control is absolutely wrong, unjust and indefensible; and that there will not be an end to social unrest until the transition is made to a joint control, with a restoration to the community of much that today is in private hands. My task seems to be that of trying to bring about the change by an evolutionary method, and avoiding revolution and its attendant evils.'

But, after all, he was only an adviser dealing with a specific series of problems. He had done what he could to educate and inspire his clients, but the results fell far short of his expectations. A couple of years later, still interested in the project to which he had given so much time and anxious thought, he was saddened to learn that the Industrial Representation Plan, which the company had introduced somewhat reluctantly, had failed because of its half-hearted acceptance by the management. Here was an example of well-designed machinery rendered inadequate by unwillingness or inability to run it properly.

XII

Mackenzie King's commitments as an industrial counsellor engaged every minute of his time till May 15, when, as had been arranged with Rockefeller, he was to sail for England to carry on further studies in labour relations. His venture into this new profession had been a success. On his way back from Colorado in March 1919 he wrote to Rockefeller: 'I do not recall ever having entertained feelings of greater satisfaction than those I am experiencing at the moment with respect to what has been achieved. I am entirely satisfied and very much delighted.' His clients, too, were well satisfied. And the representation idea had been made to work, not only in the industries in which he personally had shaped the plans, but also in a host of other industries. More than two hundred firms in the United States, he was to learn later from a report of the National Industrial Conference Board, were governing their industrial relations by some form of employees' representation.

Financially, too, it had been a rewarding experience. His 1918 income from various sources was substantial. From Bethlehem Steel he had received $4,000, from General Electric $3,000, International Harvester $2,000, Great Western Sugar $5,000, Consolidation Coal $1,000, Youngstown Sheet and Tube $1,000. This, with Rockefeller's retainer of $6,000, made an income from professional services of about $22,000. 'That surely is achievement in a financial way quite undreamed of. Had I wished to make money, I could have increased this considerably by going after business, all this work came to me unsought. The money will be helpful for future independence and service.'

A cheque for $1,000 from his first client was more than he had expected. He had made a trip south which occupied the better part of a week, and which, to his annoyance, had interrupted his writing. When the fee had been discussed, the president had asked if $1,000 would be satisfactory for the loss of a week: 'I thanked him cordially — I did not say it was the easiest 1,000 I had ever made in my life.'

An income of $22,000 for professional services was a substantial one in 1918, undreamed of for him. And it was the return for only part of a year's work. The first half of the year and more had been almost entirely devoted to the completion of *Industry and Humanity*. 'Even at this moment . . . I am making $1,000 a week, supplied with a Secretary and all his and my own expenses & a chance of doing even better than this on occasions.'

XIII

Mackenzie King had just finished reviewing his successes in 1918 as an industrial counsellor when the possibility of another kind of career presented itself. He could have become, if he had wished, director of the Carnegie Corporation of New York, a corporation with an endowment of over $130 million. As director he would be responsible for the expenditure of the income from this vast trust. It would mean a large measure of control of all the other Carnegie endowments, such as the Carnegie Institute at Pittsburgh, the Carnegie Institution at Washington, the Carnegie Hero Fund, the Carnegie Foundation for the Advancement of Learning, and the Carnegie Peace Foundation.

This was the opportunity that was opened to him on the last Sunday of the old year when he made an afternoon call at the home of Mr. and Mrs. Andrew Carnegie on East 91st Street. He had come to know the Carnegies early in 1917 when he had been introduced to them by his Quaker friend Allan Baker, of London, England, a member of the British House of Commons who was also a close friend of the Carnegies. Mr. and Mrs. Carnegie had taken a fancy to the young Canadian from the time of their first meeting, and he had enjoyed occasional visits with them in New York and at their summer place in Lennox. He admired them both and was especially impressed by the charm, character, and ability of his hostess. Because of her husband's advancing years and failing health she had been obliged to take on new responsibilities relating to his many philanthropic ventures. Their talk on that Sunday afternoon was necessarily a brief one, for Mackenzie King had to return to Ottawa on an evening train. Mrs. Carnegie was graciousness itself. She told him that she had an important message for him from her husband and herself, but she preferred that the definite proposal should be broken to him by their confidential secretary, John Poynton. Accordingly a meeting with Poynton was arranged immediately and the two men dined together at 'The Netherlands'. Poynton came to the point at once and told King that it was Mr. and Mrs. Carnegie's wish that he should become the director of the Carnegie Corporation. Apparently they had already expressed their wishes to Elihu Root, a close personal adviser, and he in turn had talked it over with his fellow trustees of the corporation. Both Mr. and Mrs. Carnegie, Poynton frankly told Mackenzie King, had confidence in and real affection for him. The salary suggested was $25,000. But there were other possibilities. Poynton spoke of the writing of Carnegie's life: 'Tho' not definitely so expressed I know were I to offer to do this work it would be entrusted to me and that I could have the sum of $100,000 for the doing of it, if desired.'

It was an astounding and exciting proposal. Mackenzie King was overwhelmed: 'Were I to go the world over, it is impossible to conceive anywhere, on either side of the Ocean, where an opening more attractive could be presented. To accept such an offer is a great responsibility, to reject it is equally a great responsibility.' For the moment the future took on roseate hues: 'Here is the promise of a life full of great opportunity and free from anxieties and harassments of every kind. It would mean going to live in New York, being able to have a comfortable house and library there, to meet the best people of the world, to be in touch in a commanding way with the affairs of the world on the subjects which I have most at heart, industrial peace, international peace, social well-being. It would mean fine opportunity of study and rest and enjoyment, a life of the highest kind of intellectual enjoyment and spiritual enjoyment as well, since the opportunity of helping others is what it is.' He could see that there was at least one serious drawback: 'I doubt if I should like to live continually in New York,' he told himself, 'tho' in such a position as the Carnegie one I could have a circle of inspiring friends & influences. Marriage wd. change the rest.' He was not unmindful of its promise of financial independence and what this would mean if he should ultimately return to political life: 'I could lay aside one or two hundred thousand dollars in a very short time and still be young enough to take an active part in politics & be perfectly independent.' Was it, or was it not, his life's greatest opportunity?

Sir Wilfrid Laurier, who naturally was the first one in Ottawa with whom he discussed the Carnegie proposal after he returned from New York, was impressed by the Carnegie offer, but assumed that, in spite of its attractiveness financially, it would not be accepted. When they discussed it on Sunday afternoon, January 5, Sir Wilfrid's 'last words at the door were that my future was in parliament, in Canadian politics'; but, he added, acceptance of the Carnegie offer '& subsequent rejection of 25,000 a year [in the event of a return to public life] would only make me stronger than ever.'

In New York a week later, he talked with Mr. and Mrs. Carnegie again and with several officers and trustees of the Carnegie Foundation. John Poynton spoke of the relationship as one in which he would become 'Mr. and Mrs. Carnegie's "Philanthropic son" just as Charlie Schwab was their "Business son". ' Mr. Carnegie spoke of his being with them at Skibo (their estate in Scotland), in the summer, as if the association were an accomplished fact. But Mrs. Carnegie could not have been in doubt, before their talks ended, that Mackenzie King thought of the possibility of his future as lying elsewhere. She had realized that his heart was in political life in Canada, and that it was perhaps too much to ask him to abandon it. He left feeling 'what a truly noble and fine woman' she was and that he would do all in his power to be of service to her. At the same time he felt, as he wrote in his diary, that 'my life is cast rather in the work of the world than in the secluded spots, & easy path'.

The matter was left open, since no immediate appointment was contemplated. It came up again in May when he told Poynton frankly that he doubted if he would take the position of director, not only because of his political hopes but because he would prefer to continue with his present work — he liked the freedom and the considerable opportunities it afforded. He had given most of his life and thought to problems affecting labour, and he felt he should adhere to this 'so long as opportunities presented'.

This was the end of the Carnegie episode. The invitation in itself was a tribute, a recognition of worth; his unwillingness to accept it, a proof of his determination to hold to the course for which he had prepared himself, either in politics, if the Canadian electorate would accept him, or in the field of industrial relations. That decision reflected the fact that money-making in itself held a very unimportant place in his thinking, and that a life of ease in which his best abilities would not be challenged had no real or lasting appeal for him. He needed action, he wrote, for the highest expression of his nature: 'The primrose path does not make for greatness in any true sense. To be a benefactor with someone else's money is not as noble a part as giving one's own life in the service of others. It is life service that must be my part to be true to myself and my traditions.'

XIV

To Rockefeller, disclosure of the Carnegie offer had come as a shock: 'He seemed quite depressed when I told him of what had transpired.' He had assumed that competition from political quarters was no longer a major consideration; *Industry and Humanity*, which had claimed so much time and attention, was out of the way, and he was hoping that King would now concentrate on his (Rockefeller's) own work. Instead, he was faced with competition from another and unexpected source. He was disposed to disparage the offer made by his chief rival in the field of philanthropy. He understood, he said, that the Carnegie Corporation was mostly a 'holding' corporation, and that the part of director would not demand all that King was able to give. 'He thought public life was the one extreme in strain, that the C.C. was the other extreme . . . That my present work seemed the biggest field of service.' It seemed clear that both Mr. and Mrs. Rockefeller would prefer to see him go into politics rather than into the Carnegie Corporation.

It was not long before they got down to bargaining, in a spirit of amity, about their future business relations, such matters as allocation of time between the Rockefeller and other interests, guarantees of remuneration, place of residence, and participation in Canadian politics. On Mackenzie King's part there was no thought of any permanent commitment unless, of course, his hopes for a future in Canadian public life were dashed irretrievably. So long as these hopes were kept alive, he could deprecate the American way of life, in private of course, and contrast it with the Canadian, as freely as he liked. In the privacy of his diary, as he ruminated on the pros and cons of the alternatives facing him, he gave vent to feelings that perhaps had always been in the back of his mind: 'I doubt if I could be happy continuing indefinitely with Mr. R. & doing work for large corporations. I have never regarded the connection other than as "a stepping-stone", a means to lay aside enough "to get into the fight". Against both the Rockefeller and Carnegie connections [it sounded strangely like 'a plague o' both your houses'] I have the feeling of dislike to associations with wealth, save enough for an independent political career & to enable me to marry and have a family. I believe there is a handicap to the highest service in the industrial world thro' either of these associations.'

It was in his mind that if he returned to politics merely as a private member he might be able to continue his association with Rockefeller on a part-time basis: 'I could be his friend and counsellor still, at his hand close by.' He would, however, prefer a complete break: 'I cannot see myself a part of New York and America more than I have already become.'

Uppermost in his mind at all times was this aversion to breaking ties with his own country: 'To hold to Canada then, even if it means for a while continuing the Rockefeller connection, which I should be happier free of altogether, save for the funds it helps to supply, would seem to be wise.' His heart's desire for service in public life in Canada remained steadfast: 'To live and die honored and respected there is closer to my heart than any other ambition. To change to another country at my age is not to enjoy the peace of mind and heart which a political career in Canada would afford.'

While Rockefeller was most anxious to retain Mackenzie King's services as personal counsellor, he was probably unaware of the increasingly radical tinge King's thinking was taking on. He and some of King's capitalistic clients might well have questioned the soundness of such doctrines as he outlined in his diary:

Of one thing I am certain, and that is that the accepted practices incidental to the accumulation of wealth under existing conditions are wholly wrong, and that my part in life must be along the direction of exposing what is in error fundamentally, and in helping to bring about such changes in the relations of Labor and Capital as will ensure greater justice to the worker. I am certain in my own mind that the revolution which time will effect, and which we are at the beginning of already, is one which will wholly reverse the positions of Capital and Labor, and will give to the return upon investment in the form of capital a consideration secondary to that which is given to the conditions under which men and women are called upon to labor. Capital is entitled to a return as a reward of saving; but that should necessarily be a small return where the element of risk can be overcome. As matters now stand, Capital now robs Management, Labor, and the Community of a large part of what each ought, in any system of rewards through social service, to be justly entitled.

This would have been too strong meat for even John D. Rockefeller, Jr., but he and the Standard Oil management had confidence in King because his proposals were practical rather than theoretical; they had accepted reforms which represented a first step towards industrial democracy, and they had introduced them as if they had been their own.

It was because of this confidence in him that Rockefeller had been so anxious to retain his services. For his part, Mackenzie King was happy with the arrangements as finally worked out between them. Among other things, it had been agreed that he should make the contemplated trip to England to continue his studies there and, more important still, it had been understood that he should not be cut off from political activities in his own country.

At this very time new and exciting developments were taking place in Canada — developments with which his own interests were inextricably woven. But for the present he was committed to the trip to England. The day of his departure was fixed for May 15. As it turned out, this date, while it was not the end of his personal relations with Rockefeller, was to mark the end of his career as industrial counsellor in the United States.

CHAPTER 15

A Political Setback in 1917

During his years of work with the Rockefeller Foundation and as industrial counsellor, Mackenzie King had never lost touch with the political scene in Canada. His relations with Laurier remained intimate, and he continued to hold a place of influence in the Liberal Party. He had given a minimum of attention to the riding of North York, where in 1913 he had been nominated as Liberal candidate. In spite of the urgent appeals of his supporters to make at least an appearance in the riding, his visits were infrequent. J. M. Walton, the energetic secretary of the North York Reform Association, kept up a steady barrage of appeals which increased in volume and vehemence with every rumour of an election – and there were many such rumours – and with every flutter of activity in the local Tory organization. 'You must get here visibly,' he pleaded. 'I fear for the results if you don't appear; absence is your only danger; it is about as urgent as that you should make your appearance at your own wedding.' Time and again Mackenzie King repeated his willingness to have them choose another candidate, and each time he was reassured, as he expected to be, that his followers would give no thought to such a change. His counter-appeal to them was to make up for his necessary absence by doing more effective work in organizing themselves. He had yielded to local pressure, however, by spending the month of August 1916 with his mother and father, at a farm-house near Aurora, a visit which was interrupted only by his response to an appeal from Sir Wilfrid to speak with him at an immense recruiting rally in Sherbrooke.

In spite of his neglect of the riding, he was optimistic about the outcome of an election, and so were his North York supporters. If one were called – and normally it would have to come before October 1916 – he promised them he would return by the first train. Writing in April 1915 from Colorado, where he had been receiving reports from Ottawa, he encouraged them: 'With all that there has been of scandal, I am sure we will have no difficulty in North York, and I should not be surprised if as a party we swept the country.' At this time Sir Wilfrid Laurier himself was optimistic: the Roblin Conservative government in Manitoba had been discountenanced, and good news from every other province had convinced him that the Borden government, if Parliament were dissolved, 'would go to the country very much discredited and with the open hostility of the best elements in their party.'

II

Optimism still reigned at the end of the year, when a large gathering of Liberals met in Ottawa to discuss plans for the party's future. Mackenzie King took an important part in these discussions, and when the National Liberal Advisory Committee was set up he was active on two sub-committees, one on technical education and the other on social reform and health legislation. This committee, a few months later, recommended 'a federal measure of old age and mothers' pensions and national insurance as soon as practicable against sickness and unemployment'.

Liberal activities before the end of 1915 were obviously in preparation for an event that had to be postponed. War news from overseas was definitely bad, heavy Canadian casualties were reported, and under such conditions the Government saw good reason for not going to the country, while on his part Sir Wilfrid

Laurier was anxious to avoid any appearance of forcing an election. Sir Robert Borden had spent two months in England and France and had been appalled by the loss of Canadian lives and deeply impressed by the need of increasing the Canadian expeditionary forces. Soon after his return to Canada in September, an increase of 100,000 men was authorized, and on December 31 the objective was further increased to 500,000 men. Enlistments had been reasonably satisfactory — 385,000 Canadians had volunteered by the end of 1916 — and there was no suggestion of conscription. Continuance of the party truce was obviously desirable, and Sir Wilfrid finally agreed, in February 1916, after months of negotiations, to an extension of the parliamentary term for one year, on the understanding that no controversial measures would be introduced. Some of Sir Wilfrid's advisers were opposed to the extension, but Mackenzie King was one who encouraged it. He was impressed, as Sir Wilfrid was, with the arguments that refusal to agree to an extension would have precipitated an election, would have added to internal dissensions, and would have diverted the energies of the Government from its main responsibility in the conduct of the war. This was no time for political campaigning — on this Sir Wilfrid could readily agree with Sir Robert.

Mackenzie King had done his part in encouraging the cessation of party strife in wartime. He had helped to establish the Canadian Patriotic Fund and he assisted in raising money for its purposes. To a degree he was concerned about his neglect of North York, but 'more than all,' he wrote, 'I feel the neglect of work in connection with this war. I should like to be taking some active part, and yet, save raising funds by speaking, there is little I can with advantage turn to. Recruiting I don't like, I cannot ask other men to go to fight when I don't go myself, and to go myself, with the obligations of father, mother and Max and his family, and the opportunities of larger service to the same cause — freedom — which I have, would seem to evidence a lack of perspective.' There was actually no occasion for him to be on the defensive, as he too frequently seemed to be during the war and afterwards. This, viewed in proper perspective, became abundantly apparent in later years. It had been his lot to have other responsibilities and opportunities in a field where his special qualifications and experience were put to their most effective use in the total war effort. This had been proved by the increase in supplies of coal and steel in Colorado as a result of improved labour relations; and was confirmed by what he accomplished in other war industries.

Developments in the political world in the early part of 1917 were disturbing, for rumours persisted of an early general election. Mackenzie King was hoping that, with all its disruptive effects, it might be avoided. In view, however, of Sir Wilfrid's unwillingness to consent to another extension of the parliamentary term, it seemed to be inevitable. At the meeting of the Ontario Reform Association late in November, the Liberal candidates shared Sir Wilfrid's expectation of an early election and his confidence of victory at the polls. Mackenzie King had been reluctant to attend the meeting, but finally decided that his absence would be commented upon, and that he 'must take no chances from now on which are likely to imperil the results at the elections whenever they come'. He was beginning to share Sir Wilfrid's optimism, and his own faith in destiny was returning: 'I have paid little or no attention to the riding, but I have a feeling that there is a sort of destiny about these matters and think when the time comes the interest aroused by a campaign will outweigh everything else — what has been done & what has been left undone. It looks like a revolt of the people against the Government that is impending.'

He was not completely satisfied that Sir Wilfrid's optimism was justified, but he was impressed by it. In late November Sir Wilfrid was 'in splendid form' at a small luncheon gathering, 'quite keen on an early appeal to the people and evidently confident of being returned. . . . He scouted all mention of a Coalition before or after election.' Two weeks later he spoke of Toronto and London as being the only centres in Canada where his followers were afraid of an election in wartime. Confident of 'certain victory', he was surprised that Mackenzie King did not share his optimism: 'He told me that I was more afraid of bringing on a fight than he was.' Mackenzie King's reply was that he 'simply wanted to avoid undue haste, in the event of other matters arising which wd. not require his forcing the issue. That even peace might now come within the next 6 months & at any rate the talk of it wd. be a reason for not granting extension early in the session.' He saw the possibilities of an early peace in the announcement that very day of Germany's peace proposals, which might mean, he thought, 'the beginning of the end'. He had called on Laurier that afternoon with his Quaker friend Allan Baker. Sir Wilfrid had taken a liking to Baker, and their serious talk had ended on a lighter note with Mackenzie King's facetious remark, which Sir Wilfrid greeted with hearty laughter, that 'if Sir Wilfrid were not a Catholic he would be a Quaker'. But King and Baker were in dead earnest, and both of them cabled to Lloyd George the next day urging that any peace proposals must include disarmament and security against future wars. 'England,' he wrote in his diary, 'has a great opportunity to lead the world in disarmament now.' This turned out to be another false hope.

III

An election was becoming more and more probable. 'If I am not much mistaken,' Mackenzie King wrote in mid-December, 'if God spares me in health and strength, I will be busily occupied in public affairs next year.' Always a believer in signs, he recorded on the last page of his 1916 diary an incident which he interpreted as supporting his expectation of return to office within the next year. He had found a five-cent piece in the snow in the middle of Sparks Street and was surprised to see on it the King's head: 'If it be an omen it may mean a King's commission with sufficient to carry it out in the New Year.' An even more convincing portent was Sir Wilfrid's frequently expressed determination to force an election by refusing to grant another parliamentary extension.

It had become clear enough, even before the end of 1916, that conscription was more than a remote possibility. Recruiting on the basis of voluntary enlistment had been exceedingly slow in the latter half of the year and casualties had been heavy on the front lines. The Government had established a National Service Board in October, with R. B. Bennett as director-general. It was designed to make an inventory of Canadian manpower, and the purpose of the national registration which followed was 'to identify and keep within Canada those who could give better service at home and to identify and induce to serve in the field those who could and ought so to serve'. Registration was carried out in January and was considered by many as a first step toward conscription. Fears were expressed widely that a conscription programme would seriously reduce the manpower so necessary to maintain production in agriculture and in the munitions industries. Labour leaders were apprehensive and sought assurances from Borden, only to be told that voluntary national service was urged in order that conscription might be unnecessary. The Prime Minister added, however, that while he hoped conscription would not be necessary, if it proved to be the only effective method he would not hesitate to use it. Coupled with the national registration campaign was a stepping-up of the recruiting programme, but results were far from adequate to supply the necessary reinforcements.

IV

That was the situation when Parliament met on January 18, 1917, a session which was adjourned within three weeks to enable Sir Robert Borden to attend meetings of the Imperial War Cabinet and the Imperial War Conference in London. He left Canada on February 14, had innumerable discussions with political and military leaders, visited the battlefields and the Canadian hospitals, and did not return until May 15. During that three-month period Borden saw enough to justify his worst fears. The Canadian expeditionary force had suffered severe losses in taking Vimy Ridge and in other engagements; the Russian revolution had paralysed Russia's war effort, thus enabling Germany to concentrate on the

western front; and Germany had entered upon its intensive sub-
marine campaign. One cheering note was the entry of the United
States into the war, but it would be months before the American
armies could take the field. On the basis of his first-hand survey of
war conditions and reports from Ottawa, Borden came to the conclusion, before he left England, that 'any further effort for voluntary enlistment would provide very meagre and wholly inadequate
results'. Four days after his return to Canada he announced in
Parliament the Government's conclusion 'that compulsory military
service was necessary'.

Up to the time of that announcement Mackenzie King had been
relatively free of political concerns: 'I seem to have little heart for
politics and strife,' he wrote in February. 'I have thought much
today of going to Toronto to live in the Fall.' That, however, was
only 'a passing mood'; 'the days and outlook will lighten again'.
In the early months of the year he had several talks with Sir Wilfrid
Laurier and had taken part in a few conferences on party strategy.

Talk of conscription, parliamentary extension, and coalition was
much in the air even before Borden's return. Mackenzie King
argued with Laurier, but made no headway, in favour of a conscription measure that would apply to productive industries as
well as to military service. Sir Wilfrid was opposed to conscription
of any kind: 'I told him I thought it was a right principle though I
disliked it, but that it seemed right to give an alternative for service
in our industries. He debated this, but I urged it strongly. He
thought those who had relatives at the front favored conscription
but others didn't. — I think leadership is needed here. I urged
strongly for a constructive program.' Mackenzie King amplified
his views slightly when he wrote in his diary on the following day:
'I feel Conscription to be the only fair method in defensive necessity. I have changed my views on conscription as the war has pro-
gressed and I have seen freedom threatened. But the need for overseas service does not seem to be as imperative for Canada as more
effective use of her manpower in industries that may help the situation.'

Opposed to a general election in wartime, he pressed strongly for a further extension of the parliamentary term. 'How I hope,' he wrote in his diary after a meeting of Liberals in May, 'a general election may be avoided. Were Borden to bring in conscription, as we hear he is likely to, I think the Liberal Party should extend the life of Parliament at least six months. It will be a difficult measure to enforce and may cost his party its life. If the Liberals are wise they will put the responsibility on him and leave him the consequences.' It was at this meeting, which he described as 'trying and tense', that 'Sir Wilfrid spoke of being an old man, 75, and of it not being his business to lead if they could not agree. He brought this up several times. I felt he was making way for himself to resign the leadership if conscription is proposed and he can't get the party behind him.' Three days later King repeated his hope that the Liberal Party would see the wisdom, under the circumstances, of granting the extension: 'It would ease my mind greatly if this could be definitely decided.' Laurier, however, continued to be unalterably opposed to any further extension, and the Liberals in Parliament agreed with him.

It distressed Mackenzie King to realize that on the most important issues of the day his views did not coincide with Sir Wilfrid's and that he could make no impression on him or on the Liberal members of Parliament. Discouraged, he decided not to attend an all-day meeting of the party to be held in Sir Wilfrid's office a few days later: 'I felt to attend would mean I would oppose those present, on favoring conscription, & being favorable to an extension, and this to no end. Where one only antagonizes, and knows there is little service to be rendered, it is as well to avoid encounters with jealous men.' He knew, as Laurier's other supporters knew, that Sir Wilfrid would not insist on loyalty to himself if a higher loyalty, to conscience, dictated another course. Weeks later, in the House of Commons, he expressed no bitterness when he found himself 'estranged from friends who were just as near and dear to me as any of my own brothers . . . such an estrangement, even if it be only temporary and upon this question only, is a wrench at one's very

heart strings; but every one of my honourable friends knows that
I have not tried to impose my views upon any of my followers. I
respect their consciences.'

V

Possibilities of estrangement loomed ominously when Sir Robert
Borden announced, on May 18, that the Government would introduce shortly a Military Service Bill. This was followed, within a
week, by his invitation to Sir Wilfrid Laurier to join in the formation of a coalition government for the purpose of carrying out the
conscription programme. In such a coalition the two parties would
have had equal numbers outside the office of prime minister. With
the majority he had in the House, Borden could have secured the
enactment of the bill, but without Sir Wilfrid's agreement to an
extension of the parliamentary term he would have to call an election in October, an election in which conscription would be the
central issue. As head of a coalition government that included
Laurier, he could face an election with confidence; but he feared
that in a straight party fight, in which the one party favoured conscription and the other opposed it, Sir Wilfrid might muster enough
strength in the English-speaking provinces, in addition to his solid
Quebec following, to carry the day. Laurier might, indeed, recap-
ture the allegiance of the Liberal conscriptionists by agreeing to
submit the question to a referendum after the election and agreeing
to abide by the decision of the electorate. Even if this proposal were
not acceptable to them, Laurier could still count on substantial
strength from his other parliamentary supporters, and from Liberals and even Conservatives throughout the country who were opposed to conscription. On the other hand, many consultations had
made Laurier realize that his own party was sharply divided: a
small but influential minority advised coalition, conscription, and
extension; the majority were opposed, as he was, to all three.

Mackenzie King, who had three long talks with Sir Wilfrid in
this period, feared that an election fought on the question of mili-

tary conscription alone would result in the annihilation of the Liberal Party, and again he pressed Laurier to adopt a programme of compulsory national service which would provide for a selective draft of men either into the armed forces or into productive industries. If Borden could be induced to accept this, an election could be avoided and Sir Wilfrid's main objection to coalition and to extension would be removed. An alternative suggestion was to agree to another parliamentary extension if the Government would agree to submit the conscription issue to the people by means of a referendum. Sir Wilfrid expressed himself vigorously against all three possibilities — coalition, conscription, extension — and in favour of an election as the one thing that would clear the air and settle the conscription question once for all — all parties would submit to the outcome. He was confident of victory — though not in Ontario — if an election were called. He would be willing to announce before an election that, if returned, the Liberal Party would take a referendum, but he was sure that the Ontario Liberal conscriptionists would not accept this. Mackenzie King then threw his weight behind the referendum proposal — an immediate referendum which would permit the Ontario Liberals to express their approval of compulsory military service without repudiating Laurier's leadership. Laurier was willing to accept this solution, but was certain that Borden would not acquiesce and he questioned if the Ontario Liberals would. Mackenzie King sought to convince his friend J. E. Atkinson, of the Toronto *Star*, but Atkinson, whose paper had come out strongly in favour of conscription, refused to consider a proposal that would mean only delay in meeting the urgent need for reinforcements. That was the view, too, of the Ontario conscriptionist Liberals. Foiled in these attempts at conciliation, Mackenzie King could only plead with Laurier to avoid if possible an open fight solely on military conscription and to emphasize the need for national unity if the country were to make its maximum contribution to the winning of the war. An open fight would only intensify existing bitterness and impede the national war effort.

After a fortnight of negotiations with Borden and of conferences with his own colleagues, Laurier announced his decision – he could not join the proposed coalition because he was opposed to conscription. In his letter to Borden he added that if conscription were adopted after a referendum or an election he would 'certainly urge in every possible way obedience to the law'.

If Sir Wilfrid had agreed to coalition and conscription it would have meant, as King told W. H. S. Cane, president of the North York Reform Association, 'that Quebec would have immediately come under the leadership of Bourassa and Lavergne, who would have been able to organize the Province as a whole against not only conscription, but possibly also against further aid in the war'. Even if a referendum were called, Sir Wilfrid would have to oppose conscription. Mackenzie King would then have been in the embarrassing position of advocating an opposite view. He made a clear statement of his attitude in a letter to Thomas Urquhart on July 31: 'I have been and am in favor of the principle of conscription. Had there been a referendum I should have done what I could to help the referendum carry.'

VI

Faced with Laurier's rejection of his coalition proposals, Borden immediately entered into negotiations with four prominent Liberals. None of them, favourable though they were to conscription, would agree to accept office. The Military Service Bill was introduced on June 11 and Sir Wilfrid moved an amendment to defer further consideration of the bill until after its basic principle was submitted to the people by means of a referendum. The referendum proposal was supported by the Quebec Liberals and Nationalists, as well as by seven other Liberals who then voted for the main motion. The bill was given third reading on July 24 by a vote of 102 to 44, with eighteen Liberals, among them some of Laurier's strongest supporters, voting for the conscription measure. The introduction of the Military Service Bill and the assurance of its enactment removed all uncertainty about an election. Borden had moved, on July 17, for a parliamentary extension, which would have postponed it, but Liberal opposition was solid, and the motion was defeated by the narrow margin of twenty votes, 82 to 62.

In the four months that intervened between Borden's proposal to Sir Wilfrid and the establishment of the Union government in October, Mackenzie King's mind was in a state of turmoil and discouragement. Many factors contributed to his depression: rumours of dissension within his North York organization, violent antagonism of the Ontario press, strained relations with former Liberal colleagues, and, above all, disagreement with Sir Wilfrid on conscription, coalition, and parliamentary extension. Much has been written of the exciting political manoeuvres of the weeks and months that preceded the announcement of Union government. Little has been known of the commotion within Mackenzie King's mind as he pondered the possibility of quitting politics altogether, with all its uncertainties and only one apparent certainty — defeat. It was characteristic of him that he kept these inner thoughts to himself — but he did confide them to his diary, and to his brother in Denver in his long weekly letters.

There were times when he permitted himself to hope, as he did on July 20, after a meeting of forty-five Ontario Liberal members and candidates. The meeting, held in Toronto, had been called by a few conscriptionist Liberals who evidently expected that their Ontario colleagues would swing into line with their views on conscription and coalition. To their surprise, and indeed to the surprise of Mackenzie King and most of the others, the meeting declared, by a large majority, against conscription and coalition and in favour of an immediate general election. The meeting was solid in its expression of confidence in the leadership of Sir Wilfrid. Mackenzie King expressed himself as 'against the attempt to coerce an entire province, believing that conscription wd. lead to passive resistance, & wd. lead to a display of internal weakness. National unity regarded as the first essential.' When he visited North York the next day he found that some important members of the riding executive were strong for conscription and inclined to be opposed to the position taken by the Liberals at the Toronto meeting the day before. Their attitude was modified to some extent, however, when he explained the difficulty of Sir Wilfrid's position and the consequences of the enforcement of conscription. This was one of the days when his spirits mounted: 'I felt today that I wd. be able to carry North York & I feel I am living a full life & a useful one in the thick of politics.'

His optimism was short-lived. Sir Wilfrid was encouraged by King's report of the Toronto meeting but could not agree to his proposals, submitted in a carefully drafted resolution, that the maintenance of national unity should be the central theme of the Liberal campaign, and that the party should not be drawn into a straight fight on the moral issue of conscription. He felt rebuffed by Sir Wilfrid's response to his suggestions, but he was not completely disheartened, for he wrote: 'But for faith in the unseen future & belief in the right of the position & its ultimate triumph I wd. even yet hesitate, but I feel the "call of the blood" to go on & my whole nature answers to it.'

Disquieting news soon came from North York, however, reporting continued dissatisfaction on the part of the conscriptionist Liberals and even suggestions that another candidate might be more acceptable (an acclamation for N. W. Rowell or for some Liberal soldier in France for the period of the war). Disturbing letters of strong protest came, too, from several influential constituents, notably Thomas Urquhart (a former mayor of Toronto) and P. W. Pearson of Newmarket. Other letters reflected the mild questioning of members of his inner circle of friends in the riding. The situation was becoming, as he wrote, 'a trying one'. He felt he must hold fast to his 'convictions against leading the country into dissension. I shall tell the executive my views, if there be any question, & give them a chance to have a new candidate — in many ways it is a mistake for me to go thro' the vicious campaign that will be waged only to be misunderstood & to lose. If they will back my convictions I shall run, otherwise I shall retire without regret.'

It is striking that in almost every diary entry in these weeks in which he refers to the possibility of withdrawal from the contest, he ends up with a 'however' or a 'but' — he might have to leave the field but his deep-seated preference was to stay. 'The more I think of an election and what it means if successful,' he wrote on July 29, 'the more foolish it seems to risk separation from the Foundation work to be drawn into turmoil of the kind. If I did not feel it was "my life" and that the real purpose of it lay in public life, I would abandon the thought of running. With the obligations I have the financial worries would be I fear too exacting. Besides I get exasperated at the hypocrisies of it, but [again the 'but'] this is a reason for going in.'

Cheering news came on August 7 from Winnipeg, where a convention of rank-and-file Liberals declared allegiance to Laurier and opposition to coalition, with no clear commitment in favour of conscription. Mackenzie King saw in this an assurance of 'a solid West' and a challenge to the defecting Liberals: 'The men who have forsaken Sir Wilfrid in this crisis will rue the day yet.' He saw in Borden's continued efforts to form a union government 'a means of burying the misdeeds of five years to get Toryism into power again'. As for himself, he declared that he would support no government with Borden as leader, but would oppose it 'for all I am worth'. 'I don't look forward to the contest with any relish,' he wrote to his brother on the following day, 'but I believe Sir Wilfrid will sweep the country.'

VII

Strong pressure was applied to Mackenzie King at this time by prominent Liberals in Quebec, to induce him to take a leading part in the Ontario campaign on Laurier's behalf. S. W. Jacobs, M.P., and Senator William Mitchell pleaded with him by letter and interview, an appeal that was strengthened by their expressed conviction that his acceptance would mean ultimately his leadership of the Liberal Party when Sir Wilfrid dropped out, and by their assurance

that if he should be defeated in North York a Quebec seat would
certainly be found for him. Mackenzie King had many reasons for
not yielding to this pressure. He doubted his ability to produce
results without financial backing, without support from the press,
and without any semblance of a political organization. There was,
too, the memory of the defeat he had suffered in North Waterloo in
1911 when he responded too freely to outside invitations and lost
the seat he might have retained by closer attention to his own riding. He felt honoured by the invitation from Jacobs and Mitchell,
but it had to be declined.

Before the end of August he was feeling less inclined than ever
to engage in 'the political turmoil', but newspaper reports of the
Government's introduction of the War Time Elections Act
aroused his fighting spirit. He 'felt indignant' that the Government
should take away rights of citizenship from naturalized citizens; it
was 'outrageous' that conscientious objectors such as Quakers (of
whom there were many in North York — 'most of them Liberal')
should be deprived of the vote, and that the extension of the franchise to women should be limited to soldiers' female relatives. He
was to learn later of an objectionable feature of the Military Voters
Act which would permit men in the Canadian Army overseas who
had never seen Canada to have their ballots assigned to any constituency they pleased. His first impulse was to gird himself for the
battle. 'It makes me feel I can take part in a fight. . . . When I see
rights of citizenship invaded I feel I do not mind defeat.' But he had
to consider his other responsibilities. To his brother he wrote that
he was 'almost contemplating dropping out of politics. . . . As
respects that, however, I have been doing as I have been advising
you, just letting each day work out the problem for itself. I always
remember what Sir Edward Grey said to me, that it never does to
plan far ahead, events determine for us the course of our lives. To
be right in each step at the time it is made should be the supreme
endeavor.' One event, a few days later, helped to determine his
course. He went to a meeting of Liberals in North York still feeling
that he would gladly give up running, but the welcome he received

inspired new hope, and he wrote: 'After listening to all the speeches, seeing the genuine good-will entertained towards me and feeling the opportunity of the issue in the present compaign, I feel that here after all is my true life. . . . I believe too I can carry the riding.' He was less hopeful of the result two weeks later, but 'whatever the outcome,' he wrote to his brother in September, 'I shall be in the fight.'

VIII

In all these weeks of Mackenzie King's uncertainty and indecision, of alternate hoping and despairing, Sir Robert Borden was going ahead with his plans for a Union government. He had had little difficulty in persuading C. C. Ballantyne and Hugh Guthrie to join him, but other Liberals in the Maritimes and Ontario were harder to convince — they favoured conscription and a national government, but they had qualms about forsaking Laurier. Negotiations with outstanding Liberal leaders in the West, largely through Sir Clifford Sifton, at first raised Borden's hopes. Sifton had reported to him at the end of July that the Liberal governments of the West were unanimously in favour of coalition. But the adverse vote at the Winnipeg convention on August 7 showed that he had underestimated the strength of the resistance of the Liberal rank and file in the prairie provinces. The convention, and the Toronto meeting of Liberals a fortnight earlier, had for the moment put new heart into the Liberals. Undismayed, Borden renewed his appeal to Laurier, at a meeting at Rideau Hall which the Governor General had convened.* The appeal was unsuccessful. Laurier insisted that no government should impose conscription without a clear mandate from the country in a general election. He was confident then of a Liberal victory in a straight party fight; he would be much less confident, of course, if Borden could induce any substantial number of prominent Liberals to join a Union government.

---

* Present at this conference, on August 9, were: the Duke of Devonshire, Sir Robert Borden, Sir Wilfrid Laurier, Sir George Foster, Sir Lomer Gouin, Lord Shaughnessy, and Sir Clifford Sifton.

Realizing that his own leadership might be the stumbling-block to such a coalition, Borden then proposed to two of his close advisers (Arthur Meighen and Dr. J. D. Reid) that Mr. Justice Lyman P. Duff of the Supreme Court of Canada be called upon to form a Union government. Both of his advisers 'fiercely opposed' the suggestion. They reacted similarly when he suggested Sir Robert Falconer, then president of the University of Toronto. Sir Clifford Sifton spoke of Sir William Meredith, Chief Justice of Ontario, but in the opinion of Meighen and Reid his leadership would have been disastrous. When Sifton reported T. A. Crerar's suggestion of Sir George Foster or Sir Charles Hibbert Tupper, Borden said he 'would hold up both hands for Foster', but his colleagues would not hear of it. The last and most forceful opposition to Borden's leadership came from the four Liberals in the West, J. A. Calder, T. A. Crerar, A. B. Hudson, and A. L. Sifton, whose support had been ardently sought. Their telegram from Winnipeg on August 26, addressed to Borden, declared bluntly: 'Change of leadership essential. Suggest Foster, Beck, or Mulock.'* They added: 'Subject to satisfactory arrangements with new leader anticipate strong Eastern colleagues willing to [co-operate].' Such a proposal was, of course, completely unacceptable to Borden's colleagues, in council and in caucus — some of them were 'very violent' in their opposition. All thought of a change in leadership was thereupon abandoned.

Unsuccessful in their attempts to dislodge Borden from the Conservative leadership, the same conscriptionist Liberals turned their attention to Laurier and tried to persuade him to relinquish the leadership of the Liberal Party. They made the attempt in the first week of October. J. A. Calder was the chief spokesman for a group that included Carvell, E. M. Macdonald, Pardee, and Fielding. After the meeting, Sir Wilfrid told Mackenzie King what they had said, that 'it was impossible to win with a French leader, that the conscriptionist Liberals saw no hope of victory with Sir W. at

* Sir George Foster, Minister of Trade and Commerce; Sir Adam Beck, chairman of the Hydro-Electric Power Commission of Ontario; Sir William Mulock, Chief Justice of the Exchequer Division of the Ontario High Court of Justice.

the head. . . . Fielding said that he had strongly scouted the idea of a change of leadership, but had come to the conclusion it was necessary.' When Sir Wilfrid asked them who would be the new leader, Calder replied that 'he thought Carvell was the man the West had most confidence in, that he shld. be the man'. Ballantyne and Guthrie had already been sworn in and Rowell was under heavy pressure, but Sir Wilfrid was still hoping against hope that Rowell and the other Liberals Borden had approached would remain faithful to him. He said he did not propose to be a leader without a party, but he would gladly step down into the ranks if this were the desire of the party. He said he would consult his friends in Toronto and Montreal, but the meeting did not end without a parting shot: 'Do you mean to tell me that because of my origin I cannot be a Liberal Leader! You tell me you will not have a referendum because the people do not want it, and yet you will not allow a man to lead who represents the view the people have.' One of the friends he consulted was Mackenzie King, whose advice was that these few men had no right to speak for the party and that they should be told that if there was to be a new leader he should be chosen by a convention of delegates from all ridings in Canada. 'This,' he said, 'would soon silence the few whose conception of their own importance had turned their heads.' Nothing came of the incipient mutiny other than the withdrawal from the Liberal Party of the members of the group who had objected to Laurier's leadership. Within a week they withdrew their opposition to Borden's leadership of his party and several of them accepted his invitation to join his Cabinet. On October 12 the Union government was thereupon established, composed of nine Liberals: Crerar, Calder, and A. L. Sifton from the West; Guthrie, Rowell, and Mewburn from Ontario; Ballantyne from Quebec; and Carvell and A. K. Maclean from the Maritimes.*

---

* Ballantyne had already been sworn in on October 3 and Guthrie on October 4. Carvell was sworn in on October 13 and Maclean on October 23. George Graham gave an account of his own refusal of an offer to join the Union government at the 1919 convention — see *Story of the Convention and the Report of its Proceedings, August 5, 6, 7, 1919*, p. 140, printed by the Mortimer Company Limited, Ottawa, 1919.

IX

Even the announcement of Union government on October 12, and the virtual certainty of an immediate election, did not settle Mackenzie King's personal problem. The question in his mind, whether to run or not, had already been answered with a brave 'yes', a troubled 'no', and an agonizing 'maybe'. The final, irrevocable decision would have to be made before nomination day. The possible disintegration of the Liberal forces under Sir Wilfrid Laurier could be an argument for or against his entry into the election contest: it was a foreshadowing of all but certain party and personal defeat; on the other hand, it was a challenge to redoubled loyalty to Laurier on the part of the friends, and particularly the English-speaking friends, who remained. October 12, a day of triumph for the Unionists, was like a day of mourning for Mackenzie King: 'As I looked outside at the cold wet sleet today, it seemed a fitting symbol of the present moment. War in the world, and its anxieties, change of gov't at home with defeat of party & personal defeat virtually assured thro' the new turn of events in the coalition — my closest political friends in Toronto all against me as a consequence, Mother practically dying, suffering alone with me here. There is enough of sadness & despair in such an outlook.' It was not utter despair, for he still could descry a glimmer of light through the clouds. Day after day he recorded his varying moods of hope and discouragement: 'The campaign will be a very bitter and a very cruel one,' he wrote on October 15, '& unless some real good can be served I shall withdraw. If they [the North York executive] are behind Sir Wilfrid I will probably stay, if not I shall withdraw.'

Before the end of that week he had a new reason for not running. He had talked with George Graham and 'was disgusted to find that Pardee [Liberal Whip] & several others intended to support the Union Govt. Graham while not supporting the Union Govt. is following his usual double course, of trying to hunt with the hares & ride with the hounds, he is not supporting the govt., but is defending the Liberals in it. The truth is Mackenzie & Mann are back of all this business & their supporters are getting their constituencies so arranged as to win by acclamation. It is a hideous sort of a deal, when Liberalism stands for principle. I felt after leaving Graham I should like to drop out altogether, rather than be mixed up in such a sink of crookedness. The rottenness of politics is but too apparent.' Sir Wilfrid expressed himself as 'very disappointed with Graham & Pardee. I cannot understand Pardee, he said, he has always been friendly, but I learn that he & Jack Reid & Cochrane [two Conservative Ministers] are carving up constituencies between them. . . . He said it was trying, all this deception at his age — he was too old & should have retired long ago.'

In his mother's illness the anxious son saw another reason for withdrawal. He had declined Sir Wilfrid's invitation to leave Ottawa for a day in Toronto to discuss with Ontario Liberals the disturbing proposal of a change in the Liberal leadership: 'It is conceivable that even the future leadership of the party might depend on being present at present conferences, but the knowledge of that does not influence me in the least from being at mother's side, come what may, until the very end.' Participation in an election campaign would mean a longer separation, perhaps for six weeks: 'How I dread the absence from Ottawa,' he wrote to his sister on October 20, 'with mother as critically ill as she is. I shall welcome any reasonable excuse to drop out of the election.' If he could count on his sister coming to The Roxborough to stay with his mother, that difficulty would be met: 'Of course if you cannot arrange it, I shall simply have to tell the committee that it is impossible to leave mother alone in the condition in which she is, and ask to be relieved on the score of my private obligation.'

The possibility of victory at the polls proved no enticement; he was too keenly aware of the probability of defeat. To his North York supporters he had to feign the optimism he could not feel. But to his brother he wrote, frankly, 'I do not think there is any chance of my winning in North York and I confess that defeat at any time, with the grave misunderstanding on the part of the public generally as to the cause of it, is not something which I contemplate with pleasure. . . . If I find that the Liberal Executive of North

York feel as I do about the new Union Government, I shall probably go on with the fight, notwithstanding that it means certain
defeat. If, however, there is any appreciable division in the ranks of
the Liberals there, I shall withdraw my candidature.' Sir Wilfrid
had said to him the day before that 'he felt we were sure to lose
this time, but was for a fight'.

He turned to his old friend Sir William Mulock for advice. Sir
William, who still lived in North York, knew the riding and knew
Mackenzie King, and was far enough removed from the current
political scene to view it with some objectivity. It was a discouraging interview: 'He said the chances of election are poor, and though
he did not put it in so many words, he is of the opinion I would be
wise to drop out, that the odds are too great against me, with the
attitude of the press what it is, Sir Wilfrid's attitude what it is, the
attitude of many of our own Liberals & of the Govt. It certainly
means certain defeat to little or no purpose, since there will be no
chance to get back into parliament on a by-election; the Gov't.
won't open any seats. The campaign will be misunderstood and
expensive. Sir Wm. said "You will have to supply all the money, all
the energy, all the brains, – not one person will give one cent."
As a wealthy man, and a Liberal, were principle aught, he might
well have said, "Willy if you make the fight for principle you
speak of, I will see that the riding helps you, win or lose!" '

His talk with J. E. Atkinson of the Toronto *Star* was equally
disheartening. He told Atkinson he was ready to fight for principle
– the principle of Union government and even conscription – if
the riding were ready for such a fight, but that he would withdraw
rather than support Borden and his Union government. It was the
keenest disappointment to hear Atkinson say – Atkinson, who
had always been his friend personally and politically – that the
Star could give him no support. 'One feels what is the use!' he exclaimed in his diary. 'No single one, not even the men of principle,
ready to make a stand. It is simply courting sacrifice & political
suicide to no end to fight at the moment. I feel quite ready to retire.'
He wrote to his brother on the same day, 'I shall have little more

than a passing regret in remaining out of the present contest, though
to give up public life at this period of the world's affairs is no small
renunciation.' Though at times he could express himself so strongly,
he had no real intention of deserting Sir Wilfrid at a time when his
support was badly needed by his leader.

x

Had he withdrawn from the field at this stage it might have meant
a permanent renunciation of his hopes for the Liberal leadership;
on the other hand, his entry into the contest would do more than
anything else could to establish him as the logical successor to
Laurier. Sam Jacobs and Senator William Mitchell had prophesied
this outcome when they talked with him in August. Now, in
October, two other Quebec Liberals, the Senator's son, Walter
Mitchell, Quebec provincial treasurer, and Andrew R. McMaster,
M.P., renewed the appeal to him 'to take a leading part in Ontario'.
They evidently had strong backing from Laurier, Premier Sir
Lomer Gouin, and Rodolphe Lemieux. After his talk with Walter
Mitchell, on October 14, he felt even more assured of solid support
from Quebec, but he continued to hold back: 'Were I free to do it,'
he wrote in his diary, 'I could easily win the leadership of the Party
at this juncture — but I am not free.' The day before, he had written: 'There is a real chance for the future leadership of the Liberal
Party. . . . Most of the possible leaders have now destroyed themselves.' And the day before that, after a talk with Sir Wilfrid on the
day the Union government was formed, it was evident that he
realized the new possibilities: 'It is even possible this coming political contest might give me, despite defeat, such a place in the ranks
of Liberalism as to become a leader in a new Parliament when Sir
Wilfrid drops out. Were I not so tired & anxious I should aim at
this. As it is I shall seek to do my duty day by day and let the Future
unfold itself.'

   In the end, after weeks of painful indecision, it was Sir Wilfrid
who spoke the final word: '*You must run.*' The words were under-

lined in the diary and were followed by his own acceptance of the inevitable, 'And so it is'; also by another underlined declaration, '*I believe I can win*.' Sir Wilfrid would not give him the definite assurance he asked for, that he might count on a seat in Quebec if he were defeated in North York; that, he said, would depend on the fight he made in North York: 'If it was satisfactory to Quebec I could get anything.' Laurier did not regard conscription as more than 'a transitory issue'; the real fight should be made against the Union government: 'He repeated that if premier he cld. raise an army in Quebec by voluntary enlistment against the bitter opposition of Bourassa.' With this Mackenzie King agreed, but added that if voluntary recruiting failed he himself would support the idea of Union government and conscription. He did not need to repeat that he would not serve under Borden.

It was some satisfaction to be able to tell Sir William Mulock and J. E. Atkinson at luncheon later that week that, in spite of their advice, he had decided to contest North York: 'Sir William's eyes filled up with tears when he learned this. He felt the chivalrous side of it, with all men deserting Sir Wilfrid at this time. . . . He thought the fight will be a hard one, & he doubts that I can win. He is inclined to favor conscription.'

As one senior colleague after another left him, Sir Wilfrid suffered the severest pangs of loneliness. 'I have lived too long,' he said to his youngest disciple, who had found him 'very depressed and used up; looked quite distraught. He spoke of Fielding having come out in favor of Union gov't. and directing everything against Quebec. He said "that was the unkindest cut of all." ' When Mackenzie King told him that he had reason to believe Graham would be the next, that Atkinson had told him so, the Old Chief expressed no surprise: 'he could expect anything after Fielding . . . he had no hope of winning, but action like Fielding's wd. make Nationalists out of all the people of Quebec, the thing he had striven most to prevent.'

From that day on, Sir Wilfrid came more and more to lean on Mackenzie King as his principal adviser — outside the province

of Quebec — on election policy. The younger man had an important part, along with Sydney Fisher, in the shaping of the party
manifesto. It had been a touch-and-go matter whether he would
have any part in the campaign, but now, definitely committed, he
threw himself into the fight with energy, though not without occasional misgivings. His decision meant that he would always be
remembered, certainly by Quebec Liberals, as a man who had supported Laurier in his hour of greatest need. Had he decided otherwise, his failure to respond would also have been remembered —
but to his serious disadvantage.

XI

Having committed himself to participation in the election campaign, he had to arrange for severance of his connection with the
Rockefeller Foundation — at least a temporary severance. Accordingly he went to New York for a talk with Mr. Rockefeller. Success in the election campaign would presumably mean an end to the
Rockefeller connection. Defeat could open up the new kind of
relationship, with Rockefeller personally, which they had already
discussed. Two days in New York were enough to convince him
that he had made the right decision. On the evening of the first day
he saw George Arliss in *Alexander Hamilton*. 'The play,' he wrote
in his diary after he returned to his room at the Harvard Club,
'made me feel more than ever that politics was my right field — the
only real one for true and full expression.' He came away from
New York feeling that he had no desire to live there, 'in fact that at
all costs I should seek to avoid it':

> I have a place in Canada, a place in Canadian public life and His-
> tory. This I can never have in the United States. My opportunity
> of service in the U.S. promises to be more and more that of slowly
> advancing Labor's position within a powerful corporation, but
> being misunderstood outside, & some day being drawn into an
> attitude of antagonism to Labor. In Canada I can stand above
> both parties, Capital & Labor, & act impartially between them. It
> is my life, — my soul's interest and development that is at stake
> and to live the life of one's inner vision is the only true living.

The return to Canada on a crisp October morning was an exhilarating experience. He woke at six and watched the sunrise through the train window.

> I resolved to set my face towards public life, to throw in my whole life with Canada, and to give up for ever, if the Fates permit, all thought of future association with the States. I felt my spirit free, my soul at rest. I decided to give up thoughts of pleasure I had been cherishing & to follow Duty, to go into the fight ahead as a Sir Galahad espousing the cause of Right & principle. I was happy, happy to breathe the free air of a free country & to feel the yoke of misunderstanding of my position off my shoulders. It is Faith or Fear, and I am putting my all on Faith, with just enough of worldly wisdom to see where my livelihood for the next year or two remains secured. I have never had mental rest since the associat'n with the Rockefellers was formed, tho' it has been providential as a means to an end.

XII

An afternoon of discussion about election policy with Sir Wilfrid and three of his colleagues (C. W. Cross, Attorney-General of Alberta, Sydney Fisher, and Charles Murphy) marked the beginning of a series of daily conferences, in which Rodolphe Lemieux and Sir Lomer Gouin later took an active part. Sir Wilfrid thought his severance with the Rockefeller Foundation was a mistake, though he must have been pleased with the basic reason for it — his wish to be free of all encumbrances in the fight. King's own part in the fight would have to be restricted to North York, but Laurier assured him that if he should be unsuccessful there he could still hope for a seat in Quebec. The positive assurances which had been given to him by Sir Lomer Gouin, Rodolphe Lemieux, Sam Jacobs, Walter Mitchell, and Andrew McMaster, as well as Laurier's qualified promise, gave him new confidence in his political future: 'I believe I can carry North York, but it is well to have this assurance, as my determination is to continue in public life in Canada and to bend all my energies to that end.'

By that time nomination day had been set for November 19 and election day four weeks later, December 17. The fight was on. The basis of Mackenzie King's campaign was the Laurier manifesto, completed on November 4, which he supplemented with a pamphlet of his own, *The Two Policies*. Both documents were widely distributed throughout North York, and their arguments were the centre of the vigorous campaign he conducted. In every speech he made, his appeal was that national unity must be maintained, and internal dissension avoided, if Canada were to play her full part in the winning of the war. In Borden's policy of conscription, and more particularly in the methods of introducing and enforcing it, he saw the gravest threat to national unity. 'As to conscription,' he wrote to a college friend who had declared that support of Laurier meant support to the German cause, 'it seems to me that ... it is not a question as to whether the method is democratic or equitable — I agree with you that it is both; it is not even a question whether we should have conscription or no conscription. It is a question as to how Canada shall be united in the face of a terrible foe menacing the liberties of mankind.' If conscription were to be imposed it should be on the basis of public acceptance of it in a referendum and it should be conscription of money and resources as well as of men. If the people approved of conscription, a Liberal government would enforce it without dividing the country; if the public disapproved (as Australian electors, even the armed forces, had disapproved in a wartime referendum), the necessary reinforcements could be secured as they had been in Australia, by a vigorous campaign for voluntary enlistment. Mackenzie King had every confidence that Sir Wilfrid would do as he had said in Parliament he would do, take his coat off and go to work to see that the province of Quebec fell in line with the rest of the Dominion.

XIII

The election campaign of 1917, from its first shot, was marked by bitterness that rivalled anything Canada had known in election contests. Quebec's failure to match the other provinces in the total

war effort and its fierce opposition to the conscription programme
made the issues of race and religion inevitable. Of little effect was
Laurier's denunciation of the army's unfortunate recruiting
methods in Quebec, such as the use of anti-Catholic and anti-French
emissaries from Ontario to induce French-Canadians to enlist.
Equally ineffective was his insistence that he could raise an army
in Quebec by a fair-minded appeal to his compatriots, and that in
any event conscription should not be imposed without the consent
of the electorate in a referendum. It was more embarrassing than
helpful to him that Henri Bourassa, leader of the Quebec Nationalists, should come out with tirades against conscription. While
they helped to intensify anti-government feeling in Quebec, where
Laurier needed no such help, they had the opposite effect in the
other provinces, where Bourassa's name was anathema because of
his outspoken antipathy to any continued participation in the war.
Mackenzie King had a point, but he got nowhere with it, in con-
demning a so-called National or Union Cabinet which included
only one Roman Catholic and not a single French-Canadian. 'Win-
the-war' sentiment ran high, much of it based on honest conviction;
it took little or no account of the dangers which King constantly
portrayed of a country divided against itself, of internal dissensions
which would last for generations.

Ontario audiences, particularly in the towns and cities, could
be aroused to fever pitch by any suggestion of 'Quebec domination', by every attack on Laurier and his followers as men lacking
in patriotism and planning to take Canada out of the war. Posters
on billboards and advertisements in newspapers declared that 'A
vote for Laurier is a vote for the Kaiser', 'Laurier is the tool of
Bourassa', 'Our Victory Loan must not be handed over to Quebec
to spend'. Newspapers outside the province of Quebec (with three
notable exceptions, the London *Advertiser*, the Calgary *News-
Telegram*, and the Edmonton *Bulletin*) joined in the attack in their
editorials, cartoons, and news reports. Editorial comment seemed
to reach an all-time low in the Toronto *News* when it described
Laurier as 'a demagogue, a charlatan and a mountebank'. Even more

offensive were many letters to editors: one of them declared that 'if Laurier were to win he would win leading the cockroaches of the kitchen of Canada to victory'. Committees organized for the Victory Loan campaign of November became centres for election propaganda. Toward the close of the campaign many of the Protestant clergy in Ontario used their pulpits and their pastoral visitations for political purposes, a circumstance which led to Sir Wilfrid's wry remark, soon after the election, 'In 1896 I was excommunicated by the Roman priests and in 1917 by Protestant parsons.'

XIV

In North York Mackenzie King embarked on his campaign with more hope than assurance, but with a buoyancy that was deceiving even to himself. It was very much a single-handed effort. Outside financial assistance was not forthcoming: the funds of the federal party had never been so depleted. As for public speakers, Liberal candidates in other parts of Ontario felt they must concentrate on their own ridings, and he did not invite them. None of his former ministerial colleagues, except Sir Allan Aylesworth in the last week of the campaign, came to his aid. Even Sir Wilfrid was not approached — a letter of invitation was drafted but never sent. He himself received appeals from seven other candidates in Ontario, two in British Columbia, and still others in Quebec, for aid in their campaigns. All were declined, for he was fighting a desperate fight, as they were, and dared not budge from North York even for an afternoon or evening meeting.

This concentration on North York in the campaign, while effective, still did not overcome the handicap from which he suffered because of his neglect of the riding throughout the four years following his 1913 nomination. It was a disadvantage from which his opponent, John A. Macdonald Armstrong, did not suffer, for Armstrong, who had represented North York since 1911, was a native of the county and knew every family in it. Then, too, with the formation of the Union government and the rising tide of feeling in favour of conscription, several of King's strongest supporters threw in their lot with the Unionists. Their defection, together with the increasing hostility of the Toronto and local newspapers, and the well-organized and well-financed campaign waged on the hustings and through billboard posters and pamphleteering, all presented a challenge to Mackenzie King's fighting spirit.

When he arrived in Newmarket on November 6 and set up campaign headquarters at the old King George Hotel, the division in the Liberal ranks was all too apparent. Many old friends gave him a hearty welcome and others a definitely cold shoulder. Still others were obviously lukewarm. Grit farmers were on the whole still clear Grit, but the townsfolk, more affected by enlistments and casualties, were more susceptible to the 'win-the-war' appeals which the Tories had pre-empted for their own purposes. The women's vote, restricted by the new franchise act to relatives of soldiers, was likely to go Unionist. The government was counting on the support of North York men and women in the overseas forces, and on the votes of non-Canadians serving in Canadian battalions who under the new Military Voters Act could cast their ballots for any candidates they chose.

xv

Altogether, it was not an inspiring outlook. It was not long, however, before Mackenzie King infused some spirit into his co-workers and encouraged them to believe in the probability of a Liberal victory in North York and even the possibility of a Liberal sweep throughout the country. He radiated good cheer in the scores of meetings he addressed and in his talks with farmers and townsfolk in their homes, on the roadside and at street corners, and at picnics and teas. On several occasions he faced the organized hostility of groups of returned soldiers, transported in bus-loads from nearby Toronto hospitals for the obvious purpose of disrupting his meetings. At the largest of these meetings, after earlier speakers had been howled down by catcalls and mock cheering and lusty singing, he succeeded in getting not only a hearing from his tormentors but in the end a round of applause that showed their admiration of his courage and adroitness, if not agreement with his argument.

Throughout the whole campaign he gave the impression of being a 'happy warrior', although secretly he was a very worried man, knowing as he did that if the worst came to the worst, party and personal defeat might well mean the end of all his political hopes. Victory for himself in North York and defeat of the party as a whole would surely establish him as the logical successor to Laurier, as Leader of the Opposition; if he were to suffer personal defeat and the Liberal Party were returned to power, he could still hope for the future leadership. But in the end the worst did come to the worst: when the ballots were counted on December 17 (his forty-third birthday) Armstrong had 3,364 civilian votes against his own 2,832, a majority of 532, which was increased to 1,078 when the overseas ballots (584 to 38) were counted. In the country as a whole the Liberal Party had shared the same fate; the percentages were almost the same. Borden's party was returned with 153 out of the 235 seats in the Commons.*

For all the good fight he had fought, he had lost, and for the moment it seemed that he had finished his course politically. But only for the moment. He had fallen in 1911, had struggled for months and years to re-establish himself in the political world, but had not succeeded. In 1914 he had changed his course and within three years, in a new and entirely different career, had reached heights that could be regarded as the summit of any man's ambition. Yet he still preferred politics. In 1917 an opportunity had come to return to the political field and to continue what he regarded as his true life-work. His defeat may seem to have marked another downfall politically, but his stand in that election turned

---

* The total Liberal vote in the country was 763,371 out of 1,821,164, approximately 42 per cent. Of the 82 Liberal seats 62 were in Quebec, 10 in the Maritimes, 8 in Eastern Ontario, and 2 in the Prairie Provinces.

out to be the solid basis of ultimate triumph. Deep impressions had been made by his insistence on the right of the people to say whether they wanted conscription or not, and what kind of conscription — whether, as he advocated, conscription of wealth as well as of manpower or merely conscription of men. Equally impressive had been his holding out for policies that would maintain national unity, particularly in time of war. He had been genuinely incensed by what he regarded as an unwarranted violation of human rights by a Union government that was creating disunity, a so-called national government that represented only a part of the nation. He had shown complete faith in Sir Wilfrid Laurier, and his loyalty to him when other Liberal leaders were deserting him was something that Laurier's friends, both French and English, would always remember in his favour.

CHAPTER 16

Ultimate Triumph—
the Convention of 1919

At the end of 1917, after his spectacular but unsuccessful campaign in North York, Mackenzie King was not utterly cast down; he was still unwilling to abandon his hopes for the political career to which he had just returned. He would carry on the fight, but not in North York — at least not until the next general election, and that might not be for another five years.*

In the meantime, if he sought immediate entry into Parliament, the fight would have to be in some area other than North York. His thoughts naturally turned to the province of Quebec; surely one of the sixty-two seats now held by Liberals could be opened for him. Had not Sir Wilfrid assured him before the campaign that if his fight in North York were satisfactory to Quebec, he 'could get anything', and from at least five leading Liberals in Quebec had he not been given the same undertaking without qualification? It was a grievous disappointment, on the day of reckoning and in succeeding months, that all these assurances of his Quebec col-

---

* At the next general election, in 1921, he did contest North York again and won the seat by 1,055 votes, a majority almost equal to Armstrong's majority against him in 1917; it represented a turnover of more than two thousand votes.

leagues fell within the category of 'election promises' — they were soon forgotten.

In a conversation at the end of February Sir Wilfrid had told him that he had made up his mind to retire from the leadership; he would go through this session, but that would be the last. He was too old, he said, too exhausted, and, besides, his race and religion were against him. When King spoke to him about his getting into Parliament himself, Sir Wilfrid declared that 'a seat in Quebec was "the last thing" to be wished for, that to sit for Quebec was to have everyone against one'. What Mackenzie King thought of such a reply is revealed in bitter words in his diary:

> I felt that he recognized no obligation to try to find me a seat or to compel it; that, in other words, he had let me make the fight for him in Ontario, but it had served his purpose, & that was all there was to it — this use of men is something I despise ... I sort of despised him in my feelings recalling that he knew the extent of the sacrifice I had made for him & the promise he had given me, also Gouin & Lemieux. I shall put them all to the test before I decide on a counter move, but action of this kind makes me feel I will be wiser to consider a move to the United States & beginning a larger work there, tho' God knows my heart has been most in Canadian politics. Much will depend on Miss "X".

Discouraged as he was by the unjust treatment he felt himself to be receiving, he turned back to writing his *Industry and Humanity*. This was finally completed in September of the same year. He continued, too, with the surveys he was making for several large industries in the United States and went to New York for frequent consultations with Rockefeller. One of these consultations involved a lengthy visit to Colorado. These persistent appeals from Rockefeller contrasted sharply with Laurier's apparent indifference. Repulsed on the one hand and courted on the other, he was at times tempted to yield to the flattering pressure, forsake politics, and establish himself in his new profession. The prospect would have been more enticing if he could have established himself in a home of his own in New York, with the wife who had been chosen but had not yet been won. He was still determined, however, that he would make no binding commitments that would interfere with a return to politics.

Not to be taken too seriously, but still worthy of mention, was his fleeting consideration in midsummer of the possibility of a seat in the British House of Commons. It had occurred to him at least once before, in 1912, when he wrote with some assurance of his chances of becoming, some day, leader of the Liberal Party in Canada and 'for that matter a leading figure in politics in England if I wished it'. In 1918 the possibility crossed his mind again (he was writing at the time about the Whitley Councils in England): 'The thought flashed through my mind that this book might open the way to my obtaining a seat in the British Parliament. It is too much to be hoped for, but something I would welcome at any cost if the chance were offered. It may come out of this visit to England.' It was only a passing thought, perhaps better described as a midsummer night's dream. He was exaggerating when he wrote 'at any cost', for he would not have considered it for a moment at the cost of a leading part in Canadian public life.

This was in July; as it turned out, the trip to England was postponed for nearly a year, and by that time political prospects in Canada had brightened; with the Liberal convention only weeks away, his whole interest was then in the Canadian scene.

II

September 1918 marked the beginning of a new chapter in the story of Mackenzie King's rise from the depths of 1911 to the heights of 1919. It was not a very auspicious beginning: 'Certainly,' he wrote on September 17, 'the Liberal Party in Canada today is at a low ebb.' On that day he had been called to Sir Wilfrid's office, along with about fifteen other leading Liberals, to discuss party organization and future policies. In his record of the meeting he had little to say about the matters discussed, but he had bitter comment to make on the attention Sir Wilfrid paid to George Graham, who had voted against him on the Military Service Bill, and E. M. Macdonald, who had declined to run as a candidate in Nova Scotia in the December election. King felt they were being treated as returning prodigal sons, to the disadvantage of the son who had remained faithful. He wrote:

> When I saw both Graham and Ned Macdonald present it was apparent to me that Sir W. is simply trying to hold us all together. Keep as many around him as possible. He is bound to get Graham back, I cld. not but feel a little resentment on what seems to me an effort to have Graham & Macdonald given a preference to me, or at all events at my being kept out of the House till they are taken in, in view of their treachery and double-dealing last election, & my faithfulness to Sir Wilfrid & his promises & the promises of others to me. I confess at times I feel Sir Wilfrid lacks a sense of honor in many things, that he is just playing the game to suit himself & is now more or less indifferent to real reform and the country's needs. He seems too tired to do anything that requires initiative & progress. He relies almost wholly on his own personal charm & 'tricks of the game' which he knows thoroughly. His continued flattery of men disgusts me at times. He invited me to lunch at the Chateau with himself & Robb, Senator Ross & Mr. Fisher. Tonight he had Ned Macdonald ... to dinner. I felt in a way that it was hardly worth while coming in [from Kingsmere] for the day, that it was all a game just to hold on to George Graham & Ned.

III

Sir Wilfrid would have more to say later about George Graham, but in the meantime — indeed the next day — overtures were made to Mackenzie King which could have opened the way to a seat in the House of Commons and a portfolio as well. The offer, if it was an offer, came before he had time to recover from his pique of the day before, and unfortunately it came from the wrong side of the House. The opportunity to re-enter Parliament, which he would have welcomed at almost any cost, was one he could not bring himself to grasp. It was a 'feeler' rather than an outright invitation, but it bore all the marks of a genuine proposal which would be implemented if willingness to accept were indicated. Sir Clifford Sifton, whom Sir Wilfrid had often referred to as 'the real prime minister in the Union Government', made the approach when they talked privately at the luncheon table at the Rideau Club on September 18. King had just exchanged greetings with Sir Robert Borden and four or five of his colleagues, and Sir Clifford invited him to lunch with him. Sifton lost no time in coming to the point:

> When we were seated he said 'I was talking with a gentleman & your name came into the discussion. He was saying how impossible the present Minister of Labor was, & how great was the need for a change. It is not an office that a Labor man or a lawyer can very well fill; it needs an expert. I said King is the only man, he is properly trained etc.' He said he did not know whether I would be available or care to go into the Government. 'He agreed you were the right person (or words to that effect).' Sifton then went on, 'You know before you took the active part you did in the last campaign it was decided you were to be offered a portfolio, not Labor but more important, the Minister of Civil Re-establishment, getting all the men of the Army back into civil life, seeing to their education etc. The work has since been given to a Committee because the right man was not available for the Ministry but that was to have been yours.' Sifton then continued, that the work wd. have to be done yet, he did not know whether I wd. care to go into the Government or not. The Liberals in the Govt. were the only active men in it. Outside of Dr. Reid, the Conservatives had few men that were doing anything.

King was sure that the 'gentleman' Sir Clifford referred to was Sir Robert Borden; he was non-committal in his reply:

> I told Sifton about my work of late & my forthcoming book on reconstruction. I said neither yes nor no to the 'feeler' he put out, but agreed that the work was certainly not a politician's job.

Thinking it over after the conversation, he could see that under

certain circumstances he might be justified in at least flirting with
the idea:

> It is quite apparent that I have only to say to Sifton I will go into
> the Cabinet to be offered a portfolio forthwith. Should Laurier
> treat with Graham and Ned Macdonald ahead of me, I should feel
> very tempted to do this at once — as a Liberal in protest against
> men who are mere politicians — & go into the Cabinet for *con-*
> *structive* work, after having fought the Government on the Elec-
> tions Act, go in as a Liberal. If my book brings me prominence, &
> my trip to England gives me the needed experience, & there
> should be a public demand, I might feel it a patriotic duty to ac-
> cept an offer were it made. In any event, I shall wait & see how
> matters develop. Each year now brings us nearer the point when
> the question of Leadership of the Liberal cause comes up. It was a
> satisfaction to have been told there was a place for me in the
> Union Government & that I lost it only by supporting Sir Wilfrid,
> & to know that after my opposing the Government, I could now
> join it as a Minister by saying the word. I believe my book will
> bring me the place I need in the public estimation & I have only
> to wait for all things to work together for good.

Had the 'offer' been seriously considered, there is no doubt that
Mackenzie King would have followed his customary practice and
discussed it immediately with Laurier, but over a month elapsed
before he even told him of the conversation with Sifton. The Old
Chief took it in his stride; he 'said he did not think it was true that I
was slated for the Unionist Cabinet but he believed the Government would be ready enough to take me now'.

IV

In that interview, and in another later in the week, Laurier showed
signs of returning confidence in the youngest of his chief lieutenants. King spoke frankly of the disappointment it had been to him,
after the campaign, that 'the first offer of a seat in the House & a
position in the Cabinet should come to me from the men I had
fought & opposed'. Sir Wilfrid rose to the occasion: 'I am not sur-

prised Sifton should want you, he is an able man & knows brains &
he wd. like to have you in his Cabinet for it is his cabinet.' Laurier
went on to tell him that, as for a seat in Parliament, he had said to
different friends 'that if the campaign Mackenzie King had made in
North York had been known in Quebec he could get a seat anywhere'. He added that he had spoken to Lemieux and would speak
again to Sir Lomer Gouin: 'I know he was very definite in his
promise to you for I was there. At that time we expected to win.'

He then made more definite suggestions as to the best way to
effect an opening. One way would be to make political capital out
of the book, which was written and would shortly be published;
he could make a speech in Montreal setting out the new policy
of industrial reconstruction, alluding to William Lyon Mackenzie
and Papineau as having fought the same battles. That would be
something for Quebec and would create enthusiasm.

Warmed up to his subject, Sir Wilfrid went on to speak of even
brighter prospects: 'No man in Canada has your chances today. I
am getting to be an old man and must drop out. George Graham as
you know was slated for the leadership, but he is out of the running
now. He could never get the support of the wing of the party on
which we depend for power. You have it, not perhaps in the
country but among the members of the House, they will support
you and rally round you.'

Sir Wilfrid had at last said the magic word. This was not a feeler,
or an offer, or a mere suggestion. It was an assurance of Laurier's
support for the leadership, than which nothing could be more
helpful. The conversation ended on the same note:

> 'The thing we must do is for me to bring you forward all I can. I
> wd. like, for example, that you go up with me to London when I
> go to speak on November 19. I will write & ask George Gibbons
> to invite you. I will put you forward all I can' ... words to this
> effect — I replied I had not thought of leadership it was the H. of
> C. I was thinking of. Sir Wilfrid said, 'I have always said a man
> wd. find his place there. Certainly it wd. help you to be in the H.
> of C. As to other work, make all the money you can but you don't

want to be wealthy. It is what is a man's aim, what is in his conscience & his purpose. As you have said, it is govt. by Force or by
Consent. Fight against oppression, for the people or against them
this goes on all the time in one form or another, that is Liberalism
or Conservatism – it is that you wish to consider with your life.'
I told him that of course that was my ideal and ambition. I said
I never doubted his own friendship for me or interest in me, but
that I doubted sometimes my own chances of a political future
unless something came soon.

Mackenzie King was so much impressed and regarded this conversation as so important that he went from Laurier's office to his own
room to record it at once.

V

Laurier's intention to retire from the Liberal leadership was made
clear when he announced, at his meeting in London on November
19, that a national Liberal convention would be held in Ottawa in
the course of the following year. There had been a constantly
growing sentiment among Canadian Liberals that such a convention
should be held as soon as possible after the war. (The Armistice
had been signed on November 11.) Mackenzie King had not been
able to attend the meeting in London – he was in Colorado
throughout November – but it was a satisfaction to him to hear
that this party gathering passed a resolution on industrial reconstruction which he had drafted at Sir Wilfrid's request. This party
endorsement of a favourite theme, the announcement of the convention, and a friendly telegram from Laurier ('hope to see you
here soon'), made him feel that he was being 'drawn toward the
inevitable goal of a life service in politics'. He had, too, an encouraging letter from Alex. Smith of Ottawa, who had been for
years a central figure in the organization work of the party and
had always had an uncanny ability to read political weather-maps.
King described him as a weathercock always turning the way the
wind blows. He could sense now that the current political winds
were blowing in Mackenzie King's favour and he thought King

should be prevailed upon to take advantage of them. In the mood of the moment King could be 'prevailed upon' without much pressure. 'Everything considered,' he wrote while still in Colorado, 'I have decided when I return to Canada this time to definitely take up the work of Leadership in Liberalism in my native country.' His decision was reinforced by the knowledge that his financial investments were at last sufficient to ensure freedom and independence in a political career and by his confidence that the programme of industrial reconstruction set forth in his book, now in the publishers' hands, would add to his prestige and would no doubt become a basic part of future Liberal policy.

Most reassuring of all was the encouragement he had received from Laurier in private conversations. For obvious reasons Laurier's endorsement of King and his disparagement of Graham could not be repeated in public at this stage or even committed to writing. They were sufficient, however, to influence the shaping of King's personal plans for the immediate future. Back in Ottawa, in his review of the year's progress, he recorded that 'twice with his own lips Sir Wilfrid has told me that he wished me to be his successor; that it was a matter now of only arranging "the time and the occasion".' Support was apparent from other members of the Liberal hierarchy and from none more enthusiastically than from Sydney Fisher, who told him that he had Quebec solidly back of him and was stronger in the other provinces among the Liberals than any other man. 'There is no question,' King wrote, 'that the leadership of the party is mine if I care to go in for it.' Both Sir Wilfrid and Fisher discussed with him steps to be taken toward securing the leadership. Fisher thought he should not go abroad, as he had arranged with Rockefeller to do. Sir Wilfrid thought it would make no difference and that he would be unwise not to take the chance.

VI

Laurier's task at the end of 1918 was to surround himself in the House of Commons with outstanding Liberals of real fighting spirit; even those who had deserted him in 1917 (or most of them) would be welcome. If he could add to the strength he already had from Quebec by inducing Fielding to move from the cross-benches to the Liberal side, and by finding seats for such former Cabinet ministers as George Graham and Mackenzie King in Ontario, Frank Oliver in Alberta, and E. M. Macdonald in Nova Scotia, he would have the nucleus of a strong government. W. R. Riddell, then a judge in the Supreme Court of Ontario, was one of several outsiders he approached. As to the leadership, whatever his thoughts were he did not disclose them publicly. Any sign of favouritism on his part at this stage, when he was trying to restore harmony, would have led only to discord. Each potential candidate, whatever stand he had taken in 1917, should, Laurier was determined, have his opportunity between now and the convention, and at the convention, to prove his worth. Any expression of preference by Laurier at this time might indeed work to the disadvantage of the favoured one. Rumour had it, early in 1918, that Mackenzie King was Laurier's choice, and Charles Murphy (who was favourable to King at that time) pleaded with Laurier to do what he could to scotch the rumour; it would 'destroy King', he thought, and would weaken Laurier's chance of reuniting the party. E. M. Macdonald was disturbed by a report that in a private conversation Sir Wilfrid had said that a seat would be found for Mackenzie King in Quebec, and that expressions he used had suggested King's possible future leadership. Sir Wilfrid assured him that 'there never was any mention at all of Mackenzie King's future leadership'. When A. B. Aylesworth recommended Henri S. Beland for the leadership, Laurier replied that no one in the ranks would be more acceptable, but that his French origin was against him: 'No Roman Catholic French Canadian,' he declared, 'should ever try to lead the Liberal Party again.' Rodolphe Lemieux, who entertained some leadership aspirations himself, suffered from the same disadvantage as Beland. W. S. Fielding and George Graham would not be disqualified on this score — one was a Baptist, the other a Methodist — but their apostasy was too recent to justify so early an acceptance of either as leader, however desirable it might be to welcome their restoration to full membership in the party.

Mackenzie King had none of these counts against him — he had enthusiastic support in Quebec — but in Ontario there were influences that were working against him. If pro-King sentiment outside of Quebec had been more favourable, or if King had been a Member of Parliament at the time, Laurier might have expressed himself more freely, but he was still unwilling to say in public what he had said in private conversation. 'Were you in Parliament,' he said to King frankly shortly after Christmas, 'I should resign the leadership at once.' That was the third declaration of the kind and the substance of it was repeated by Hon. Walter Mitchell, who told King early in January 1919 that he had heard Sir Wilfrid say to Sir Lomer Gouin that 'were King in Parliament I should resign the leadership in his favor tomorrow.' Guest of honour one night at a banquet at the Montreal Reform Club, King had made a stirring address on industrial reconstruction. Sydney Fisher, S. W. Jacobs, Walter Mitchell, Senator James W. Domville, and others were greatly impressed and assured him that he had a solid Quebec behind him and that he was the only man acceptable to the Liberals in Parliament. Two Quebec members offered to resign their seats in his favour, and he was told he could have his choice of two others, one of them Maisonneuve, then represented by Rodolphe Lemieux who was member for Gaspé also. J. A. Woodward, a railway union man, president of the Fifth Sunday Meeting Association of Canada, was all for arranging a series of addresses on the same theme across the continent; he assured King he would have the railway men from the Atlantic to the Pacific at his back. The summit of his political ambitions, it seemed, was at last coming within sight. With these assurances, culminating, he hoped and expected, in an immediate nomination for Maisonneuve, the party leadership would be all but a certainty, the approval of a national convention a foregone conclusion. Against any possible mishap, however, he still carried the insurance of the offers he had received from Rockefeller and Carnegie at the end of the year; indeed, negotiations with his New York friends continued while he discussed future political prospects with his friends in Montreal.

VII

Leaving Montreal for New York almost immediately, he had no opportunity to improve his chances of early action on the Maisonneuve front. Most of the next five weeks were spent in studies of the labour problems of several companies in the mid-western states, with scarcely a thought of Canadian politics. He did exchange letters with Sir Wilfrid and was pleased particularly with one letter that urged him, 'please come back'. The letter added: 'I would not speak too positively, but it is sufficient to remember that, at this period of all periods, things are moving fast. . . . Your better course is to stay in Canada, and to deliver as many speeches as you can, without waiting for an official candidature.' King had told him of his further talks with Rockefeller, but made it clear where his preference lay: 'My heart and will are with my own country, and only the lack of opportunity of service there at all comparable with that which lies before me through the connections I have formed here would lead me to take any step which might mean a permanent severance of my life relations with Canada.' Laurier's reply was encouraging; again he advised speaking at every opportunity and even accepting Woodward's proposal to make a tour of the Dominion: 'Your speech in Montreal has produced a great impression, even more with the thinking men than with the crowd, and the oftener you speak on that line, the better it will be not only for the country but for yourself also.' To be in the limelight in that way would, in Laurier's opinion, have more effect than the recognition he would get by winning a nomination to Parliament. For all that, he urged his Quebec lieutenants to act with more dispatch in arranging for the opening of the Maisonneuve seat. He also pressed his Ontario colleagues to arrange for a meeting in Toronto. 'Your presence there,' he wrote, 'is indispensable.' That letter was written exactly a week before Sir Wilfrid's death.

VIII

Mackenzie King was in Youngstown, Ohio, on Monday, February 17, when he learned from a small item in an evening newspaper that Sir Wilfrid had suffered a paralytic stroke on Sunday and was sinking rapidly. He took the first train for Ottawa; it was after midnight and, unable to get a berth, he sat up in the smoker till 4:30. At Buffalo he read in the morning paper that Sir Wilfrid had died on Monday afternoon.

In Toronto, before taking the night train to Ottawa, he had talks with such good friends as R. R. Cromarty, P. C. Larkin, Main Johnson, and J. E. Atkinson. All of them looked upon him as Laurier's logical successor, although Atkinson would have preferred N. W. Rowell. Editorials and special articles in newspapers all across the country reflected the genuine sorrow of a nation at the passing of a great Canadian who had held the affections of friend and foe alike. They also reported every scrap of gossip and conjecture about the four men who might be considered in line for the succession: Fielding, Graham, W. M. Martin of Saskatchewan, and Mackenzie King. A poll of public opinion at the time would probably have shown King's name at the top of the list. Not his only qualification, but an important one, was his record of support of Laurier in 1917.

'I am glad,' King reflected on his return to Ottawa, 'that before his death Sir Wilfrid on three different occasions made plain to me his desire to have me succeed him in the leadership — and that he had under way at the time of his death the opening of Maisonneuve to that end.' True enough, there was no written or public confirmation of Sir Wilfrid's preference, but 'he had gone far enough to make his wishes known . . . he was spared having to reveal his hand in public, having to choose between lifelong friends and supporters'. No such assurances had been given to Fielding, or to anyone else, but rumours were current after Laurier's death that he had admitted privately to his wife that the election of Fielding as his successor might serve to bring back conscriptionist Liberals into the party fold. If Fielding were chosen — and at this time there seemed little likelihood that he would be — his tenure would be brief, for he was then over seventy.

King was satisfied in his own mind that neither Fielding nor Graham could be a serious contender. 'The Liberals of Quebec,' he assured himself, 'will never take as a leader any man who "betrayed" Sir Wilfrid at the last election. All the Liberal members of the Union Government & Graham & Fielding, have only themselves to thank for the position in which they find themselves today. They failed in a moment of crisis, at a time of great need. They left their leader when the popular tide was rising against him.' His own record was clear in this respect. 'This begins a new chapter in my life,' he wrote, 'a chapter of great responsibilities & I believe great opportunities. Had Sir Wilfrid lived there is no question that his guiding hand would have secured me the leadership of the Liberal Party at the convention in June. In his death I lose a political father as well as a great leader. The thought uppermost in my breast is one of peace & rejoicing that I remained true to him when he was true to Liberal principles. That loyalty will secure me the leadership in the end. . . . That stand will not be forgotten and on it, and on Sir Wilfrid's known preferences will turn the choice of the new leader.'

For Mackenzie King it was a sad farewell on personal as well as on political grounds. His 'political father' had been a personal friend as well, one for whom he had genuine affection. There had been occasional differences between them, particularly when the impetuous younger man could not induce his leader to take the immediate action he wanted. But their disagreements were short-lived and soon forgotten. In their religious experiences they were far apart, but not because one was a Roman Catholic and the other a Protestant. Each of them had a deep regard for the church of the other. Indeed, Mackenzie King coveted for Sir Wilfrid a firmer faith in his own church and its doctrines, while Sir Wilfrid could think of himself as potentially Quaker or Unitarian. The more spiritually-minded man of the two was unhappy that the other should so concentrate on things that are seen, 'which are temporal', to the neglect of things not seen, 'which are eternal'. This was his mood as he looked for the last time on his departed friend: 'I could not but wish that Sir Wilfrid had had more of faith in his life. I believe he was an agnostic. . . . I wished that he had had deep religious conviction. He had a great love for humanity, but it was not a belief in God or immortality. That is where our natures failed to meet, where we failed to come into closest & intimate communion. It made a difference in my feeling as I looked upon him lying there.' His mood changed, however, as he reflected on the essential goodness of the man whose loss he mourned: 'He had all that the world could bestow upon a man of its honors, praise & in some measure of its scorn & betrayal, his greatness was that he remained true to the humble people, & that he could stand against the world for a conviction. This will give him his place in the chivalry of God.'

The possibility of his succeeding Laurier, not only as Leader of the Opposition, but as member for Quebec East, was suggested by Quebec friends even before the week was over. If that could be arranged immediately it would be an honour that any potential successor to Laurier would have coveted; the nomination itself would have high prestige value in the contest for the leadership. It was soon made clear, however, that the Union government had no thought of accommodating the Opposition by the early calling of a by-election in any constituency; indeed it was nearly eight months before the necessary writs were issued — and that was about two months after the Liberal convention.*

IX

With the possibility of the Liberal convention being held in June Mackenzie King was strongly tempted to cancel engagements already made in the United States. But if his political hopes were not realized it would be necessary to return to his work in the industrial

---

* In the by-elections in October, Quebec East returned Ernest Lapointe by a large majority, and Mackenzie King was elected by acclamation in Prince County, Prince Edward Island.

field. He would take on no new engagements – his main objective must not be interfered with – and when Rockefeller urged him, late in February, to spend two or three weeks in completing one already begun he protested: 'Any prolonged absence from Canada just in the present crisis would be most embarrassing to me personally, and would be commented on by friends in the Liberal Party who are urging my name as one to be placed in nomination for the leadership . . . the present moment is a very critical one, both as concerns the future of the Liberal Party in Canada and my own life and its relations to the cause of Liberalism.' His final decision was to complete his work for several American companies, but to leave himself enough free time for speech-making in Canada and frequent contacts with political friends. His address to the Empire Club in Toronto early in March, the first of a series on the same theme, 'The Four Parties to Industry', was received enthusiastically, and he was thrilled by the same kind of response when he spoke to the Canadian Clubs of Montreal and Quebec and to other non-political as well as political organizations. He had every reason to feel encouraged, but he could not rid himself of misgivings about the future: 'I wish I felt equal to the task. What I need most is physical exercise. I am not myself, too morbid and introspective. How I wish I were married happily. That is what is most needed now, & it would make all the difference as regards the future. . . . Apparently things are at 6's & 7's in the party. The job of leading the elements that make up the Opposition today would be a terrific task. The intrigue on every side is frightful. Clearly it is well to leave everything to better itself. How wise I am to think of the task I cannot say.' Four days in Toronto as the house guest of J. E. Atkinson and his wife gave him opportunity to talk with influential Liberals and others, and to pay a hurried visit to North York. The day in North York was one of 'nervous strain and anxiety and doubt as to the wisdom of again going into the political arena. Nothing but a belief in the destiny of the situation causes me to do so, & the duty that I believe I shall be able to perform. But I am losing confidence in my own ability.'

Quebec City gave him a warm welcome toward the end of March that should have lifted his spirits to the point of exultation. He had suffered agonies at the prospect of speeches for the Canadian Club, the Reform Club, the Young Liberal Club, and a meeting which the Trades and Labour Council had arranged. One of them was to be his first address in French. After they were delivered he was justified in feeling that there had been no grounds for his worst fears — standing applause and cheers greeted him on each occasion. He was deeply moved by the enthusiastic acclaim of an audience of 1,500 workingmen at St. Sauveur Hall when the president of the Trades and Labour Council welcomed him in an address in French. Fortunately he was able to reply in French in a brief speech he had prepared for such an emergency.

Particularly pleasing, the next day, were the assurances of a deputation that the labour vote would be his if he would stand for Quebec East; it could be a joint nomination. His feelings of warm admiration for the French Canadians were confirmed and enhanced by his new first-hand contacts: 'I find a refinement and charm of manner & sympathy about the French-Canadian that our English-speaking Canadians lack.' He himself lacked the ability to speak freely in French or to understand it — his French speeches, never long, were always written first in English and he relied on friends for translation and coaching in pronunciation. It pleased him greatly to read a comment in the Quebec *Chronicle*, a Conservative newspaper, that his pronunciation and accent were good. 'I wish I could understand and speak French & cannot too much regret not having studied it the year I was abroad. My feeling at the moment is to go to France for a month between now and the summer & live with a French family and practise French after being in England for a time. This if the Govt. doesn't open a seat.' The Government did not open a seat, but the crowded schedule of his overseas trip in the summer, and the whirl of political activity immediately after his return, left no time for private studies.

In all his conversations with political leaders in the spring of 1919, Mackenzie King was conscious of the danger of entangle-

ments with representatives of business interests whose views on
tariff and other policies he could not share. Above all things he
must not permit himself to be under obligation to such avowed
protectionists as Sir Lomer Gouin, the premier of the province, and
Sir Charles Fitzpatrick, the Lieutenant-Governor, who had been
Minister of Justice and Chief Justice of the Supreme Court of
Canada. They honoured him for his support of Laurier and his
stand against the Union government; they were close enough to St.
James Street and the C.P.R. to ensure that influences from these
quarters could be exercised on his behalf in any campaign for the
leadership. That, however, was not the kind of support King
wanted. When Sir Charles suggested a week-end in Quebec with
Sir Lomer and himself for 'a tripartite chat', from which 'much
good might be accomplished', Mackenzie King declined; he feared
that such a relationship would be productive of more harm than
good. One thing Fitzpatrick had in mind was disclosed a month
later when he admitted frankly, in a talk in Ottawa the day King
left for England, that 'he was desirous of being the power behind
the throne in a new Liberal administration; in his own words to be
"the Sir Clifford Sifton" of the new organization. . . . He thought
that perhaps in the future there should be a joint English and
French leadership, as in the days of the Baldwin-Lafontaine,
Hincks-Morin administrations etc. etc. He believed the C.P.R. influence would be with such an administration. They were strongly
opposed to the present Unionist combination.' He went on to say
it was unwise, with the Liberal convention only weeks away, for
King to make the trip to England. He was taken aback by the
reply: 'I explained that I was indifferent about the leadership, and
certainly would not wish it if it had to come through manoeuvring
on my part, or if there was otherwise than a united party. I was
going away, amongst other things, to avoid entanglements with any
faction or group.' Perhaps Sir Charles took with a grain of salt this
declaration of independence, this indifference to the leadership.
But he was shocked that a prospective and probable successor to
Laurier should so express himself just when prospects were bright-

est for the achievement of one of his highest ambitions.

Mackenzie King had already told Sydney Fisher he would 'prefer being in the House as a member, rather than leader, for a while'. He would gladly stand aside for Fisher, he said, but, he added quickly, having in mind possible Liberal Unionist candidates, he would not stand aside for another. Fisher (then in his seventieth year, and even at that slightly younger than Fielding) agreed that no Unionist should or would be chosen — 'he thought the chance would come to me'. Fisher had entertained hopes that he himself might succeed Laurier, but he conceded now that the leader should be a younger man 'who could afford to lose this election and win the time after, as Laurier did when made leader'.

To be elected as a private member, particularly for Sir Wilfrid's riding of Quebec East, might be better than to be chosen for the leadership: 'I should almost incline toward the former,' he wrote to his brother. 'There is a fine independence that goes with simply being a member, and if I secure the seat . . . I shall feel wholly indifferent to the leadership.' He was thinking, of course, of only the immediate future; as a private member he would have opportunity to demonstrate his qualifications for leadership; if he could not succeed in that he would not wish the chance to lead.

The possibility of serving two masters, though only for a time, as a private member in Canada and as an industrial consultant in the United States, made momentary appeal. He could not live on a private member's indemnity of $2,500, but if he could carry on with his other work at the same time, as Rockefeller had suggested, he might be able, as he told his brother, 'to make ends meet'. He was beginning to give up thoughts of immediate leadership of the party, and to wonder whether perhaps, after all, his greatest service might not be 'to keep on with the industrial problem primarily, seeking at most a seat in Parliament to have that forum from which to speak; or possibly forgoing that altogether so as to avoid the identification with party and the handicap which it brings'. He was thinking of public questioning of his motives in whatever stand he might take on controversial issues. His conscience was clear, but at times he could not help 'feeling that the public regard me as a self-seeker in going into public life'. He missed the sympathy and interest which his father and mother had shown in his career: 'Much of the interest I had in public affairs was due to the pleasure and pride which I knew they felt in the work.'

X

His lack of close attachments, his sense of deep loneliness, had no small part in curbing enthusiasm for a new life that would be so demanding. 'Unmarried,' he wrote to his brother, 'I hesitate to take on the awful burden of leadership of a party and the conflicts of public life alone.' 'Being all alone,' he had written earlier, 'I would gladly drop out of the whole business. . . . It is too unfortunate for words being alone just at this time of my life; it causes me to lose ambition in everything.' The mood of introspection and doubt was upon him when he wrote: 'I sometimes wonder if being so much alone, and with my thoughts so inwrought with the grief and sorrow and strain of recent years, I am not living far too much in the past, and [have] more or less unfitted myself for the kind of all-round outlook which is so essential to wise leadership.' He could think of many reasons why he should not be the new leader of the Liberal Party. 'I realize more than all else,' he wrote at the time of Laurier's death, 'my limitations for so great a work, my short-comings in the past. I should have been reading history, studying politics, & above all watching my every thought & word.' Not only had his reading been too circumscribed, he felt, but everything he had been doing in recent years had been done in haste, 'leaving little in the way of intellectual capital of a kind likely to be of service in public affairs': he had been in Parliament for too short a time, out of Canadian politics too many years, and a good deal out of touch with the movements in political life. 'Moreover,' he confessed, 'when I see the jealousies and selfishness of many of those prominent in political circles, I feel I should like to be rid of the business altogether.' The numerical strength and morale of the party had never been lower: the new leader would have to take over an enterprise that was closer to bankruptcy than it had ever been; it would mean a much more difficult and trying life than any other he could be drawn into. He was concerned too about his health: 'Unless my mental health picks up within the next few months, nothing in the world would induce me to take on the strain of leadership. I have been too much run down with mental strain to cause myself to risk breaking under it. I could be of no service to the party, to the country or myself unless in decent mental and physical condition.' His financial condition was another reason for his reluctance; he had built up some reserves in four or five prosperous years, but hardly enough to guarantee the kind of financial independence he felt a political leader should enjoy: 'It would be hell itself to lead a political party and be dependent on politics for a livelihood.' Summing up all his misgivings, he wrote to his brother: 'To tell the honest truth I am daily coming to be in grave doubt as to the wisdom of my thinking of any leadership at this time.'

These, then, were important considerations which explain in part the attitude of indifference to the leadership which he had frequently expressed and his obviously sincere declarations that he would have 'neither rejoicing nor heart-burning in the outcome whatever it may be'. But there were still other considerations. He had told Fitzpatrick that he was 'more than happy in his present work and relationships' and had before him 'splendid openings in the United States'. 'If not chosen leader,' he had observed earlier, 'I shall be free of worry, having extra time for study etc. and [be] better off financially.' (This was the day he had received assurances from Rockefeller of an income of at least $25,000 a year.) He had unusual aptitudes for work in both fields, political and industrial, and would find personal satisfaction in either, though the political, with all its uncertainties, made stronger appeal than the other with all its likelihood of an assured future.

Another explanation of Mackenzie King's apparent lack of concern about the leadership, probably the most important of all, lay in his belief that the whole course of his life was, in a very special way, being determined by invisible forces beyond his control or any human control. He was Calvinist enough to believe in predestination; he was realist enough to apply the doctrine to the circumstances of his own life. With him it was a conviction that God had a unique mission for him 'to help work out His will in the world', to take an important part in the public life of Canada, to be a leader, and eventually to be the country's prime minister. Over and over again throughout the years he had reaffirmed his confidence in his own destiny, recognizing in every advance a manifestation of the Providence of God, and in every setback a testing of his faith. The 'Unseen Hand' and the ministry of his guardian angels were but synonyms for the Providence of God. 'There is a divinity that shapes our ends' was an often-repeated quotation. A week before Laurier's death he had written to his brother, 'It looks as though Destiny has intended me to continue to carry on the fight which grandfather commenced so bravely on behalf of the common people in their struggle against autocratic power.' He had a profound belief in 'that power which erring men call chance', but he was not among the erring ones; to him there was no such thing as chance: in this ordered universe every person, every happening, a falling leaf, the position of the hands of the clock in his study, had secret meaning for the discerning eye and ear and mind. Religious overtones are discernible even in the worldly phrase he used in April, referring to his future political prospects: 'I am simply leaving matters to decide themselves.' There were times, of course, when faith weakened and pessimism reigned; times when destiny seemed to need a helping hand to remove mountains or to prevent seemingly unnecessary delays; times, too, when he felt he must take thought for the morrow, fearing that the morrow might fail to take thought for itself. But basically his philosophy was one of trust that, without any manoeuvring or pulling of strings on his part, all things would work together for good — for, to complete the scriptural quotation, he had loved God and was one of them 'who are the called according to His purpose'.

Instead, therefore, of flinging himself headlong into a campaign for the leadership, his course would be one of wise inactivity. The choice, if it came to him, should be 'that of the people themselves and not [because] of any influence directly or indirectly exerted by myself or any fictitious advantage enjoyed'.

These were the underlying convictions that made him refuse to resort to any manoeuvring to win a prize which, none the less, he coveted. Unless, of course, standing still or forsaking the scene of battle altogether could be interpreted as manoeuvring, as part of a subtle strategy designed to put his rivals and their supporters off their guard. Unfriendly critics, presuming to understand the workings of a mind which few could ever fathom, could see only this as a possible explanation. In their opinion he was playing a game of 'hard to get', adopting a pose of indifference, planning to keep himself more or less under cover in order to avoid the attacks which would certainly be made upon him if he were much in the limelight. At the crucial moment, they were saying, he would emerge as a dark horse. In all this there may have been more than a modicum of truth: he himself recognized the advantages of a course that would keep him from being a target in the centre of pre-convention controversy. This may well explain his decision to absent himself from Canada for the ten precious weeks immediately before the convention, at the very time when Liberal minds would be subject to influences, now one way and now another, as they thought about the biggest issue at the convention, the choice of a new leader. Otherwise, how explain the fact that he was able to leave for England and the Continent for an unhurried visit, there to talk with friends abroad about matters unrelated to Canadian politics, with industrialists and trade unionists about joint control of industry, and with political leaders about plans for industrial reconstruction! And this after ten weeks spent in the United States, interrupted by only a few days in Toronto, Montreal, and Quebec City, where he talked with keen interest about the possibility of a seat in Parliament, and with apparent indifference about the leadership of the Liberal Party! In his public addresses at this time his theme was always 'The Four Parties to Industry', but no one could miss the political significance of these appearances. Going overseas, however, meant giving up opportunities for even occasional personal contacts with political friends who were willing to help and who wished he would be less reluctant about helping himself. What a way, they thought — and many said so frankly to him — what a way to conduct a campaign! Had he submitted such a programme to public-relations experts of that day they would have laughed at his naïveté. Elections, they would have told him, are won by campaigns and campaign funds and organization — not least, organization. There should be an advisory board of big names, a campaign committee representing every province, syndicated articles in the press, floods of pamphlets, personal canvasses in every polling division of the Dominion, and, above all, personal appearances of the candidate in cross-country speaking tours. Mackenzie King did not consult the public-relations experts. He had not been much impressed by those who reminded him that to be out of sight might quickly lead to being out of mind, but he was most anxious that the Liberals of North York should not forget him. He visited them and found that they were eager to have him accept again the nomination for the riding. They were evidently under the impression that he was thinking of Quebec, and were relieved to find that he had not committed himself. The warmth of their reception greatly cheered him: 'It is when I see the confidence that men of *this* type have that I feel drawn to politics.'

In spite of this apparently detached attitude to politics, his ambitions for the leadership were never for a moment forgotten. 'I have a feeling that so far as the leadership of the party is concerned, it will look a good deal more dignified on my part if I get out altogether and make it plain to the country that I am not seeking the position and that if it comes it must seek me.'

XI

Throughout April and until the very day of the sailing from New York on May 15, indeed up to the time of the convention in

August, Mackenzie King held to this intention not to lift a hand to further his candidature for the leadership. He made no arrangements with anyone in Canada to look after his interests in his absence; he set up no organization. It was a disappointment to keenly interested friends to be left in doubt whether he would run or not and, during his absence abroad, to receive no letters from him suggesting things that might be done or even inquiring about his own prospects. His detachment from the Canadian scene was apparent, too, in his conversations with Britishers about their affairs, his hungry interest in experiments in industrial democracy in the plants he visited and the industrialists and trade unionists he talked with, his unhappy brooding as he viewed the battlefields and devastated areas of France and Belgium. He kept a detailed record of his movements, his interviews, and his thoughts about what he had seen and heard. In that record all references to his own political prospects occupied only a few paragraphs out of nearly two hundred single-spaced typewritten pages. He was living in another world — the Old World — absorbed by its problems and their solution, forgetful of his own problems in the New World. He deliberately avoided discussion of party leadership, as when his friend Sir Campbell Stuart expressed the opinion that 'the Liberals ought to stand a good chance in Canada at the next election'. Stuart's curiosity was not satisfied: 'I felt that this remark was just in the nature of a draw and did not pay much attention to it.' Nor did Stuart get much more response when he remarked that he understood the choice of leadership was between Calder and King. The reply was brief: 'I told him I was not taking any part one way or the other; that I had important work along industrial lines to do, and unless there was some very strong demand to be of service in helping to reconcile the different factions into which our country was divided — French and English, East and West, Labour and Capital — that I could be of service in, I should not wish to be in politics.'

When he met General Sir Arthur Currie, he spoke freely about Canadian politics, though not about the leadership question. Currie was a man of his own age, forty-three; he was still in command of the Canadian overseas forces, and had just made a memorable speech at the Mansion House on 'the future relations between the Dominions and the Motherland'. Mackenzie King was 'greatly taken' with General Currie's personality, his modesty and reserve in speaking, his calmness and poise. He saw in him unusual political potentialities: 'I feel perfectly confident that he has a big future ahead of him in Canada. Of all the men I have met, he seems to me more likely than any other to become a prominent political figure, and I should not be surprised to see him Prime Minister of Canada some day. I intend to use what influence I have to keep him allied with the Liberal Party, because I feel that he is a true Liberal and has the principles of Liberalism at heart.' Before the end of their long conversation, Mackenzie King sounded the General on his thought of engaging in Canadian politics, and got the impression that he was not going to take any position for the present. He was satisfied with the answer and advised Currie to be 'very guarded about not touching politics again until he had been in Canada long enough to size up the situation for himself . . . that he could afford to wait until after the next election; that any Government would want to include him, and that he had better reserve himself for the place where he found it most desirable from his sympathies and beliefs to be.' Currie deprecated the way in which, in politics, all the men on one side were spoken of as all right and the others as all wrong: there was also too much that was abusive in the attitude of men toward each other. With this Mackenzie King agreed and commented that 'unless some of us who have a higher conception of politics kept in there would be no deliverance from this kind of thing . . . he would have to raise our politics to a higher level.'

It is plain from all his records in diaries and correspondence that he was not attempting anything in the way of remote control or influence from his constantly changing headquarters overseas. He had 'neither hopes nor expectations,' he wrote to his brother on June 23, 'as to what would happen at the convention. . . . It is possible that the labor unrest of the West may cause some of the

Party to be disposed toward my leadership, but I know so well the part which corrupt influence and jealousy play in politics and in the control of political situations that the thought of leadership does not present itself to my mind as more than the barest possibility. Were I in Parliament I should feel almost certain of the position; but having no seat, I can well see wherein it will not be difficult for interests with which I have never been allied to keep matters otherwise controlled.'

XII

As his sojourn in England was nearing its close his schedule was crowded with engagements. He did give some thought to the timing of his return. To himself he admitted that the convention was 'too important in its possible significance to take any chances on. I feel therefore it is best to be in Ottawa a little in advance of the meeting, and to learn something of the lay of the land and possible developments before the Convention is held.' Ten days in Ottawa, he had said before he left Canada, would be enough. Having this in mind he approved of a reservation that had been made for him on the *Adriatic*, due to sail from Liverpool on Monday, July 14. It so happened that I, his secretary, without consulting my chief and without realizing that I might be playing the part of a guardian angel, booked an alternative passage on the *Aquitania* for Saturday, July 12. Faced with the choice a few days before the sailing dates, Mackenzie King expressed preference for the later date, since it would give him another week-end in England. He yielded, however, to what seemed to be a whim of his secretary and left it to me to do whatever I liked. Passage on the *Aquitania* was thereupon confirmed, and when the ship sailed on the Saturday the two Canadians were aboard; we reached New York on July 20. Had we waited for the *Adriatic* the delay would have had disastrous effects: a strike of longshoremen, called during that week-end, postponed all sailings from English ports for a fortnight; we would not have reached Halifax until the afternoon of August 4.

With Ottawa a thousand miles away (a rail journey of twenty-eight hours, given the best of train connections) Mackenzie King might have reached the capital in time for the tail-end of the convention. He would have missed completely the important sessions of the 140 members of the national committee. This had been convened on July 31 and met daily. He would have missed also the important meetings of the special committees which decided what resolutions should be placed before the convention and who should sponsor them. Worst of all, he would have missed the golden opportunity which came to him as sponsor of the report of the Committee on Labour and Industrial Relations. Had his arrival been delayed he would have had no place on the committee, no part in its discussions or in the drafting of the resolution which represented the core of the eloquent speech he made before the convention as a whole. All this would have been lost — all this and the leadership too — had destiny not intervened and brought him safely to port on July 20 instead of August 4.

XIII

When he arrived in New York he wrote to his brother, 'I am going on to Ottawa tonight so as to have a fortnight clear to prepare for the convention. . . . I still have little expectation of being chosen leader, but have decided, if the choice comes my way, to accept it. If it passes to another I shall be wholly content.' Once he arrived on the scene in Ottawa, however, he experienced a remarkable but understandable change of attitude. He could be a relatively disinterested observer miles away and months away from the impending conflict, but here and now, with the challenge of battle and the plaudits of friends ringing in his ears, and the taste of possible triumph in the air, his fighting spirit was aroused. The speech he made on the labour committee's resolution was the outstanding speech of the convention. It was not a blunt appeal to the delegates to cast their votes for him; it was rather a declaration of policies worth fighting for, the condemnation of Tory practices that should be fought against, from which the obvious inference might well be that he was the man to lead them in such a fight. The glowing tribute to Laurier with which he concluded had in it no suggestion of himself as a worthy or unworthy successor, but it served to remind his hearers that he was one man who had remained true to Sir Wilfrid in his hour of need. His peroration was one that stirred the hearts of the faithful and moved them to prolonged cheering, an ovation that seemed the harbinger of certain victory. It was a dramatic *coup de grâce* and the sense of drama was heightened by the contrast between this outburst of eloquence and the silence which for months had preceded it. An attempt to shorten his address by insisting on the observance of a fifteen-minute rule had been made by Hartley Dewart, acting as chairman at that session, but 'I kept on despite his efforts to stop me — I felt I was entitled to a few words to Sir Wilfrid's memory'.* It was common talk at the end of the convention and afterwards that Mackenzie King's fighting speech marked the turning of the tide in his favour.

In spite of this acclaim from the floor of the convention, Mackenzie King still had his doubts about the outcome on the morrow. Four names were placed in nomination (Alexander Smith, K.C., because of his lifetime of service to the party as an organizer, received a complimentary nomination and withdrew his name immediately): W. S. Fielding, George P. Graham, W. L. Mackenzie King, and D. D. McKenzie (chosen acting leader in the House after Sir Wilfrid's death). Sydney Fisher's name was not included — he had decided, the night before, to drop out. Had a public-opinion poll been taken throughout the country before the event, it would undoubtedly have shown Fielding well in the lead. For days the newspapers had been full of reports of a Fielding 'boom' and editorial support was strong for him. All but two of the eight Liberal provincial premiers were known to be Fielding supporters; the two exceptions were Bell of Prince Edward Island and, prob-

---

* This speech and those of the other candidates (two of them also exceeded the time limit) were reported verbatim in *The Story of the Convention and the Report of its Proceedings, August 5, 6, 7, 1919.*

ably, John Oliver of British Columbia, whose first choice would be
King; Graham, it became obvious, would have the support of Hartley Dewart, then leader of the Liberal opposition in Ontario. The
Liberal-Unionists who had returned to the fold were naturally in
favour of either Fielding or Graham. They were none too sure,
however, that Fielding would stay in the running, for he had been
playing a game, as King put it, of 'not being in — then being in'.

In Ontario Mackenzie King could rely on substantial support
from the rural areas and from many elements in the labour movement, from North York and North Waterloo ('the men who knew
me best'), and from the rank-and-file Liberals who had admired his
stand with Laurier against the Union government. But against this
support he had to measure in Ontario the undoubted strength of
what he derisively termed the political machine controlled by the
federal and provincial organizations. 'The old gang', 'the machine
politicians', 'the Mackenzie and Mann crowd' — his descriptions
stopped only at the edge of profanity — these forces were arrayed
against him in support of George Graham. Since many of them had
been sympathetic to the Unionist cause, their votes, if Graham were
eliminated in the early balloting, would probably be transferred to
Fielding.

In the Maritimes and the western provinces the relative strengths
of the four candidates were difficult to assess. Two of them (Fielding and McKenzie) were Nova Scotians, the other two were from
Ontario; two (King and McKenzie) came within the category of
Laurier Liberals, the others (Fielding and Graham) had fraternized
with the enemy in the 1917 election, but not to the point of accepting invitations to join the Union government; two of them were
sixty years of age (Graham and McKenzie), while Fielding was
just over seventy and King not quite forty-five. In the West Mc-
Kenzie was virtually unknown; Graham had no following west of
Ontario, but his genial personality was of the kind that was
supposed to appeal to westerners; Mackenzie King was reasonably
well known because of his success in dealing with industrial disputes in the prairie provinces and Oriental immigration problems

which were of special interest to British Columbia; Fielding, a national figure since 1896 (he had been premier of Nova Scotia for twelve years before that), was recognized by the West as architect of the policy of reciprocity with the United States, ill-fated but still popular in the western provinces. It could be anyone's guess how the four candidates would fare in the first balloting of the eastern and western delegates, equally uncertain how in subsequent ballots, if McKenzie and Graham were eliminated, Fielding and King would fare as second choices.

As for Quebec, some division had appeared in the solid support that King's friends had counted on. 'The Quebec delegates were for me from the outset, except the Quebec protectionist group who were headed by Sir Lomer Gouin and the group around him at Quebec, including Taschereau, Paradis and others who had given me such a hearty welcome there some months ago.' A move had been made in a caucus of Quebec delegates in favour of Quebec abstaining from voting: 'This, Ernest Lapointe, in a smashing speech, destroyed completely, only the mover and seconder supported the motion. Then the caucus put the "protectionist" group to the wall and declared open revolt against the Quebec leaders et al. The province almost solidly agreed to stand by me, Fisher was accorded no place. This caused Fisher to drop out Wednesday night.' Fisher's unwillingness to retire earlier had been an embarrassment, for King had been counting on him to watch his interests. Every vote for Fisher would be a vote less for King. A. B. Aylesworth had intended to nominate Fisher and W. T. R. Preston had been conducting a one-man campaign for him in Ontario and elsewhere. When Fisher made his last-minute decision not to run, Aylesworth transferred his allegiance to King, and it was he and Fisher who moved and seconded his nomination. Up to that time — and this was only hours before nominations closed — no arrangements had been made to ensure King's nomination; he himself, in keeping with his policy of *laissez-faire*, had taken no steps to secure a nominator, although he had been urged to do so by Quebec friends.

Mackenzie King received a staggering blow when he made an evening call on Lady Laurier the day before the voting. He had felt sure of her support, and was shocked to find that she had been telling others that it was Sir Wilfrid's wish that Fielding should succeed him. 'She told me that was what he had said, Fielding for a time, then me.' This was, to him, almost unbelievable: 'Undoubtedly Sir Wilfrid would have preferred that, had Fielding remained true, but he told me with his own lips on three occasions that he wished me to succeed him. So I knew his wish.'

It was a difficult thing to know what was going on in the minds of the hundreds of delegates (949 voted on the first ballot, not as members of provincial blocs but as individuals). Some were as secret as the ballots they subsequently cast; others outspokenly and honestly committed themselves to particular candidates; still others were outspoken but dishonest in their declarations of loyalty. One instance of such hypocrisy occurred when, in one of the many little groups that huddled together in the grounds of Lansdowne Park before and after the sessions and during intermissions, one prominent delegate (in his own opinion a potential Cabinet minister) held forth in unprintable language about the calamity that would befall the party and the nation if Mackenzie King were chosen. It was only chance that the object of this vituperation, unaware that he was under attack, edged into the group only to be greeted by a cheer of welcome from the speaker, an embrace, and an enthusiastic cry of 'You're the boy for us, Billy'.

XIV

Faced with all the uncertainty that is a part of any election and at the same time oppressed by the certainty of formidable opposition in the central provinces and more than a suspicion of intrigue, Mackenzie King questioned within himself whether he really wanted to be the final choice of the convention. This state of indecision lasted to within hours of the taking of the vote. To one person at least he confided his doubts: 'I spoke long with Walter Mitchell and expressed to him honestly my feelings which were that I should like to win on the first ballot, but was not anxious to win out. I was thinking of the strain and all the hate of public life, I was hoping that Fielding might win & I might get into Prlt. & there make good and succeed later to the leadership if worthy.'

These were his thoughts when he retired at two-thirty for a sleep that lasted only till six o'clock. His first impulse on waking was to reach for his book of devotional readings, *Daily Strength for Daily Needs*, to see what 'message' it might have for him on this momentous day, what augury for good or ill it might reveal, what word that could be interpreted as divine guidance. He was not disappointed. Opening the book at random (it was a practice of his) he was rewarded by the appearance of several significant passages, one of them from the Old Testament: 'Ye shall rejoice in all that ye put your hand unto.' But even more reassuring and inspiring were the words that leaped to his eye when he opened the book at the page for that very day, August 7: 'If thou canst believe, all things are possible to him that believeth', and 'Nothing shall be impossible unto you'. Emerson's words were there: 'When Duty whispers low, *thou must*, the youth replies *I can*'; and Carlyle's 'Know that "impossible" has no place in the brave man's dictionary.... Brother, thou hast possibility in thee for much: the possibility of writing on the eternal skies the record of an heroic life.' This was the revelation he was looking for. He was always resentful of any scoffing of 'unbelievers' so blind as not to see, as he did, that the divine will could be revealed through such commonplace acts as the opening of a book. Copying out these passages in his diary he addressed himself to the sceptics in words of stern admonition: 'Look ye who doubt, and say whether or not ye believe there is a God who rules the world!'

All through the day the haunting words of his little book were in his thoughts. But other thoughts, of questioning and doubt, crowded into his mind as the time approached for the taking of the vote. Ballots for the first vote were distributed and collected and while they were being counted delegates continued to speak on

various resolutions. At the completion of Colonel Ralston's address
on soldiers' civil re-establishment, the chairman interrupted the
proceedings to announce the result of the first ballot. Before the
announcement was made, Mackenzie King and presumably others
on the platform had had advance word of the result. 'I felt a
momentary qualm,' he wrote later on, 'not a feeling of elation —
but of depression — at the thought that I was likely to win —
wondering if I could measure up to the task, being conscious fully
of my limitations and many imperfections.' Then came the official
announcement: King had received 344 votes, Fielding 297, Graham
153, McKenzie 153. King's lead over Fielding was narrow enough,
only 47 votes. Since no candidate had received a majority of the
total votes cast, ballots were distributed for a second vote and the
result was duly reported: it showed King with 411 votes, Fielding
344, Graham 124, McKenzie 60. At this point, Graham and Mc-
Kenzie retired and with their withdrawal came the moment of
greatest suspense. Would their supporters turn to Fielding or to
King? Several more speeches on resolutions were listened to, or at
least were delivered, pending the return of the tellers. At long last
they filed in and the chairman announced the result: 476 votes for
King, 438 for Fielding, a majority of 38 votes. Mackenzie King was
the new leader of the Liberal Party in Canada.

Again, his first reaction was not one of rejoicing: 'Just before the
result of the last ballot was announced, I sat quietly waiting on the
platform. . . . I turned to look at Sir Wilfrid's picture which was at
the back of the stage and beautifully illuminated; the eyes were
looking straight down upon me. I thought of his words that he
wanted me to succeed him, and I felt — tho' still wishing I might
be saved the choice — happy in the thought I had made an honor-
able run — I shall win or, rather, I shall be chosen. There was no
thought of winning in my mind.' The majority when it was announced was better than he had anticipated but, he wrote, 'I was
too heavy of heart and soul to appreciate the tumult of applause.'
His thoughts were of the members of his family, whose presence
he could feel, much as he felt in later years when he believed even

more implicitly in his ability to communicate with the souls of the departed. He wrote on: 'I thought, it is right, it is the call of duty. I have sought nothing, it has come, it has come from God. . . . It is to His work I am called, and to it I dedicate my life. This dedication I made to God in my heart as I sat there and heard the returns.'

With mingled feelings of sadness and satisfaction Mackenzie King could look back on the collapse of 1911 – the collapse of a promising political career too soon cut off – and the years of frustration which followed. He would never be able to forget his fruitless efforts to secure again a foothold in politics, the indifference of friends, the bitterness of hopes dashed again and again – all culminating (or so it seemed at the time) with the debacle of 1917. Family ties had been broken with the death of his sister, his father, and his mother in three successive years. His only brother was hundreds of miles distant, and mortally ill. At this moment of triumph he was alone. Oppressed by the overwhelming need he felt for love and companionship, for some close personal relationship, he wrote that night in his diary, 'I need a wife – God will send the right woman to me to share my life & to work out a realization of the high purpose in view. My faith is strong. My belief is sure.' But the Providence which had guided him to political victory vouchsafed no answer to this prayer. Even his strong faith and sure belief, supported by sporadic but earnest efforts, accomplished nothing; his life of unmarried loneliness stretched on for another three decades, to the end of his days.

Nevertheless, in other spheres life had offered him much. The political defeat of 1911 had opened the way to a new career which began with his first association with the Rockefeller Foundation and the remarkable personal relationship with its president, John D. Rockefeller, Jr., which grew out of it. The warm friendship between the two men, which continued throughout their lives, had led to opportunities to widen his scope as an industrial counsellor, and in this new career – though of necessity it was his second choice – he had quickly risen to the top, by his own sheer native ability and hard work. Through this work and through his *Industry and Humanity* he had made notable contributions to the movements toward industrial self-government and post-war industrial reconstruction. He had suffered defeat in 1917, it is true, but even this had had its compensating advantages, for it was his loyalty to Laurier throughout that campaign that won him his victory at the 1919 convention. Thus, while his personal life remained incomplete, the leadership of the Liberal Party was now to give him, at last, after many vicissitudes, the opportunity to take the place in the public life of his own country for which he had always and so deeply longed. The long strain over, he was able to write in his diary: 'I feel a great happiness . . . as if I had found my life work at last.'

Notes

Each item in this list consists of a page-number (in roman type), a line-number (in italic type), and a source. The line given is the line in which the quotation or reference ends. Dates refer to Mackenzie King's diaries, unless otherwise explained.

CHAPTER 1

Pages 18-45

19 *21* Feb. 18, 1901
26 *The Secret of Heroism.* Fleming H. Revell Co., New York, 1906
20 *25* Feb. 8, 1901
21 *10* Sept. 2, 1901
22 *29* Jan. 4, 1904
23 *5* Sept. 10, 1906
15 Feb. 14, 1904
25 Feb. 21, 1904
24 *6* Mar. 3, 1904
20 Oct. 12, 1904
25 *10* Oct. 19, 1904
20 Nov. 18, 1904
23 Mar. 3, 1908
26 *25* Dec. 17, 1904
28 *2* Nov. 4, 1905
27 Jan. 2, 1906
31 Feb. 3, 1906
29 *8* Apr. 23, 1906
30 *8* Aug. 31, 1906
32 Dec. 4, 1906
31 *5* Jan. 1, 1907
31 July 25, 1907
32 *27* July 25, 1907
33 *27* Aug. 27, 1907
34 *5* Aug. 27, 1907
9 Oct. 9, 1907
24 Sept. 7, 1907
30 Sept. 28, 1907

35 *5* Sept. 4, 1907
28 May, 4, 1908
36 *4* Sept. 9, 1908
11 Aug. 29, 1908
15 Sept. 2, 1908
18 Sept. 6, 1908
22 Sept. 9, 1908
25 Sept. 12, 1908
37 *8* Sept. 17-21, 1908
16 Sept. 17-21, 1908
29 Oct. 30, 1908
38 *19* Dec. 5, 1908
40 *5* Feb. 4, 1910
15 Dec. 6, 1909
41 *31* Dec. 15, 1909
42 *20* Jan. 18, 1911
31 Jan. 26, 1911
43 *16* O. D. Skelton:
Life and Letters of Sir Wilfrid Laurier. Vol. II, p. 370. O.U.P., Toronto, 1921
23 A. R. M. Lower: *Colony to Nation*, p. 430. Longmans, Toronto, 1946

CHAPTER 2

Pages 46-64

46 *10* Sept. 24, 1911
47 *8* Sept. 25, 1911
26 J. W. Dafoe:

Laurier: a Study in Canadian Politics, p. 136. Thomas Allen, Toronto, 1922
48 *7* Sept. 25, 1911
21 *Ibid.*
32 *Ibid.*
49 *22* Sept. 30, 1911
30 Nov. 9, 1911
50 *7* Jan. 16, 1912
15 Mar. 2, 1912
30 Dec. 2, 1908
51 *25* Mar. 2, 1912
52 *26* J. W. Dafoe, *op. cit.*, p. 139
53 *11* Sept. 30, 1911
24 *Ibid.*
54 *3* Nov. 17, 1911
11 O. D. Skelton, *op. cit.*, p. 371
55 *14* Feb. 27, 1904
23 Feb. 29, 1904
56 *16* Jan. 16, 1912
57 *2* Feb. 8, 1901
5 Mar. 6, 1912
12 May 7, 1914
58 *2* Sept. 25, 1911
18 Oct. 23, 1911
23 Oct. 10, 1911
59 *10* Mar. 16, 1912
22 Oct. 26, 1911
60 *10* Oct. 23, 1911
26 Nov. 16, 1911
61 *6* Nov. 21, 1911

28 Dec. 14, 1911
62 *3* Dec. 20, 1911
33 Feb. 16, 1912
63 *9* Mar. 18, 1912

CHAPTER 3

Pages 65-91

65 *22* Jan. 12, 1912
66 *10* Feb. 29, 1912
20 Dec. 17, 1911
67 *32* Dec. 31, 1911
69 *2* Sept. 24, 1911
8 W.L.M.K. to
Violet
Markham,
Oct. 11, 1911
11 *Ibid.* Dec. 11, 1911
21 Oct. 13, 1911
70 *1* Sept. 24, 1911
3 F. A. Acland to
W.L.M.K.,
Sept. 2, 1912
15 Sept. 24, 1911
23 Sept. 24, 1911
71 *29* Sept. 25 and
Oct. 23, 1911
72 *14* Mar. 15, 1912
74 *10* Oct. 31, 1911
23 *Ibid.*
75 *2* *Ibid.*
31 *Ibid.*
76 *15* *Ibid.*
23 Nov. 14, 1911
30 Dec. 11, 1911
77 *12* *Ibid.*
32 W.L.M.K. to
Violet
Markham,
Feb. 13, 1912
80 *21* W.L.M.K. to
Mrs. John King,
Dec. 9, 1912
81 *32* Oct. 24, 1914
82 *16* Mar. 15, 1912
23 Jan. 1-14, 1919
83 *35* Sept. 24, 1911
84 *9* Jan. 25, 1911
17 Jan. 28, 1911
85 *10* Oct. 31, 1911
16 Dec. 31, 1911

30 Jan. 14, 1912
86 *13* Jan. 17, 1912
30 *Ibid.*
87 *8* *Ibid.*
25 Jan. 19, 1912
88 *5* Jan. 21, 1912
29 Feb. 5, Mar. 4, 12,
1912
34 Mar. 14, 1912
89 *29* May 2 and 4, 1914
90 *11* May 11, 1914
17 May 10, 1914
27 May 12, 1914
91 *1* *Ibid.*

CHAPTER 4

Pages 92-114

92 *8* W.L.M.K. to
Violet
Markham,
Mar. 5, 1913
19 May 12, 1914
93 *20* Jerome D.
Greene to
W.L.M.K.,
June 1, 1914
94 *3* C. W. Eliot to
W.L.M.K.,
June 1, 1914
33 Jerome D.
Greene to
W.L.M.K.,
June 3, 1914
95 *6* Oct. 10, 1914
96 *28* June-December,
1914, pp. 9-15
97 *34* *Ibid.*, p. 15
98 *11* Jerome D.
Greene to
W.L.M.K.,
June 9, 1914
27 *Ibid.*
99 *6* June-December,
1914, p. 20
26 *Ibid.*, pp. 24-5
32 *Ibid.*, p. 24
100 *11* *Ibid.*, pp. 25-6
20 *Ibid.*, pp. 26-7
28 *Ibid.*, p. 27
31 *Ibid.*, p. 27

101 *6* W.L.M.K. to
D. M. King,
July 8, 1914
15 D. M. King to
W.L.M.K.,
July 21, 1914
102 *35* Violet Markham
to W.L.M.K.,
June 11, 1914
103 *17* June-December,
1914, p. 17
20 *Ibid.*, p. 23
25 *Ibid.*, p. 43
104 *9* Dec. 4, 1914
29 June-December,
1914, pp. 34-5
105 *29* *Ibid.*, p. 36
106 *16* *Ibid.*, pp. 46-7
29 J.D.R. Jr. to
W.L.M.K.,
June 23, 1914
107 *3* June-December,
1914, pp. 48-9
27 *Ibid.*, p. 37
108 *15* D. M. King to
W.L.M.K.,
Oct. 29, 1914
28 René Vallery-
Radot: *The
Life of Pasteur,*
Vol. II, p. 222.
Constable,
London, 1911
29 Oct. 6, 1914
109 *15* Answers to
Questionnaire
of U.S. Com-
mission on
Industrial
Relations, Dec.
1914
30 Dec. 1, 1914
111 *21* Dec. 13, 1914
28 Nov. 19, 1914
112 *7* Nov. 5, 1914
12 Nov. 25, 1914
20 Nov. 17, 1914
33 Oct. 4, 1914
113 *1* Oct. 17, 1914
30 Dec. 3, 1914
114 *2* Dec. 8, 1914
9 Dec. 16, 1914

CHAPTER 5

Pages 115-125

117 *30* Raymond B.
Fosdick: *John
D. Rockefeller,
Jr.: a Portrait,*
p. 151. Harper,
New York, 1956
118 *10* Jan. 6, 1915
120 *2* Mar. 25, 1915
121 *25* Testimony before
sub-committee
of Congressional
Committee on
Mines and
Mining, April
6, 1914, p. 2887
122 *6* M. D. Foster to
J.D.R. Jr.,
April 29, 1914
32 Mar. 3, 1915

CHAPTER 6

Pages 126-146

127 *5* Sec. of Act of
Congress
creating U.S.
Commission on
Industrial
Relations, Aug.
23, 1912
130 *4* Dr. Charles
McCarthy to
Jerome D.
Greene, Oct. 8,
1914
22 Oct. 15, 1914
131 *25* Jan. 12, 1915
33 Jan. 15, 1915
132 *6* Jan. 14, 1915
27 Jan. 12, 1915
133 *7* Jan. 24, 1915
16 Jan. 25, 1915
17 Jan. 18, 1915
21 Jan. 26, 1915
26 Fosdick, *op. cit.,*
p. 157
29 Jan. 25, 1915
134 *2* Jan. 25, 1915
10 Jan. 26, 1915

17 Jan. 21, 1915
26 Jan. 27, 1915
135 *20* Jan. 27, 1915
137 *10* Jan. 25, 1915
32 Jan. 27, 1915
35 Fosdick, *op. cit.,*
p. 148
138 *17* Jan. 25, 1915
33 *Ibid.*
139 *10* *Ibid.*
140 *3* *Ibid.*
17 *Ibid.*
29 *Ibid.*
141 *6* Jan. 27, 1915
13 Jan. 25, 1915
142 *2* Jan. 28, 1915
19 Jan. 26, 1915
143 *8* Jan. 28, 1915
19 Fosdick, *op. cit.,*
p. 94
144 *10* *Ibid.,* p. 158
29 Jan. 27, 1915
145 *7* *Ibid.*
22 Feb. 2, 1915
146 *5* W.L.M.K. to
J.D.R. Jr., Feb.
9, 1915

CHAPTER 7

Pages 147-161

147 *17* W.L.M.K. to
J. D. Greene,
June 9, 1914
148 *6* J.D.R. Jr. to
W.L.M.K.,
Aug. 11, 1914
21 J. F. Welborn to
J.D.R. Jr., Aug.
20, 1914
27 W.L.M.K. to
J.D.R. Jr., Sept.
21, 1914
149 *3* Jan. 16, 1915
10 J. F. Welborn to
J.D.R. Jr., Aug.
20, 1914
18 Mar. 2, 1915
150 *3* Jan. 27, 1915
9 Feb. 23, 1915
24 Feb. 20, 1915
31 Feb. 25, 1915

151 *4* W.L.M.K. to
J. D. Greene,
Mar. 1, 1915
13 Mar. 2, 1915
25 *Ibid.*
152 *5* Report of Seth
Low Commis-
sion, Feb. 23,
1916
8 Feb. 27, 1915
11 Mar. 4, 1915
31 Mar. 15, 1915
153 *4* Feb. 27, 1915
154 *25* *Ibid.*
32 *Ibid.*
155 *12* Mar. 1, 1915
25 Mar. 2, 1915
156 *15* Mar. 19, 1915
32 Mar. 23, 1915
157 *6* Report of Com-
mission on
Unemployment
and Relief,
Mar. 28, 1916
28 W.L.M.K. to
Starr J.
Murphy, Apr.
19, 1915
158 *11* *Ibid.*
16 Apr. 21, 1915
159 *4* Apr. 23, 1915
28 Testimony of
J.D.R. Jr.
before U.S.
Commission on
Industrial Re-
lations, New
York, Jan. 25,
1915
160 *8* W.L.M.K. to
J.D.R. Jr., Feb.
12, 1915
161 *25* May 8, 1915

CHAPTER 8

Pages 162-174

163 *12* F. A. McGregor
to C. O. Heydt,
May 10, 1915
29 May 3, 1915
164 *14* Sept. 8-11, 1915

165 *11* May 17-25, 1915
15 Ibid.
166 *14 Ibid.*
21 Ibid.
170 27 Testimony of
W.L.M.K.
before U.S.
Commission on
Industrial
Relations,
Washington,
May 25, 1915
35 New York *Times,*
May 29, 1915
171 *12* New York
Tribune, May
29, 1915
172 *12* George P. West:
Report on the
Colorado Strike
(1915), pp.
166-7
173 *16* W.L.M.K. to
J.D.R. Jr., Dec.
18, 1915
19 Ibid. Dec. 28, 1915
174 *13 Ibid.* Nov. 6, 1915
26 Selig Perlman:
*A History of
Trade
Unionism in the
United States,*
p. 238. 1937

CHAPTER 9
Pages 175-189

175 *8* J.D.R. Jr. to
W.L.M.K.,
Aug. 9, 1915
176 *1* Sept. 8-10, 1915
177 *13 Ibid.*
184 *6* Selekman and
Van Kleeck:
*Employes' Rep-
resentation in
Coal Mines,* p.
27. Russell Sage
Foundation,
New York,
1924. See this
volume for full

discussion of
Plan for coal
mines.
185 *29* New York *Times,*
Oct. 5, 1915
186 *32* Report of Seth
Low Commis-
sion, Feb. 23,
1916
187 *19* Ben M. Selekman:
*Employes' Rep-
resentation in
Steel Works,* p.
44. Russell Sage
Foundation,
New York,
1924. See this
volume for full
discussion of
Plan for steel
works.
27 Ibid., pp. 197-8

CHAPTER 10
Pages 190-198

190 *16* J.D.R. Jr. to Mr.
and Mrs. John
King, Oct. 14,
1915
21 Jan. 29, 1915
191 *1* Fosdick, *op. cit.,*
p. 154
193 *2* Dec. 4, 1914
11 Mar. 4, 1915
24 W.L.M.K. to
Violet
Markham, un-
dated (Feb. or
Mar. 1917)
194 *1* June-December,
1914, p. 41
14 Ibid., pp. 38-9
23 Jan. 16, 1915
195 *5* Jan. 15, 1915
11 Jan. 16, 1915
27 Feb. 21, 1918
196 *15* Feb. 27, 1918
22 Apr. 6, 1918
29 Apr. 13, 1918
197 *30* Fosdick, *op. cit.,*
p. 161

198 *4 Ibid.,* p. 198

CHAPTER 11
Pages 199-214

199 *22* Testimony of
W.L.M.K.
before U.S.
Commission on
Industrial
Relations,
Washington,
May 25, 1915
200 *24* Feb. 27, 1915
201 *6* Sept. 7, 1915
13 Ibid.
203 *12* Sept. 15, 1915
204 *16* Sept. 13, 1915
26 Denver *Post,* Oct.
5, 1915
206 *27* Selekman, *op. cit.,*
pp. 327-8
207 *16* Jan. 25, 1919
23 Ibid.
208 *9* W.L.M.K. to
J.D.R. Jr.,
Mar. 4, 1919
26 Sept. 29, 1919
209 *7* Raymond B.
Fosdick to
W.L.M.K.,
Sept. 19, 1919
21 W.L.M.K. to
J.D.R. Jr., Oct.
6, 1919
31 J.D.R. Jr. to J. F.
Welborn, Oct.
25, 1919
210 *7* W.L.M.K. to
J.D.R. Jr., Oct.
25, 1919
28 Report of Royal
Commission,
Sept. 1919. See
Labour Gazette,
July, 1919
211 *12* Proceedings of
National
Industrial Con-
ference, Ottawa,
Sept. 15-20.
King's Printer,

Ottawa, 1919
23 Ibid., p. 71
36 Ibid., p. 72
212 22 Ibid., p. 73
35 Selekman and
Van Kleeck,
op. cit., pp.
393-4
213 15 Bulletin 1267,
U.S. Dept. of
Labor, Dec.
1959, p. 9
18 Leo Wolman:
Growth of
American
Trade Unions,
1880-1923, p. 41.
1924
26 Herbert Harris:
American
Labor, p. 139.
1938
214 5 See Arthur M.
Schlesinger, Jr.,
The Coming of
the New Deal,
pp. 144-5.
Houghton
Mifflin, Boston,
1959

CHAPTER 12

Pages 215-229

216 19 W.L.M.K. to
J. D. Greene,
Jan. 24, 1916
217 6 J. D. Greene to
J.D.R. Jr., Apr.
14, 1916
9 J.D.R. Jr. to
J. D. Greene,
Apr. 17, 1916
19 Report of
W.L.M.K. to
Rockefeller
Foundation,
May 10, 1916
219 4 June 26-July 1,
1916
33 Oct. 13, 1916
220 9 Dec. 16, 1916

221 1 Feb. 10, 1917
18 Apr. 26, 1917
21 Jan. 9, 1917
223 22 Mar. 7-9, 1917
224 6 Oct. 30, 1917
225 18 Dr. George E.
Vincent to
J.D.R. Jr., Dec.
27, 1917
34 Feb. 21, 1918
226 22 Feb. 17, 1918
227 21 Sept. 16, 1918
35 R. MacGregor
Dawson:
William Lyon
Mackenzie
King: 1874-1923,
p. 252. Univer-
sity of Toronto
Press, Toronto,
1958
228 20 Oct. 14, 1918
229 7 Oct. 16, 1919

CHAPTER 13

Pages 230-246

231 16 Bruce Hutchison:
The Incredible
Canadian, p. 39.
Longmans,
Toronto, 1952
233 25 Industry and
Humanity, p.
207. Houghton
Mifflin, Boston,
1918
35 Ibid., pp. 512-13
234 9 Ibid., pp. 492-3
16 Ibid., pp. 515-16
28 Ibid., p. 432
235 18 Ibid., pp. 432-3
23 Ibid., p. 379
29 Ibid., p. 380
236 8 Ibid., pp. 380-1
16 Ibid., p. 388
27 Ibid., pp. 382-3
237 19 Ibid., pp. 186-7
30 Ibid., pp. 178-9
238 11 Ibid., pp. 179-80
239 3 Ibid., p. 56
9 Ibid., p. 73

18 Ibid., p. 327
240 13 Ibid., p. 419
25 Ibid., pp. 419-20
241 4 Ibid., pp. 344-5
21 Ibid., p. 350
242 3 Ibid., p. 346
18 Ibid., pp. 346-7
32 Ibid., pp. 347-8
244 20 Violet Markham
to W.L.M.K.,
Feb. 22, 1919
30 W.L.M.K. to
Sidney Webb,
July 11, 1919
245 8 Nov. 4, 1918
246 10 Nov. 11, 1918
14 Jan. 1-14, 1919

CHAPTER 14

Pages 247-278

247 20 Feb. 17, 1918
248 2 Feb. 19, 1918
20 W.L.M.K. to
D. M. King,
Feb. 27, 1918
31 W.L.M.K. to
Violet
Markham,
Mar. 6, 1918
249 13 Apr. 6, 1918
19 Apr. 13, 1918
250 21 Apr. 27, 1918
33 Ibid.
251 2 June 3, 1918
11 Apr. 24, 1918
25 Aug. 29, 1918
252 11 June 3, 1918
24 June 26, 1918
253 3 July 26, 1918
22 Aug. 10, 1918
32 New Republic,
Aug. 10, 1918
254 17 Aug. 12, 1918
255 6 J.D.R. Jr. to
W.L.M.K.,
Sept. 18, 1919
256 2 Richard H. Rice
to W.L.M.K.,
Sept. 29, 1919
33 Nov. 30, 1918
257 23 Oct. 30, 1918

258 *15* Harold F.
McCormick to
W.L.M.K., Oct.
30, 1919
19 Earl Dean
Howard to
W.L.M.K.,
Feb. 7, 1922
259 *10* Nov. 4, 1918
36 *Ibid.*
260 *20* *Ibid.*
28 *Ibid.*
261 *9* *Ibid.*
35 W. L. Petrikin to
W.L.M.K.,
Nov. 4, 1919
262 *16* June 3, 1918
263 *12* J.D.R. Jr. to
W.L.M.K.,
Nov. 9, 1918
264 *5* Jan. 17, 1919
15 Jan. 25, 1919
265 *6* Feb. 7, 1919
28 *Ibid.*
266 *7* *Ibid.*
20 W.L.M.K. to
J.D.R. Jr.,
Feb. 10, 1919
267 *11* Feb. 14, 1919
32 *Ibid.*
268 *22* R. W. Stewart
to W.L.M.K.,
Oct. 7, 1919
29 W.L.M.K. to
D. M. King,
Feb. 10, 1919
31 *Ibid.*, Mar. 23,
1919
269 *26* Apr. 12, 1919
35 Apr. 12-15, 1919
270 *9* Feb. 1, 1919
23 Apr. 15, 1919
36 Apr. 16, 1919
271 *19* W.L.M.K. to
J.D.R. Jr.,
Mar. 23, 1919
272 *3* Dec. 17, 1918
10 Aug. 30, 1918
17 Nov. 23, 1918
273 *29* Jan. 1-14, 1919
274 *10* *Ibid.*
14 *Ibid.*

18 *Ibid.*
26 Feb. 19, 1919
33 Jan. 14-21, 1919
275 *8* *Ibid.*
16 May 15, 1919
30 Jan. 1-14, 1919
276 *11* Jan. 14-21, 1919
34 Jan. 1-14, 1919
277 *5* *Ibid.*
14 *Ibid.*
36 Jan. 29, 1919

CHAPTER 15

Pages 279-309

279 *16* J. M. Walton
to W.L.M.K.,
July 3, 1916
280 *13* W.L.M.K. to
J. M. Walton,
Apr. 19, 1915
18 Laurier to W. S.
Fielding, May
6, 1915
27 Ottawa *Citizen*,
July 21, 1916
281 *33* June 27-9, 1916
282 *26* Nov. 22, 1916
32 Nov. 29, 1916
283 *6* Dec. 12, 1916
18 Dec. 13, 1916
22 Dec. 14, 1916
28 Dec. 31, 1916
284 *9* *Robert Laird
Borden: His
Memoirs*, p. 609.
Macmillan,
Toronto, 1938
285 *10* Borden's Memoirs,
op. cit., p. 698
15 Feb. 21, 1917
28 May 9, 1917
35 May 10, 1917
286 *14* May 15, 1917
17 May 18, 1917
29 May 17, 1917
287 *3* House of
Commons De-
bates, July 24,
1917. Quoted in
Borden's
Memoirs, p. 704

288 *28* J. E. Atkinson to
W.L.M.K.,
May 28, 1917
289 *6* Laurier to Borden,
June 6, 1917
12 W.L.M.K. to
W. H. S. Cane,
June 11, 1917
290 *34* July 20, 1917
291 *8* July 21, 1917
19 July 23, 1917
35 July 24, 1917
292 *12* July 29, 1917
23 Aug. 7, 1917
293 *10* Aug. 8, 23, 1917
25 Sept. 6, 1917
33 W.L.M.K. to
D. M. King,
Sept. 10, 1917
294 *5* Sept. 15, 1917
18 Borden's Memoirs,
op. cit., p. 734
25 *Ibid.*
295 *20* *Ibid.*, p. 742
29 Oct. 6, 1917
296 *22* *Ibid.*
297 *20* Oct. 12, 1917
298 *5* Oct. 19, 1917
10 Oct. 23, 1917
18 Oct. 9, 1917
27 W.L.M.K. to
Mrs. H. M. Lay,
Oct. 20, 1917
299 *4* W.L.M.K. to
D. M. King,
Oct. 15, 1917
23 Oct. 20, 1917
34 *Ibid.*
300 *3* W.L.M.K. to
D. M. King,
Oct. 20, 1917
20 Oct. 14, 1917
23 Oct. 13, 1917
30 Oct. 12, 1917
301 *13* Oct. 23, 1917
21 Oct. 26, 1917
33 Oct. 27, 1917
302 *23* Oct. 29, 1917
34 Oct. 30, 1917
303 *16* Oct. 31, 1917
33 Nov. 3, 1917
304 *18* W.L.M.K. to J.

Murray Clark,
Nov. 22, 1917
306 *10* See O. D. Skelton,
op. cit., pp. 537
and 544

CHAPTER 16

Pages 310-345

311 *7* Feb. 27, 1918
22 Ibid.
312 *10* Jan. 17, 1912
16 July 18, 1918
313 *25* Sept. 17, 1918
314 *34* Sept. 18, 1918
315 *20 Ibid.*
27 Oct. 20, 1918
316 *8* Oct. 22, 1918
317 *9 Ibid.*
27 Nov. 23, 1918
318 *1 Ibid.*
5 Ibid.
30 Dec. 17, 1918
(written Jan. 5,
1919)
319 *7* Laurier to E. M.
Macdonald,
Jan. 12, 1918
9 Laurier to
W. R. Riddell,
July 4, 1918
21 Murphy to
Laurier,
Jan. 13, 1918
25 E. M. Macdonald
to Laurier,
Jan. 9, 1918
26 Laurier to E. M.
Macdonald,
Jan. 12, 1918
31 Laurier to
Aylesworth,

July 8, 1918
320 *11* Jan. 1-14, 1919
(written
Jan. 14)
15 Ibid.
321 *13* Laurier to
W.L.M.K.,
Jan. 27, 1919
19 W.L.M.K. to
Laurier,
Jan. 30, 1919
25 Laurier to
W.L.M.K.,
Feb. 3, 1919
31 Laurier to
W.L.M.K.,
Feb. 12, 1919
322 *18* Feb. 18-22, 1919
30 Ibid.
323 *11* Feb. 18-22, 1919
22 Ibid.
324 *15 Ibid.*
325 *10* W.L.M.K. to
J.D.R. Jr.,
Feb. 24, 1919
28 Mar. 7-8, 1919
35 Mar. 15, 1919
326 *20* Mar. 28, 1919
30 Ibid.
327 *32* May 12, 1919
328 *4* Mar. 4, 1919
9 Ibid.
18 W.L.M.K. to
D. M. King,
Mar. 4, 1919
27 Ibid.
329 *5 Ibid.*, Apr. 13,
1919
13 Ibid., Mar. 26,
1919
18 Ibid., Apr. 2, 1919
23 Feb. 18-22, 1919

32 W.L.M.K. to
D. M. King,
Apr. 13, 1919
330 *10 Ibid.*
15 Jan. 1-14, 1919
17 W.L.M.K. to
D. M. King,
Apr. 13, 1919
22 May 12, 1919
27 Mar. 3, 1919
331 *17* W.L.M.K. to
D. M. King,
Feb. 10, 1919
332 *4* W.L.M.K. to
D. M. King,
Feb. 21, 1919
333 *24 Ibid.*, Apr. 13,
1919
30 Ibid., Apr. 2, 1919
334 *33* May 31, 1919
335 *13* May 30, 1919
29 Ibid.
336 *8* W.L.M.K. to
D. M. King,
June 23, 1919
15 June 21, 1919
337 *22* W.L.M.K. to
D. M. King,
July 21, 1919
338 *15* Aug. 5-9, 1919
340 *15 Ibid.*
23 Ibid.
341 *9 Ibid.*
342 *5 Ibid.*
30 Ibid.
343 *9 Ibid.*
33 Ibid.
344 *5 Ibid.*
20 Ibid.
345 *12* Aug. 10, 1919

Index